MASTERING
WINE

MASTERING
WINE

TOM MARESCA

BANTAM BOOKS

TORONTO • NEW YORK • LONDON • SYDNEY • AUCKLAND

MASTERING WINE

A Bantam Book / November 1985

Library of Congress Cataloging-in-Publication Data

Maresca, Tom.
  Mastering wine.

  Includes index.
  1. Wine and wine making. I. Title.
TP548.M333 1985   641.2'22   85-47648
ISBN 0-553-34202-9 (pbk.)

Published simultaneously in the United States and Canada

PRINTED IN THE UNITED STATES OF AMERICA

FG   0 9 8 7 6 5 4 3 2 1

This book is gratefully dedicated
to
the daring palates
and unflinching taste buds
of
The Kamikaze Tasting Squad

# Acknowledgments

This book could not have been started or finished without the help of many friends and associates. Cathy Cashion helped lay the groundwork for it, and Susan and Tim Benthall led me to refine the idea. The good will and good palates of my volunteer tasters were indispensable, and hearty thanks go to Barbara, Bruce, Carey, Charlotte, Donna S., Donna W., Frank, Joan, Mary Lou, Nancy, Nick, Nino, Shirley, Susan, and Tim. Every stage of this project, from conception to consumption to completion, was aided and abetted by my wife, Diane Darrow.

Thanks are also due to many generous and efficient people in all branches of the wine trade, without whose cooperation this book could not have been completed. There are more of them than I can decipher from my scribbled notes, but among those whose aid showed clearest are Mr. Don Poretz of Almadén Vineyards; Peggy Schochet of Buckingham Wile; the staff of the Champagne News and Information Bureau; David Milligan of Chateau and Estate Wines; the Christian Brothers Winery; Mireille Guiliano of Clicquot, Inc.; Patrick Séré of Dreyfus Ashby; Mary Lyons and the staff of Food and Wines from France; Bill Juchet of the Joseph Garneau Company; Robert Fairchild and David Bass of The House of Burgundy; Philip Di Belardino and Eric Solomon of International Vintage Wine Company; Mary Mulligan of the International Wine Center; the staff of the Italian Wine Center;

Charles Mueller and Gerard Yvernault of Kobrand; Carolyn Martini of Louis M. Martini; Monarch Wine Company, Inc.; Frank De Falco and Niki Singer of Niki Singer Inc.; Eric Fineman of Paramount Brands; Fiona Morrison of Paterno Imports; Bonny Birnbaum of Peartree Imports; Angela Seracini of Pepsico Wines and Spirits International; Annamaria Lepore of P. L. Imports; Rolar Imports Inc.; Marsha Palanci of Schieffelin & Co.; Barbara Edelman of Joseph E. Seagram & Sons; Louis Bonaccolta of Trebon Wine and Spirits; Joseph Victori Wines, Inc.; Lucio Sorré and Sharon Piech of Villa Banfi; Michael Eisenberg of Vintage Wine Merchants; Carm Tintle of Vinum Communications; Julie Ann Kodmur of Frederick Wildman.

Finally, a huge thank-you to my agent Felicia Eth and my editor Peter Guzzardi for their enthusiasm, their encouragement, and their expertise.

Tom Maresca,
Bottomley-under-Barrel,
1985

Contents

# Read This First

This is a do-it-yourself wine book—a teach-yourself project.

Its first premise is that wine is fun.

Its second is that most people would rather drink wine than read about it or take classes about it.

Its third premise is that drinking wine is the only effective way to learn about wine anyway.

And its fourth premise, to let you in on everything all at once, is that most people don't plan to become connoisseurs—at least not at the start. They want to learn enough about wine to be able to enjoy it—to stay calm when the wine list winds up in their hands, to avoid sweaty palms when someone asks them what they think of the wine, to be able to relax and enjoy a sip when the wine finally gets into the glass.

Enjoyment is the premise of this book, and your own preferences, your own likes and dislikes, are all the tools you need to learn as much as you want about wine. Our procedure is going to be very simple. You taste wines in pairs, and the wine you like better in each pair will point the way to your next pair. Like leads you on to like, and you increase your wine knowledge and your wine pleasure at the same time. No terror, no anxiety, no questions you can't answer. The questions don't even have wrong answers. Whatever you say in response to "Which wine did you like better?" is bound to be right.

I've set up for you a whole gamut of wines, all arranged in pairs. There are thirty-nine pairs in all—red wine, white wine, rosé, and sparkling wine—thirty-nine steps to solving the mystery of wine. They start from relatively simple and popular wines and gradually move up a scale of complexity and distinctiveness.

You don't have to taste them all at once. You don't even have to taste them all. You'll follow the path of your own preferences through the book, and at your own pace. If you want, you could conceivably work through all the wines in this book in a month or less—even a few days if you could go at it full-time. But if you prefer, you can also stop at any point you like and resume tasting in a week, a month, a year. It's entirely up to you. You can taste alone or with your spouse or steady, with family or with friends. You can be solemn if that's your style or flip if you like—that's entirely up to you, too.

All you have to do is taste the specific wines named in each pair and, after you and I have talked them over, decide which of the two wines pleased you more. That choice will lead you on to a pair of related wines so that you can sharpen your sense of the qualities you liked. I've deliberately chosen the first handful of wine pairs to display fairly sharp contrasts so that you should have no trouble at all tasting real differences between them. Later on, when you're narrowing down your range and really trying to focus on very specific elements you enjoy, the wines within the pairs will be more similar to each other and the differences between them subtler—but by that time you'll be subtler, too, and a lot more experienced at tasting and enjoying.

Yes, you'll need practice enjoying. For many people, wine is an ordeal rather than a pleasure. It's so fraught with anxiety that they approach it not merely seriously but also tensely.

That's where I come in: what I'm going to do is write this book as if it were a conversation between us. I'll do and say everything I can—bad jokes and all—to put you at ease, to keep you interested, to keep you focused. I'm going to talk you through these wines exactly as I would if we were sitting across the table from each other. As far as I am concerned, there is one subject on which you are an indisputable authority: your own taste. Why drink a wine someone else thinks you should like rather than one you actually do like? Your own taste is going to be the key that unlocks the whole world of wine for you, because you're going to learn from what you like, with me on the sidelines cheering you on.

If you are already started with wine, or are not interested in the entry-level wines, or prefer particular kinds of wine, you can use this book to suit yourself. The book is organized so that each tasting concludes with directions for following three separate paths. You can simply follow your own preference: if, after the third tasting, you prefer the Jadot Beaujolais 1983 to the Paul Masson California Zinfandel 1982, you can skip to the tasting on page 74. Or you can choose to follow a special class of wines—those made from a noble grape variety such as Cabernet, for instance. Or you can explore the wines of a particular country.

Even more simply, you can just proceed through this book in sequence, page by page, pair by pair, ignoring the choices entirely. Because the overall sequence of the wine pairs in this book graduates from simple to complex just as the preferential sequences and varietal sequences and national sequences do, anyone, beginner or not, can simply taste the wines in the order of their presentation, work straight through the book, and come out the other end with a good amount of wine lore assimilated.

At any point in the book you can freely switch from one of these methods to another. Say, for example, that you are going along the trail of your own preferences and come upon a wine that really excites you—a German Riesling, for instance. You can at that point either continue on the path of your preferences or explore the other wines made from Riesling or explore German wines. You could either resume your original trail later on or just continue along your new track to its end. The book is designed to be helpful in any of these ways.

Whichever of these routes you choose, here's what you can get out of this book:

- a survey of and firsthand acquaintance with the major classes and classifications of dry dinner wines
- a painless introduction to wine terms, each presented in a situation in which it is immediately understandable because you are at that moment experiencing what it means
- practice, right from the start, with all of the seemingly mysterious and sophisticated techniques of wine tasting and wine analysis
- direct knowledge and experience—not descriptions, but the actual tastes—of most of the major kinds of dinner wines available in the United States
- a chance to explore your own taste in wine and find out what you really like, free from any pressures or constraints.

If you are shy or embarrass easily, you can work through this book entirely by yourself. But if you'd rather, there is no reason you couldn't make the whole process into a festive social occasion. By gathering a few like-minded friends, you can turn your tasting sessions into predinner cocktails and finish the wines (and an important part of your lesson) at dinner. That even has the advantage of letting you divide the cost of the wines so no individual is very much out of pocket. (Just for the record: most of the wines included here are quite reasonably priced.) Even if you really feel that you know absolutely nothing about wine, this book is designed to let you teach yourself to enjoy it, or—to put it more accurately—to let you find out how very easy wine is to enjoy and how very well equipped you already are to understand and enjoy it.

Despite all the myths, Americans have no need to feel any inferiority about their knowledge of wine. Perhaps about their consumption of it and their capacity for it, but not their knowledge. The simple fact of the American marketplace forces a certain amount of knowledge on us: we can—and every day are solicited to—buy wine not only from all over the United States but also from Canada, Argentina, Chile, France, Italy, Spain, Greece, Yugoslavia, Hungary, Germany, Austria, Portugal, Romania, Israel, Cyprus, Algeria, South Africa, and Australia, not to mention nongrape wines from China and Japan. Just to hold onto our dollars we have to learn to say no in several languages.

If you had grown up in a small city in France or Italy or Spain or any other of a number of wine-growing, wine-drinking countries, you would never have had an anxious thought about wine in the entire course of your life. As a matter of routine you would have drunk with your meals whatever wine was made in your locality, without ever wondering whether it was a good vintage or not. For your wedding or graduation or the birth of your child, you would have provided Champagne if you could afford it, and if not, whatever sparkling substitute your region offered.

Maybe, if you went to the big city or to a fancy restaurant or were trying to impress someone, you would choose a special wine—but when you did, your ignorance about wine would probably be so abysmal that you would either put yourself blindly in the hands of the restaurateur or stubbornly insist on the one or two prestigious wines whose names you knew, whether or not they were appropriate to the occasion. As for wines made in another country: the odds would be very strong against your ever having heard of or tasted more than one or two, perhaps not even that.

The average European is as uninformed about vintages and vineyards as the average American. The only difference between an American and a European is that we are intimidated by wine—maybe justifiably so, considering all the choices we're confronted with—and a European usually isn't. A European assumes wine as his or her birthright, so to speak, because the European has grown up with it. Most of us haven't. Wine on the table at every lunch and dinner is not yet an American tradition, though we can hope it will become so soon. Neither do we have the kind of communal or collective dining facilities, like British clubs, that allow the less-than-wealthy access to a well-stocked cellar.

By and large, American restaurants don't help, either: though things are slowly improving, the vast majority still have pathetically inadequate wine lists. Worse yet, even good restaurants with decent lists charge a criminal markup on wine, so high in some cases that you'd think the restaurateur was being paid off by the temperance lobby to discourage wine drinking. More troublesome still, even the most conscientious restaurants find it very hard to maintain a cellar of properly aged wines—the overhead and cash tie-up are simply prohibitive—so most Americans never have the opportunity to taste a mature wine at its peak of perfection.

Because of that, a lot of wine instruction starts at the wrong place for the beginning American wine drinker. Many, perhaps most, books and courses assume that the reader or student already enjoys wine, already knows something about it, and is working on developing a degree of connoisseurship or refining an expertise. They never say so explicitly, but that implicit bias shows clearly in the speed with which they pass over the mass of popular wines from which most Americans begin their acquaintance with wine.

That in itself might not be too serious a flaw if it were not usually compounded with two others—the failures to differentiate clearly, first, between what a trained palate discerns and what a beginner tastes, and second, between the ideal taste of a wine and the reality of its average market specimen's flavor. Too often those very real distinctions are completely blurred. The student tastes nothing remotely like what the instructor describes, assumes that the fault lies in his or her own insensitivity, then either gives up on wine entirely or sticks with Hearty Burgundy. In either case, there is a real loss both to the apprentice wine drinker and to the world of wine.

The unspoken assumption of traditional wine lore is that the taster already knows or will instantly recognize the flavor of greatness in wine. The unfortunate truth is that most Americans have never tasted a mature claret, or a great Burgundy, or an old Hermitage, and would probably not be able to recognize its greatness or understand what made it great if they had. Only a few very fortunate individuals who are blessed with the wealth that allows them to buy a—let us say—1945 Château Latour have ever tasted such wine. And fewer still are blessed with the extraordinary palates and palatal memories to learn from one bottle alone the standard that such a wine may teach. For most Americans, that bottle of Latour would be a dead waste. To learn wine tasting from great examples like that, you need to have a palate already active, a memory already stored with tastes and flavors and ideas. You have to be ready, so to speak, for that wine to hit you dead center and rearrange all your previous taste experiences around itself.

People who learned wine and wine tasting that way started at the opposite pole from where most Americans begin. There is a whole new crop of potential wine drinkers in the United States who are right now poised on the edge of wine, hesitant either to immerse themselves or to stay dry. Most of them have to learn wine from the ground up, working with what they can afford, moving tentatively from soft drinks and hard liquor and watery beer to domestic jug wines and inexpensive imports. And the wine courses and the wine books skim over in the first two pages or two minutes as unworthy of serious attention a whole class of wines that the jug-drinker hasn't even tried yet! Even the drinker who has made the plunge finds precious little help in his or her first faltering attempts to figure out what makes a Liebfraumilch different from a Zeller Schwarze Katz, or a New York Champagne different from a Spanish Champagne from a French Champagne.

What You Need to Know

What do you need to know about wine to read this book?

Nothing. Zero. Zip. Zilch.

What is the one essential rule for learning about wine?

Don't be buffaloed.

No matter what you may have heard, nobody "knows all about wine." No matter what great feats of recognition a few extraordinary palates are capable of, there isn't an expert in the world who can't be fooled in a blind tasting at least some of the time. Besides, that kind of expertise is totally irrelevant to most people's lives. It's the vinous equivalent of running the four-minute mile: most of us are content to admire it without seriously aspiring to do it. Most people who want to learn about wine wish to do so not to turn their lives into a constant process of testing nor even for social points or one-upmanship: they simply want to enrich their lives by bringing something enjoyable into it. That is the best reason for learning about wine.

To become as much a connoisseur as most people ever aspire to, all you need do is discover what your personal tastes in wine are and develop confidence in your judgment. That's why nowhere in this book are you going to see any wine described as "better" than any other wine. The best wine is the wine you like best. That is one of the bedrock, working assumptions of this book.

If at the end of this book you've decided that you really prefer the simpler, less expensive wines with which the book begins, terrific! Think of the money you'll save over the rest of your life! More to the point, you'll have the knowledge and the confidence of having tried other wines and knowing why you like the ones you do, and you'll have the language to explain those preferences to anyone who really wants to know.

There is nothing to embarrass anyone in a preference for simple pleasures. The embarrassment that people feel about wine comes

- from not knowing what they like
- from fearing that they don't know what they ought to like
- from fearing that they don't like what they should like
- from fearing that there is something wrong with what they do like because it is too inexpensive or too popular or too unsophisticated or too whatever.

That is nonsense. The greatest enemy of wine is the wine snob. I drink all sorts of wine, of every conceivable level of quality, character, and cost, and I find that there are few wines I cannot enjoy if they are presented in their proper setting.

Naturally, I have my own preferences, wines I think of as "better" than other wines. You will, too, as soon as you have enough tasting experience. But what I mean by "better" is, simply, more pleasing to my personal taste and more conformable to the standards applied by wine professionals—which, in fact, are not very standard at all. My taste and those unstandards are completely irrelevant to most of the rest of the world.

It may be that such professional measurements will eventually become important to you. Ninety-nine percent of the wine professionals in the world and 100 percent of the gifted amateur connoisseurs did not become so by a cold-blooded, logical decision, but because at some point in their lives they drank a wine that just stripped their taste buds bare and made them stand up and cheer. After that, they became knowledgeable about wine simply by pursuing what they loved. Anyone can do the same thing the same way.

After all, the upper limit of what you can learn and enjoy about wine is simply the limit of what you can taste, what your palate and nose can perceive. If you've got the palatal equivalent of perfect pitch, or of the perfect ninety-nine-mile-an-hour pitcher's arm, you are going to taste and enjoy more and more acutely than the rest of us mere mortals. Your analysis and description of the taste of wines will be more complete and more precise than ours—but your preferences will still be every bit as subjective.

 # Rules of the Game

Wine in America is 50 percent romance and 50 percent pseudoscientific jargon—a bundle of unrealistic attitudes in a glossy high-tech package.

People think of wine in itself as complicated and of wine expertise as a sign of sophistication. Few people label themselves connoisseurs, but everyone loves being thought one. We shy away from the word, but we love the idea it conveys—the glamor; the discreet, worldly wisdom; the easy, offhand mastery of arcane lore. "Oh, yes," you say, smiling at your obviously wealthy, fashionable, admiring dinner companion and simultaneously nodding approval to the reverently attentive wine steward, "the Pichon-Lalande 1967. A pretty little claret, isn't it?"

So the romantic fantasy runs. The other side of wine in America is all Brix and pH, measures of residual sugar and acidity and alcohol. Experts earnestly argue the precise differentiations between the effects of new or old wood on Cabernets and Zinfandels and Chardonnays from one current superstar winemaker or another—California's updated version of Abbott and Costello's "Who's on first?" routine. We learnedly discuss the significance of climatic variations in zones I, II, III, IV, or V in Napa and Sonoma and Monterey and the Alexander Valley. We have university courses to teach us everything from wine making to wine smelling, vinification to appreciation. Kits are available to help us analyze odors, charts to help us pin down colors, a whole lexicon of special terms from "ascescence" to "vinosity" to help us speak correctly of wine.

We do everything with wine, it seems, except drink it and enjoy it. That's too simple for our complicated world. In an environment like this, it's all too easy to forget that all you really need to enjoy wine is a mouth.

The only secret of wine expertise, at least as far as tasting is concerned, is to pay attention. So this book is set up to prod you to think seriously about what you are tasting.

For most people, it's easier to distinguish and identify flavors and aromas when comparing two wines than when dealing with one in isolation. For that reason, you will taste a pair of wines at a time. The wines in each pair have been chosen both because they should be available just about anywhere in the United States and, even more important, because they clearly reveal important wine characteristics and components.

Since these pairs have been chosen for particular reasons, I urge you to try to obtain the exact wines specified. If a particular wine should be unavailable, a younger vintage of the same wine will always make the best possible substitute.

Information about the importers or distributors of most of these wines is provided throughout the book. That should facilitate your local wineshop's ordering any of them for you if they are not in stock. In the Appendix, I also include a very limited number of reasonable approximations should such substitution be absolutely necessary. But remember, no two wines taste exactly alike, and using substitutes will make it more difficult for you to get the clear-cut distinctions we're both after.

The paired wines should all be available throughout the United States. This doesn't mean that you can walk into a neighborhood mom-and-pop liquor store and expect to find them all. The odds on your finding every one of them even in a large wine shop are fairly long, given the vast number of wines on the American market. You may have to make a few phone calls or even have your dealer order one or two of them for you. That is rarely a problem. By far the most common difficulty you are likely to encounter in gathering these wines is the lazy shopowner who tells you there is no such wine and tries to sell you instead whatever is on hand. Be polite but firm. Give your dealer all the relevant data—you'll find everything you need in the pair entries—and tell him or her to consult the latest edition of *Beverage Media* to find out what company to call for any particular wine in your area.

One last preliminary assurance. I'm not going to bombard you with jargon. The necessary wine terms—you'll have to take it on faith for a little while that some are necessary—will be introduced only in a context where they are immediately relevant and where you will have (I hope in your glass or on your tongue at that very moment) a vivid example of what the term really means. Only by tasting wine can you learn anything about wine, and only by experiencing the precise sensation the wine terms are intended to denote will you understand that some pretentious-sounding words are really very exact. Should you come across a term whose meaning you're unsure about, the index will show where its principal explanation can be found.

 # What You Need to Have

At its most basic, all you absolutely need to use this book are wine, two glasses, and a corkscrew. That is bare bones, but it will still let you perform the basic task, tasting the wines. If you want to get the most out of this undertaking, however, here's a list of suggested paraphernalia:

- A good corkscrew (Screwpull is the best on the market)
- Clear, clean glasses, preferably tulip- or bowl-shaped, and preferably one for each wine to be tasted
- Paper cups or a bucket for spitting and pouring out waste
- A white tablecloth (to let you better see the wine's color)
- A pitcher of water and water glasses (for rinsing mouths and, if necessary, glasses)
- Note pad or tasting sheets and pencil for each taster
- Some good, fresh, crusty bread
- *Un po' di formaggio:* a little bit of an honest cheese—nothing too strongly flavored, and especially nothing sweet
- Some paper napkins
- The wines

That's not so bad, is it?

What You Have to Do

At first, deliberate tasting is a very strange activity, and most people feel self-conscious about it. After all, your mother spent all those years teaching you to eat quietly and to close your mouth while you're chewing, and here all of a sudden you're expected to slurp and burble air into your mouth and slosh wine around in your cheeks and spit and God knows how many other things Mom would most definitely not have approved of. For a sophisticated activity, wine tasting sure seems to get off to a low start. It's no wonder so many apprentice tasters feel awkward.

Tasting all alone is a good way of avoiding the self-consciousness, but it deprives you of the benefits of other people's reactions—and it is almost certain that no two people are going to respond exactly the same way to a pair of wines (more about this and how it affects this book's descriptions of wine flavors later).

The optimum tasting situation would involve two, three, or four—rarely more—individuals who are at roughly the same stage of knowledge or ignorance, appreciation or curiosity. More important, they should be comfortable enough with each other so that embarrassment or shyness won't be a factor: better to taste alone than in a group where you can't say honestly what you think, because the whole point is to come to know your own taste.

Tasting with a small, congenial group not only lets you see how widely reactions to the same wine can vary but it also helps you discern elements in the wine you might otherwise overlook. Each taster can help teach the others and be taught in turn. And group tasting also has the practical advantage of spreading the cost of the wines so that nobody is out of pocket for any large sum.

In group tasting, you will be using everybody else (and they will be using you) as a foil/comparison/contrast to your own experience. For this reason, no one should say anything about any wine until everybody has finished jotting down his or her remarks about it. Sorry if that sounds antisocial, but it's too easy to be persuaded—and to convince yourself— that you taste or smell something you actually don't, so it's important to get your own impressions firm before you hear anybody else's.

On p. 16 is a sample tasting sheet. You can make as many copies of it as you think you'll need, or simply have your tasters copy out its categories onto blank sheets of paper. Its format is deliberately simple to focus your attention on the factors that matter most about a wine: its appearance, its aroma, and its flavor. You'll notice there's space for overall comments: this is because, surprisingly often, tasters find them- selves saying quite glowing things about the components of a wine that on the whole they don't really care for, or making disparaging comments about aspects of a wine that they like a lot *in toto*.

You'll also notice there are no numbers, no points to be assigned, no mathematical games to be played. Just words, and your job is to find the right ones. This is in part to generate sympathy for my job, but mostly to force you really to think about what you're smelling and tasting. Numbers seem to be exact, but in fact they allow you to slide over a lot of important details.

TASTING NOTES

PAIR NUMBER _____   TASTER _____

Wine 1: _____   *Wine 2:* _____

APPEARANCE: APPEARANCE:

AROMA: AROMA:

TASTE AND TEXTURE: TASTE AND TEXTURE:

OVERALL IMPRESSION: OVERALL IMPRESSION:

In spite of
             my remarks above, I prefer Wine _____
Because of

The actual process of tasting involves what you will come to think of as the "infamous s's": see, swirl, smell, sip/slurp, savor/slosh, and spit. Not a prepossessing bunch, but a lot of fun when you get to know them.

See: Look closely at the color of the wine: How would you describe its shade? Is it clear? Is it brilliant? Is it attractive? Tilt your glass slightly and look closely at a thin edge of the wine. Is the color true to the end? Or does it fade off? Or does it show other tints there?

Different wines have different color patterns, and as you come to know wine better, this will be a useful clue to you about how well a particular wine has been made or how well a particular bottle is holding up. Initially it won't tell you too much beyond whether you find the appearance of the wine attractive, but prettiness is also one of the pleasures of wine, so don't ignore it.

Swirl: With a gentle wrist motion or even gentler forearm motion, slowly start the wine circulating around the glass. You do this to release the aroma of the wine by bringing more oxygen in contact with it. Remember, gentleness is the key: too much exuberance leads to wine stains on the walls, the guests, and the precious self.

The much-revered ancient Greeks, when they weren't being wise and venerable, used to unwind after dinner with a wine-swirling game. The rules were simple: a large bowl was placed in the middle of the floor, and seated guests tried to swirl their remaining wine out of their cups and into the bowl. This only goes to show that even the ancient Greeks weren't impressive all the time, and anyone is entitled to look a little silly where wine is involved.

Smell: After you have swirled the wine, put your nose right down in the glass and draw in a long, deep breath. Don't worry about what it looks like: if anybody is there with you, they ought to be doing the same thing at this point. The crucial thing is that as you are breathing in, you are concentrating as hard as you can on what you are smelling. Use your nose as you've never used it before. Think about the traces of things you recognize in the wine's aroma. Nuts? If so, what kind? Fruit? Vanilla? Violets? Earth? Grass? This is where you really have to work, because smell is a major factor in our enjoyment of wines. Even what we call flavor is mostly made up of smell. And literally hundreds of different aromatic elements have been identified in wine, while most of us nasally impoverished humans recognize only a few of them.

Many wine aromas change in the glass, developing and/or fading as the minutes pass. This is why so much fuss is often made about exactly when to uncork and whether to decant a very old or very fine wine. Contact with oxygen releases the aroma, but too much contact with oxygen will also kill a wine—everything it has will literally vanish in air. So go back to a wine every now and again to smell it anew. Any young wine that disappears like that after, say, twenty minutes in the glass is a badly made wine.

Sip/slurp: Take in a small amount of wine—not a whole mouthful—with as much air as you comfortably can. That's where the slurp may come in. The point of the air is, once again, to get maximum flavor out of a small amount of wine so you can taste everything that's in it. A small amount of wine keeps alcoholic intake to a minimum, because alcohol will eventually tire and numb the palate, and you want to be fresh for the next wine or wines.

Savor/slosh: Let the wine run slowly over the entire surface of your tongue. Move it about both sides of the mouth. Expose it to every surface you've got that's capable of sensation.

This need not look silly, and it can be done very quietly. People who sit in posh restaurants and ostentatiously *chew* their wine (usually with wine steward or captain in patient attendance) are doing so not because they must but because they want you and everyone else in the restaurant to know what they are doing. The difference between true wine connoisseurs and such performers is the difference between people who do what they do out of sheer love and people who haven't the slightest idea of the worth of their activity unless it's noticed by an audience.

The action of tasting shouldn't look or sound like a mouthwash commercial, but don't rush it, either. Again, concentrate on what is actually going on in your mouth. Are you tasting one flavor, or many? All over the mouth, or in different parts? Are several flavors present at the same time, or do they succeed each other? What kind of flavors are they? Related to the aroma, or very different? What do they taste like? Fruit? Nuts? Tobacco? Minerals? Grass? Be as specific as you can—and remember to taste both with and without a bit of food, and note carefully how the wine changes. If you've never done anything like this before, you're going to be amazed by how many different things you become aware of.

If you're tasting with a group, you're also going to be surprised by how very different each individual's description of the same wine's flavor can be. Don't let this bother you, not even if everybody in the group says the wine tastes like plums and you're all alone insisting it tastes like asparagus. If it tasted like asparagus to you, it tasted like asparagus. That's all there is to it. The important questions are, Did you like it? Or did that asparagus flavor put you off? Once you know that, you can also know, for example, that there are other wines made from this same grape, or vinified the same way, and the odds are you're going to find them tasting something like this wine, and you'll like or dislike them accordingly.

All this holds true for my own comments about the wines, when you come to them. Just because I describe something I found in a wine doesn't mean you have to experience exactly the same thing. There's a fifty-fifty chance you will or you won't. That's not important. The important thing is to develop and sharpen your own taste.

To help you do that, I will provide you with some reactions to the same wine you are tasting, comments and descriptions made by varying groups of nonprofessional wine tasters—people at more or less the same level of wine knowledge as yourself. You may be surprised by some of these comments. I know some of them surprised me. But they should help you to get over any lingering doubts or self-consciousness about your own reactions and also provide you with a makeshift frame within which you can locate your own response to an individual wine. And every now and again I'll tell you what connoisseurs look for or hope for in the very best examples of a particular kind of wine.

I've deliberately avoided anything like a statistically significant sampling or a rigorous, scientific gathering of reactions, in order not to risk intimidating you into feeling that you had to taste exactly what other people had described. All the comments I have included are intended simply to help you come to know your own palate better by letting you know what other tasters of skills similar to yours have tasted and what professionals look for as standards for the breed. But I cannot say this too often: all that matters are what you taste and how you react to it.

Spit: It means what it says. Spit no matter how much you like the wine. Why? So you won't get sloshed, that's why. Obviously, the more wines you plan to taste at one sitting, the more important this becomes.

Remember, too, that even though you spit every mouthful, you still absorb some alcohol directly through the mucous membranes that line the mouth, so it is possible to get a bit tiddly—and considerably more, if your tolerance for alcohol is low—without actually drinking a drop.

After you spit out the wine, once again concentrate. Does its flavor persist in your mouth? Does a component of its flavor, or a new flavor element, persist in your mouth? This is what is called a wine's finish (congratulations! you've just learned your first piece of wine jargon), and it, too, is an important part of a wine's overall effect and pleasure. Most beginners with wine have a bit of trouble discerning the finish without actually swallowing, so for that purpose it may be a good idea at first to let a little of the wine slide down your throat. But after you get used to really paying attention to the sensations in your mouth, you won't find that necessary.

Professional tasters always spit out their wine, so no matter how distasteful this may seem to you, it's actually got quite a lot of professional prestige attached to it. Your mom may think you unmannerly, but your fellow wine drinkers will recognize real sophistication when they see it. If you plan to taste only one or two pairs of wines at a sitting, you can certainly skip the spitting if you wish to—it's not crucial where the number of wines remains small. So suit yourself. Either way, you win: swallow and enjoy the wine, or spit and look impeccably professional.

Don't worry about memorizing this sequence of steps. I'll go through them with you in detail in the first tasting, and after that I'll remind you of them at appropriate places. After you've done them a few times, they will come naturally to you. The watchwords are relax and enjoy.

Let me stress that each time you taste a wine try to taste it with a little bit of food. This runs counter to almost every other wine-tasting method, but I strongly recommend it. Have something along with your wine, even if it's only a nibble of a mild cheese, because—unless you are very unusual—that is the way you are going to consume most of the wines you'll have in your lifetime. And food changes wine—in some cases, very dramatically.

That fact is what lies behind the ancient piece of wine business lore that says, "Buy on apples, sell on cheese." Acidic foods like apples strip bare every flaw and blemish in a wine. Fat foods like cheese bring out all that is best in them. Similarly, all sorts of food differently affect the way wine behaves. Some wines that do not seem impressive when tasted only against other wines simply blossom alongside food. And many wines that do very well in formal judgings fail miserably with food. Many a huge, high-alcohol wine has won a gold medal because it has the effect on the judges' palates of a double martini: you simply can't taste anything else after it.

There is a not-so-apocryphal story of a California winemaker who was proudly displaying his medal-bedecked, 18-degrees-of-alcohol (that's 36 proof for you whiskey drinkers), 6-degrees-of-residual-sugar, late-harvest Zinfandel: a monster Zin, as they call it in California, for which he was also charging a monster price. When asked what kind of food you would drink such a wine with, he answered—with a straight face, mind you—"It's terrific with peanut butter."

After you have finished all of the "infamous s's" and after you have finished jotting down your comments, proceed as follows: if you are tasting alone, turn at that point to this book's comments on the wines you just tasted and use them to refine your own perceptions. Retaste step by step with the book if you find that that helps you. If you are tasting in a group, thoroughly discuss the wines among yourselves before turning to the book's comments. Go through each wine category by category as they appear on your tasting sheets—appearance, aroma, taste, etc. Then and only then look at the book's comments. As I have said before and will remind you many times again, you laid out your hard-earned money for this book to sharpen your taste in wine, not to defer to mine or anybody else's.

With the exception of the first flight, where I will conduct a guided tour, these basic tasting procedures remain the same throughout the book. The initial few sets of wine have been chosen to present fairly sharp contrasts and to introduce the basic terms and concepts you will use through the rest of this book. For that reason, I urge beginning tasters especially to taste the first four pairs in sequence. Your preferences there will lead you to subsequent groups of wines, different groups according to your preferences in each pair, and so on through the book. What you like will be leading you on to more complex examples of related wines or related kinds of wines. If at any point you can't make up your mind—if you either like or dislike both wines of a pair—go on to either or both of the next sets: strong preferences are almost bound to make themselves felt pretty quickly.

Leftover wine shouldn't be a very great problem. If you're tasting at the cocktail hour, I urge you to complete the tasting process by drinking the remaining wine with dinner. Otherwise, if you tightly recork the bottles, most wines should hold pretty much unchanged for a day or two; whites should be refrigerated. If the wines do change, it will usually be for the worse, unfortunately—but that, too, is part of the learning process.

What You Need Not Do

To taste the wines as fully as possible, it would be wise to approach them with your mouth and nose and eyes as fresh as possible. For this reason, many professionals taste only in the mornings. There is also a mystique that claims that everyone can taste more accurately in the morning; all of us who awaken slowly and ineptly know just how much hogwash that is. In any event, for most people, morning tastings are going to be difficult at best, impossible at worst. Don't worry about that, but do pay attention to your own metabolism and your bodily clock. Try to block out for tasting a time of day when you are normally alert and energetic, whenever it may fall, and try to schedule all your tastings for that same time. Many people find early evening convenient.

Try to keep your palate fresh for tasting. I'm obviously not urging you to fast all day if you're tasting in the evening (your palate would still get stale anyhow), but at very least, don't try to proceed directly to wine tasting from wolfing down a deli-special pastrami, salami, and Swiss cheese hero with peppers and onions and coleslaw and Russian dressing: it won't work.

This is also true if you are a smoker: sure, your palate has made the adjustment and you can taste wine just as well as a nonsmoker; nevertheless, your judgment will be skewed if you've been smoking heavily immediately before tasting. As for smoking during tasting: if everyone in your group also smokes, it might be okay in moderation, but it can very easily get tricky. If there are nonsmokers present, anyone smoking during the tasting will make it impossible for them to smell anything other than the smoke and will seriously impair their tasting ability.

Other things that will also skew the functioning of your taste buds and interfere with your perceptions: alcohol and sugar, alone or in combination. A cocktail before the tasting (people do stranger things) will diminish your ability to discern flavors, as will heavily sweetened foods. In fact, if you are a sweets eater of more than average dimensions (take that how you will), you will have trouble coming to appreciate many very fine wines: you will find them too dry, perhaps even sour. You can make things easier for yourself by gradually drying out your palate: reduce the amount of sugar you consciously add to things, and start avoiding the kinds of food that have already been laced with sugar before they come to you. Sugar is a palate-killer: it masks the flavors of other elements in a wine or a dish, and it seems to have almost addictive effects on some people, so they find anything without sugar insipid.

Setting Up the Board

Now is the time, for convenience' sake, to provide yourself with all the wines you're going to need for your first tasting or two.

Remember, these tastings can be conducted at your own pace. You may choose to do one pair of wines at a sitting, or two, three, or four. You can do even more than that at one time if you choose, but you'll find that your ability to concentrate gets increasingly impaired as you go along. Even if you are conscientiously spitting out every mouthful of wine, you're bound to lose both mental and physical sharpness. You won't quite be able to pick up the aroma, flavors will be more blurred and vague than at first, and the words to describe them won't come as readily.

If you're doing this sort of thing for the first time, you might want to start very gently—say, two pairs of wines at most, and if that goes well, you could consider trying three or four pairs the next time. But don't push beyond your physical limits—which is good advice for most situations, but especially where alcohol is concerned. I'm not even being moralistic here so much as pragmatic. Go beyond your capacity, and you're just wasting your time and money.

My policy in working with you through this book is going to come pretty close to total disclosure, so let me start off on the right foot by telling you that you are here, on the verge of your first tasting, about to commit an oenological heresy. (Do you like that word "oenological"? All it means is "having to do with wine," but do you notice how I let you get this far along before I sprung one of those on you? A man can smile and smile and be a villain.)

Your crime—maybe it's mine—consists in tasting red wines before whites, as all of you were innocently just about to do. Conventional tasting and teaching procedures always put white wines before reds for the usually very sound reasons that white wines are for the most part lighter-bodied, less alcoholic, and less markedly flavored than red wines. That means that tasting red wines before whites in the same tasting session would all but make the white wines disappear.

We're starting off with red wines, however, because none of those reasons applies to our case. First and most obviously, we're not tasting reds and whites at the same sitting. Second, I like red wine better (total disclosure, see?). Third and most important, you can learn more about wine faster from red wines than from whites.

Because the flavors of red wines are both more distinct and more varied than those of whites, it's easier for any taster, beginner or experienced, to pick out individual tastes and characteristics, and it's easier to come to grips with concepts like balance and maturity in wine. On the other hand, precisely because the flavors of white wines are more subtle than those of red wines, it makes sense to approach white wines after you've gained some tasting experience and have a better idea of how to taste and what to taste for.

One last piece of information. For reasons that are totally obscure to me, any number of wines grouped together for tasting are known as a *flight*—just like darts—so our pairs are really, in technical wine jargon, flights of two. Got that? If so, get ready to earn your wings. *Avanti!*

RED WINES

OPENING MOVES

Red Wines:
The First Flight

ROBERT MONDAVI TABLE RED 1982
AND
VILLA BANFI ROMAN RED NV

I'm going to walk you through the tasting of this first pair of wines step by step so you get a good, clear sense of what your tasting procedure is going to be throughout the book. So for this one time only, read my golden words as you are actually performing your various tasting maneuvers. In all the flights that follow this one, I'll ask you to read only the preliminary remarks (if any), then to taste and take your notes, and only after that to look at what the book has to say.

Okay: you've provided yourself with glasses, water, a little nibble, pads, pencils, good lighting and the two bottles of wine named above. Now get your corkscrew and pull the corks or, in the case of the Roman Red, unscrew the cap.

First lesson: cork both is and isn't essential to wine. For wines designed to be drunk young, as both of these bottles are, modern bottling techniques can seal a bottle so efficiently that cork closure is not necessary. That screwcap on the Roman Red is keeping its bottle just as airtight as is the cork on the Mondavi Red, perhaps even more

That's a Corker

Cork became the standard stopper for wine somewhere in the late seventeenth or early eighteenth centuries, just about the same time that glassblowing techniques had progressed enough for bottles to become the standard wine containers. Now that technology has made many other materials available for the same purpose, we are starting to see wine in cans (so far unsuccessful—the wine tastes metallic) as well as wine in cartons; various metal and plastic stoppers are also being tried on wine bottles. For the time being, cork has the upper hand. However, right now, there is a big argument among wine professionals about whether the long corks that traditionally seal the finest wines are really the best material for that purpose. Some people swear by cork; because it is slightly porous it allows the wine to breathe and develop over a long period. Others argue that that is exactly what's wrong with cork: any oxygen at all is bad for wine and will eventually kill it. If you want to see what oxygen does for wine, leave a glass of one of these testers out overnight and then taste it: compare your reaction then to the notes you'll be taking in just a few minutes.

One final note: a wine is said to be "corked" or "corky" when it either smells of cork rather than wine, or it smells stale, old, and sour. This is usually the result of oxidation, which in turn can result from a soft or crumbling cork. This is the reason wine stewards make so great a show of presenting you with the cork they have just extracted from your bottle of wine: so that you can see it is sound. In the case of most young wines, this is hardly necessary, since the cork will not have been in the bottle long enough to have deteriorated.

so. The difference, however, lies in the public mind: people associate corks with quality wines, screwcaps with more plebeian drinks. But if you're going to explore the complicated world of wine, the first really serious lesson you should learn is not to be impressed by packaging. A badly made wine in a fancy bottle is just a badly made wine that costs a lot. A well-made wine in a no-frills presentation is often a bargain. Shop for good wine: don't buy glitzy packages and, above all, don't buy labels.

Back to business. Pour a little bit—no more than two ounces, and even one ounce is sufficient—of each wine into a glass. You can always pour more wine if your tasters need it, but most people find this quantity ample. Also, you will want to swirl the wine in your glass, and until you get the knack of that, a smaller amount of wine can spare you quite a few lurid stains.

If you're not sure how much an ounce or two of wine comes to in the glasses you're using, take a standard bar jigger (shot glass to most people), fill it with water, and pour it into one of your wine glasses. That should be 1½ ounces of liquid precisely. If you have lived a life so temperate that you don't own a shot glass, 2 ounces equal ¼ cup equal 4 tablespoons equal 12 teaspoons—and bless you.

Always pour in the same direction, especially if you are tasting several wines or several pairs of wines. Most people find it easier to keep track of their wines if you arrange them like print on a page, moving progressively (or regressively, depending on your point of view) from the left to the right. This is wine advice, not political advice.

Now is the time to put the "infamous s's" to work: see, swirl, sniff, sip, savor, and spit. Celebrate and cerebrate. Those last two are constants.

First see. Look at the color of the wines carefully. It's a good idea if you can contrive a uniform white background to do this best. If you don't mind risking a tablecloth, that would obviously be ideal. Otherwise, you can make do with the sheet of paper on which you will write your comments.

First of all, any wine should look pleasing to the eye. Its color should be bright and clear, and it ought to look somehow lively. This may sound crazy, but a wine that looks dead usually tastes dead. The difference is hard to verbalize but is as apparent to the eye as the difference between a sleeping dog and a dead dog.

Wines that look cloudy or muddy are, if not dead, dying; they will almost certainly be marred by off-flavors. If one of the wines in front of you looks like that, go no farther: return the wine to the dealer and try another bottle.

Of the two wines before you, the first, the Mondavi, is a clear ruby, while the Roman Red is visibly lighter in color, almost strawberryish. Its appearance prompts you to expect it to taste lighter than the Mondavi, while the Mondavi by contrast looks as if it ought to be weightier or fuller, somehow heftier to correspond to its deeper color. As it turns out, although such correlations are by no means guaranteed, they work out often enough so that color can provide a usable clue to the character of the wine in the glass.

The shade of the Mondavi Red, by the way, is pretty close to a textbook example of what wine jargon means by describing a wine as ruby. Remember the shade and the term: both will be getting a lot of use.

A professional taster, in examining the color of a wine, will always tilt the glass to about a 45-degree angle to make a thin lip of wine for the light to pass through. What you look for in that lip is whether the color of the wine is true all the way out to the edge, whether it thins and fades, or whether bands of other colors appear. In more complex wines, those bands of color can be important indicators of the wine's maturity or youth, how fast or how slowly it is developing. For relatively simple wines like Mondavi Red and Roman Red, however, this shading of color is neither apparent nor important. So, if you like, you can practice looking professional—and professionally—by tilting your glass a little and regarding it judiciously. While you're having fun, just don't forget to jot down your notes on the colors you see.

All right, now swirl and smell. Gently rotate the wine in the glass. The idea is simply to get it moving and expose a bit more surface to the air to liberate the aroma. Now really concentrate on what you are doing. Bring the glass close to your nose and take a long, deep whiff, just as if you were savoring the aroma of fresh-baked bread. Put the glass down, think for a few seconds about what you've just smelled, and jot down your impressions right away. Trust your first impressions, even if they seem silly or irrelevant.

If the smell seems fruity, force yourself to be more precise. What kind of fruit? or at least, What color fruit—red like cherries or strawberries? White like pears or bananas? If it smells to you like growing things, what sorts of growing things? Fresh grass? Flowers? A woods after a rain? Herbs? If so, which? Spices? If it smells of earth—wet soil? Dry, dusty soil? Chalk?

Be as detailed as you can, and if you wish, take a few more sniffs—but remember that our noses overload very fast. You've probably noticed that when you first enter a new olfactory environment—a florist shop, say—the scent of flowers forces itself on your attention; then after a minute or so you aren't even aware that the flowers have scent unless you bury your nose among them. That's why your first impressions are so important in analyzing the aroma of a wine.

Don't be embarrassed by anything that occurs to you about the scent of wine. Smelling is not a test—at least not of *you*—and even if it were, there are no wrong answers. What you smell is what you smell, and that is all there is to it. So if one wine smells to you like horse manure and another like maple syrup, just jot those impressions down.

Smelling attentively and analytically does not come easy to us human beings. Because of the relative weakness of our smelling apparatus and our lack of experience in identifying and classifying smells, this is going to be the area where the greatest divergence of opinion—or at least of description—is going to take place.

I say "at least of description" because you may very well discover here that several of you are using different words to say the same thing about the wines or are using the same words to denote different things. The latter case is by far the most confusing aspect of describing wines—or anything else, for that matter.

For instance, if there are four of you, the odds are very strong that at least two will use the word "musty" (it seems to be a popular word among beginning wine tasters) in describing one of these wines' aroma. The odds are also strong that one of you will mean the Mondavi Red and the other the Roman Red. There's an even greater chance that what at least one of you means by "musty" is not the traditional definition of stale or mildewy but something more akin to the smell of overripe fruit, fruit on the verge of fermenting, perhaps combined with a slight smell of earth.

In fact, neither of these wines has a pronounced scent nor a very complicated one, so you've been put very much upon the stretch here. Most people tend to find that both aromas seem to share, in slightly different proportions, elements of earth and of generalized fruit—an unspecific scent that at most leans toward sweet fruits such as berries rather than acid fruits such as apples.

Let me underline that you should not be distressed if what you smelled was nothing like what I just described. Everybody's sense of smell is different. Everybody's way of linking specific smells with specific objects is different. The crucial thing at this stage is smelling atten-tively, thinking about what you're smelling, and thinking about the language you're using to express your thoughts. "Earth" and "fruit" are two very important wine terms, and you are beginning to learn the concepts behind them and to see how what might before today have seemed totally vague to you can have a concrete meaning. That's not bad, considering I haven't even let you taste a wine yet.

Now we're ready. Take a big sip or a small mouthful, with a lot of air. Don't worry about the noises you make. Let the wine flow all over your mouth and tongue, and pay attention to what sensations you are getting from it and where they occur in the mouth. Is there a prickle on the tip of your tongue? Is there astringency (a contracting sensation) at the sides of your tongue or on your cheeks? Are you getting flavor only at the front of your mouth, or at the back, or all over? Finally, what flavor? What does it taste like? Is the flavor similar to the aroma or different? Think of the categories we used: fruit, growing things, earthy flavors. Do any of these fit here?

Don't forget to spit. And don't forget to write down your thoughts.

Now for the great wine instruction heresy: take a bite of food and do the whole thing once more, tasting all over your mouth. Does food change the wine's flavor? If so, how? Once more, be as specific as you can, and make your notes as detailed as possible. Memory is untrustworthy, especially when alcohol is involved.

A few things about the action of these wines on the palate can be stated as fact—which means that about 90 to 95 percent of you ought to agree with them. First, the two wines have a different feel on the tongue. The Mondavi Red feels heavier, bigger somehow, and definitely soft in comparison to the Roman Red, which feels lighter and thinner; some people will even detect a slight spritziness, a sensation as if the wine were the slightest bit carbonated, in the Roman Red. The French call this sensation *pétillant;* Italian wines possessing it are called *frizzante.*

This entire package of weight and feel of the wine is what is meant by the *texture* of a wine. Notice especially that what we are talking about here are tactile sensations: lightness, heaviness, thinness, and softness are what the wines *feel* like on the tongue. They aren't tastes or flavors at all: they're pressures, textures, surface sensations. Taste again if you're not sure of any of this.

If you were really paying attention when you tasted, most of you will have noticed that the preponderance of the taste of the Mondavi Red came on the back and sides of your mouth, while most of the taste of the Roman Red came from the center of the tongue and felt as if it were higher in the mouth than the flavor of the Mondavi. Go back and taste again, if you wish, to see if this isn't so.

The upper edges of the tongue are the primary receptors for sourness, the sides of the tongue for saltiness, the back the primary locus for bitterness, and the tip for sweetness. So the Mondavi Red is making the greatest impact on your sensors that read saltiness and bitterness. The Roman Red, on the other hand, is striking those sensors that pick up sourness, normally in wine a product of acid.

Both wines are by any sane definition dry—that is, wines with no perceptible residual sugar. The sensation of sweetness that different tasters can receive from either wine is purely a function of their differing combinations of fruit and acid, not to mention the hundreds of other "trace elements" that are found in even the simplest wine. Depending on your sensitivity to these different factors, you are going to find the Roman Red anything from bright, light, and lively to thin and astringent, even vinegary, because what you are reacting to is the combination of fruit and acidity in that wine. The taster who finds the Roman Red bright and lively is by the same token likely to find the Mondavi Red flabby and overly fruity, even sweetish, with a different sort of astringency of its own (the result of tannin, which we talk about in a little while). Conversely, tasters who prefer the Mondavi will in all likelihood do so because they find it mouth-filling, smooth, and relatively fruity. For them, the Roman Red may be too light and sour.

Mondavi Table Red wine is produced by the Robert Mondavi Winery, one of California's most innovative and prestigious. It makes sound and often distinguished wine at every level, from simple table wines like this one up to and including prestige varietals.

Roman Red is produced by Villa Banfi, an American importing firm that now has extensive grapegrowing and winemaking operations of its own in Italy. It imports just about every level of Italian wine from simple to complex, from blended table wines like this to fine single-vineyard bottlings.

That ends our first red-wine-tasting session. There are several ways for you to proceed from here.

If you plan to follow the trail of your own preferences through the book, no matter which of these two first wines you liked better, you should at this point proceed straight on through the next three flights,

Chemicals in Wine

Wine, like any other organic product, is a construct of naturally occurring chemical components. Fermentation is not only a natural process but also a chemical operation. Yeasts attack grape sugars, digest them, and convert them into alcohol and several different kinds of acid. A good many other by-products result from both this process and the other components of the grapes themselves. Because of this, there are as many different naturally occurring minerals and chemicals in wines as there are in, say, bread or pickles, and for much the same reasons.

In modern winemaking, science and technology play an increasingly important part at every stage, from protecting the vines from parasites to cultivating selected strains of yeasts, from manipulating the musts (grape liquids resulting from pressing) to bottling the wine in an oxygen-free environment. Most of this leaves little if any trace in the finished wine. The introduced trace element that the wine drinker is most likely to encounter is sulfur dioxide (SO_2), and that most often in white wines, where it is used to discourage wild yeasts and pave the way for the desired strain. Sulfur is also sometimes used to clean wine barrels. Any perceptible level of sulfur in the aroma or especially in the taste of a wine indicates flaws in the winemaking. This is far more likely to occur with white wines than with reds.

in order to equip yourself with some basic tasting categories, concepts, and terms. Otherwise, if you are
Following the wines of the country:

Wine 1, Mondavi Red: go to Flight 3.

Wine 2, Villa Banfi Roman Red: go to Flight 2.

Just for the record, at this point there is no way here to follow any particular grape variety because both these wines are pretty miscellaneous blends. Later on in the book, however, a varietal approach will become possible, and I will give you appropriate directions. Happy trails to you, as Gene Autry used to say.

Red Wines:
The Second Flight

BOLLA VALPOLICELLA 1982
AND
JABOULET "PARALLÈLE 45" CÔTES DU RHÔNE 1982

You're going to taste these two wines, as you will all the others from this point on, exactly as you did the first pair: pour an ounce or two in each glass, look at it carefully to gauge the color and limpidity, swirl it to free the aroma, then smell and assess that, and finally take a good-sized sip, taste attentively, and spit. Take a nibble of food and taste again. Remember to take your notes promptly at each step, because each succeeding sensory stimulus can smudge the clarity of the one that preceded it. You're going to get sick of reading reminders like this before you've finished with this book, but what we are trying to instill here are new—and it is to be hoped permanent—patterns of attention.

The only change you'll make from Flight 1 will be that you'll complete the whole tasting procedure on your own first before coming back to see what the book has to say about the wines. If you are tasting as a group, make sure to discuss among yourselves your responses to these wines before going on to read my comments on them. Try to sort out your terms and clarify as much as humanly possible that you all mean the same things by the same words. For instance, if some of you are using terms such as "tart" or "acidic," are you describing two different things or only one? A dictionary may come in handy to resolve amicable disputes.

Push each other for some details. If you like a wine, why? What is there about it that pleases you? If you describe an odor or a color as lovely or as displeasing, why? What about it appeals or offends? You don't all have to agree about your responses to the wines, but you should all have a good idea of why you are reacting as you do.

If you're ready now, perform the ritual of the "s's" and make all your notes. Take your time: wine tasting is a leisure activity (or so I'm told). After you've made all the comments you want about these two wines, check back here to see what some other people like you have tasted in them.

Appearance. The Valpolicella and the Côtes du Rhône present as sharp a color contrast as did the Mondavi Red and Roman Red (Flight 1). The Rhône wine shows a deep ruby, almost but not quite purplish, while the Valpolicella is a pale red, certainly not pale enough to describe as a rosé, but nearing that; moreover, it has orange or amber highlights or glints. Both wines are limpid and attractively clear.

The differing colors suggest depth and lightness, respectively. Both are characteristic of their kinds of wine—that is, these are exactly the shades that good examples of these kinds of wine ought to show. Let me underline that for you, since people sometimes think that the Valpolicella's relative paleness or (less often) the Rhône's relative depth of color indicates a poorly made wine, either watery on one hand or coarse on the other. Not so; a Valpolicella is always lightly colored and a Rhône always deeply colored because of the vastly different grapes from which they are made. A Valpolicella as dark as the Rhône or a Côtes du Rhône as light as the Valpolicella would be wines to worry about, but these two are right as they are.

Aroma. The Valpolicella's aroma will strike most people as light and evanescent: little hints of fruit, perhaps of mint, but delicate and not persistent. The Rhône, on the other hand, has a markedly stronger aroma, with some depth to it. It will suggest to most tasters things in the spicy, peppery, sweet-fruit range—at the extremes, perhaps raisin or a more vegetable smell. Many tasters will be surprised that the aroma is not as big as the color of the wine led them to expect.

Once again, as with the colors, these aromas are perfectly typical of these kinds of wine. Different vintages might yield some variations in strength of aroma (this particular Valpolicella strikes me as near the bottom edge of its lightness scale), but the general polarity of delicacy vs. strength that these two wines illustrate will persist.

Taste. This pair of wines offers a case study in the deceptiveness of appearances. From looking at the wines, you would expect the Valpolicella to be very light, with little to it, and the Rhône by the same criterion to be a powerhouse. In fact, the Valpolicella strikes most palates as more substantial, and the Rhône less blockbusterish, than appearances suggest.

The Valpolicella *is* light, but it does show some fruit and plenty of bright acid. How do I know that? By its effects: it's the acid that makes it feel so lively on the tongue. Try to log that piece of information in your palatal record book. It's important, since that function of acidity goes a long way to determining the character and style of a wine, especially a not-very-complex one like this Valpolicella.

Other elements in its flavor? Well, if you concentrate really hard, you may even discern hints of something like cherry in it, but nothing much more specific than that—just a general fresh-and-fruity flavor. All in all, most tasters would describe it as a pleasant, very light wine, small-bodied and straightforward.

The Rhône, on the other hand, does not deliver the big-bodied wine its color and aroma lead many tasters to expect. What you do get is mouth-filling enough but very soft in texture. There is some fully dry fruit and an astringency, most apparent in the almost bitter finish (the finish, remember, is the taste that persists in your mouth after you have spit out or swallowed the wine).

That astringency is almost certainly due to *tannin,* a substance that enters wines both from the grapeskins themselves and from wooden (especially oak) barrels, where it occurs naturally. Consequently, you'll come across tannin far more frequently in the flavor of barrel-aged red wines than in white wines, which are normally vinified in stainless steel without any skins in the musts (musts being the grape liquids resulting from pressing). We'll be talking a lot more about tannin, so take note of that astringent sensation in the finish and log it in your memory.

Tannin usually makes itself felt in the mouth by a drying, puckery sensation on the cheeks and/or a raspy sensation on the tongue and throat, neither of which—despite what that description sounds like—is always unpleasant. Tannin's taste in the purest form is reminiscent of that of overstrong or oversteeped tea, or the bitterness you get from biting into a raw acorn. You rarely find it that concentrated in any wine, but even lesser degrees of tannin can make themselves felt quite forcefully there.

Tannin is crucial in wines of any pretensions to greatness because it is one of the key elements that promote long life. Consequently, balance and harmony are also quite crucial to the success of any such wines; otherwise we would have undying tannin monsters roaming the shelves of our wineshops.

Tannin enters wine from the grapes themselves (particularly from their skins, where it occurs in widely varying concentrations according to grape variety) and from the barrels the wine is fermented and/or stored in, especially from new oak barrels. So wine makers can control, with some degree of precision, the amount of tannin presence they want to achieve in their wine by altering the containers in which that wine is fermented, stored, or aged.

For beginning tasters, the effects of tannin sometimes are difficult to distinguish from the effects of acid. Consequently, it is possible to confuse the two different sets of flavors of these wines. You experience acid as a prickly sensation, usually pleasant, and almost always all over the tongue, as if thousands of little carbonation bubbles were gently scratching it. You feel the effect of tannin as a distinctly puckering or astringent sensation, definitely unpleasant when strong. It occurs mostly on the cheeks and, to a lesser extent, at the side of the tongue.

Despite the fact that they are very different sensations, some people may experience the fruit and acid of the Valpolicella and the fruit and tannin of the Côtes du Rhône as almost the same thing. Consequently, they may describe these two wines as only slightly different versions of each other, or they may describe the Rhône as being like the Valpolicella, only more so. Don't worry if you've done this: it doesn't mean your wine-tasting career is already over. As you get more practice tasting wines, you'll start to make that distinction a lot more sharply. You'll very quickly be able to feel the difference between the drying effect of tannin and the enlivening effect of acid on your mouth. Then all you'll have to learn is how to differentiate more exactly among kinds of fruit.

Fruit is a difficult but absolutely crucial wine term. After all, all wine is made from fruit and inevitably, unless Better Living Through Chemistry has intervened, all wine must taste of fruit. But different varieties of grapes have different flavors to start with: even humble table grapes such as Concord and Thompson Seedless can show you that. The highly bred varietals that go into fine wines are even more distinctive, and the whole process of vinification and aging—especially barrel aging—can accentuate or modify, blend or isolate those differences. Grape juice always tastes like a grape; wine can taste like the whole range of fruits and many other substances as well.

So what do wine people mean when they talk about fruit? Fair question.

First, they most commonly and most generally do not mean a specific fruit, and emphatically not grapes. To call a wine grapey is often an insult: it implies a kind of excessive simplicity, even coarseness.

When wine professionals say of a young wine, as we have said of the Valpolicella and the Rhône in this pair, that "it has fruit," they mean first to compliment the wine, second to denote a quality of freshness and refreshingness, often linked with the presence of a kind of sweetness without sugar, that almost immediately calls to mind for most people a loose and unspecific idea of fruitiness.

Probably the most graphic way to describe what they mean is to remind you of the way you think of a nice, juicy piece of fruit on a blistering hot summer day. You may not even have in mind a specific kind of fruit, just a broad idea of succulence, moisture, pleasing flavor, and refreshment. That's the ideal that wine professionals are referring to when they describe wines as having a lot or a little fruit. Above all, fruit is those elements in a wine that convey to our palates and our imaginations the sensations and ideas of freshness and vitality. That is the most important meaning of fruit in wine jargon, and I think you can see how it is possible for one wine to have more or less fruit than another, or more or less vivid fruit.

Beyond that basic notion, you enter on greater complexities, because as your taste buds get sharper and your experience broader, the wines you're going to taste in the course of this book are going to get more complicated, and you will begin to be able to discern in some of our examples not simply fruit but also classes of fruit and even, perhaps, individual kinds of fruit.

In fact, the second most important use of the concept of fruit in talking about wines lies in the broad distinction between flavors that align themselves with the red fruits such as berries and cherries and those that align themselves with the white fruits such as pears, apples, and, at an extreme, bananas.

Lest you think that all this is so much hokum, remind yourself about what you already know that is just like it. Macintoshes and Winesaps and Golden Delicious and Greenings can't be mistaken for one another, but you wouldn't take them for anything but apples, either. A Green-gage and an Eldorado taste very different from each other, but both taste of fruit and both taste like plums. You can already recognize sameness and differences within the general flavor of classes of fruits: all you have to do now is transfer that ability to wine flavors.

In the two wines of this second flight I think you can readily distinguish two very different "tonalities" of fruit (I put that word in quotation marks because I'm using it loosely at the moment: it's not a conventional wine term). By that I mean that the fruit present in the Valpolicella is not simply more delicate or less pronounced than the fruit in the Côtes du Rhône but that it strikes the palate as if it were in a higher register than that of the Rhône: tenor, or perhaps even soprano, to the latter's baritone.

I know, I know: this kind of language is going to drive you crazy. You think it's the worst thing about wine, and you're right. The sad truth is, however, that that kind of language is unavoidable: we are talking here about personal perceptions that have so far resisted scientific measure-ment. No one has yet found a way to quantify what goes on in our mouths or our minds when we taste something. The French—who else?—are working on the problem, but until they come up with a solution, we are stuck with the imprecision of language. We are essen-tially driven to metaphors and figures of speech to try to convey the varying shades of what we perceive. It needs goodwill and an effort at understanding on everybody's part to make it all work.

Besides, would it really help if I could tell you that Wine A was 5.4 on a salinity scale and 3.2 pH, while Wine B was only 4.7 and 3.1, respectively?

After all that palatal palaver, here are a few facts about these two wines to balance against all this subjectivity.

Valpolicella is made from about three varieties of grapes grown in a hilly area near Verona in north-central Italy. Valpolicella should be drunk as young as possible, and specimens over four years old can be dead if they have not been stored very well. Generally speaking, it's wise to drink Valpolicella before its third birthday. In Italy it is often served chilled, not iced. Bolla is one of the largest and most reliable shippers of Valpolicella and other Veronese wines to the United States. Its wines are imported by The Jos. Garneau Co.

"Parallèle 45" is the Jaboulet firm's proprietary name for their Côtes du Rhône wine. The area in which the several varieties of grapes for this

Barolo/Barbaresco

• Milan

VENETO

• Turin

PIEDMONT

Po River

Venice

**FRIULI-
VENEZIA-
GIULIA**

ADRIATIC SEA

Chianti

Florence
•

TUSCANY

• Rome

MEDITERRANEAN SEA

Naples
•

CAMPANIA

ITALY

wine are grown lies along both banks of the River Rhône in southern France. Simple Rhône wines like this usually are pleasant to drink, with a straightforward, robust style, and they often offer very good value. Jaboulet is one of the largest and most important wine makers and wine dealers in the Rhône area. Its wines are imported to the United States by Frederick Wildman.

Valpolicella and Côtes du Rhône are both usually described as "fruity" wines, in case you needed further proof how one wine term can cover a multitude of *vins*.

You're probably thinking that this has been an awfully long discussion of the flavor components of what you thought of as only two simple, enjoyable wines. You're right. It was a very long discussion, but it's worth every word, because even though you may not have realized it at the moment, you have just acquired the essential key to understanding red wine. Congratulations.

What do you mean? What is it?

I told you. Tannin, acid, fruit. Fruit, acid, tannin. Acid, tannin, fruit.

That's it?

That's it. From the taster's point of view, tannin, acid, and fruit are the basic building blocks of dry red wine, just as you will find later that acid, fruit, and sugar serve the same function for tasters of white wine. The nature and relative proportions of tannin and acid and fruit will account for most of the distinctive flavors of the whole world of red wine. At the very least, that trio of elements will explain the large differences among the major kinds of red wine. They can describe, for example, the differences among wines made from the same kind of grapes located in different parts of the world. So from here on, every red wine tasting you do is going to force you, to one degree or another, to consider the relations of tannin, acid, and fruit in each wine.

As I said before, congratulations: you're well on your way to knowing wine.

This is the conclusion of our second red-wine-tasting session. To increase your basic wine knowledge and armory of tools, it would be best to go right on to the next flight. However, should you choose otherwise, there are several ways for you to proceed from here.

Following the lead of your own preferences:

If you liked the first wine better, Bolla Valpolicella, go to Flight 3.

If you liked the second wine better, Jaboulet "Parallèle 45" Côtes du Rhône, go to Flight 4.

Following the kind of grapes:
Go to Flight 19.
Following the wines of the country:
Wine 1: go to Flight 4.
Wine 2: go to Flight 3.

Red Wines:
The Third Flight

JADOT BEAUJOLAIS 1983
AND
PAUL MASSON CALIFORNIA ZINFANDEL 1983

Here again are two wines frequently described as fruity, so be prepared to compare them in those terms. With all of these pairs of wines, it is good strategy to seek those ways in which they are alike as well as the elements that distinguish them from each other. Since we don't have any sort of objective measurements, we've got to construct a makeshift set of yardsticks from the ideas of sameness and difference. Every new wine you learn and every new wine element you recognize extend that ruler a fraction of an inch. By the time you finish this book, you should have built your own private yardstick for measuring what you like in a wine.

Are you ready? Perform the ritual: see, swirl, smell, sip, savor, and spit.

And take notes. And talk it over. And then read on.

Appearance. Once more, we have sharp color contrasts between the two wines. Both wines, however, should be equally clear and bright, with no trace of muddiness. The Beaujolais shows a very pale ruby, really a light cherry red, almost soda-pop-looking, though definitely not as pale as a rosé. In fact, although it can appear almost faded alongside the deep ruby of the Zinfandel, this bright, clean, lively-looking wine has a fine, deep color for a Beaujolais: 1983 was an exceptionally good vintage, and its wines are more marked in every respect than Beaujolais usually are. That very dark shade of red, almost moving into purple, that you see in the Zinfandel is quite a characteristic color for that wine. The Zinfandel is a very robust grape that makes an exceptionally deeply dyed young wine.

Aroma. With these two wines, you should be able to start making some more elaborate distinctions among aromas. Both of their bouquets ought to suggest to you a pretty large assortment of components.

After you finished your visual survey, you were probably surprised that the Beaujolais had so big an aroma: it is no pantywaist wine, despite its lighter color. Most people perceive it as, in effect, *tutti frutti:* a medium-strong, distinctly fruity aroma, all ripe cherries and berries (some tasters discern apples, too). Many people pick up a pleasing earthy or stemmy undertone and a small scent of pepper as well. This is a classic Beaujolais aroma, and most tasters love it, though a few find it too soda-poppy for their pleasure.

Most people will describe the aroma of the Zinfandel as a combination of alcohol (perceived as a kind of headiness or warmth), fruit (perceived as intensely ripe grapes), spice (cinnamon, nutmeg, pepper), and earthy odors, with one or another of these predominating. Usually, for the majority of tasters, the fruit takes charge, and what they smell, though they may use differing terms to describe it, is the brambly, berryish scent that distinguishes this style of Zinfandel from almost every other wine. Overall, this particular Zinfandel has an aroma that can technically be called full, forthcoming, and absolutely characteristic of the grape variety—in other words, this, too, is a classic varietal aroma.

While most of you probably will agree about what's in the aroma, you'll no doubt disagree sharply over whether it is pleasant. It is not hard to get a consensus on the description of the aromas of these two wines, but in both cases the house divides on the question of whether they are attractive—which is a very nice illustration, if you needed one, of the limits of objective measurements of wine and the importance of plain, old-fashioned personal taste.

Varietal Is the Spice of Life

Varietal is a key word—and an overworked one—in wine jargon. Its usage derives, obviously, from a grape variety, but in wine circles it is used primarily in connection with the prestige grapes, the so-called noble varietals of Vitis vinifera (*the European wine grape as opposed to the native American Vitis* labrusca).

Important red varietals include Cabernet Sauvignon, Merlot, Pinot Noir (*all three cultivated in both France and California*), Zinfandel (*California*), and Sangiovese and Nebbiolo (*Italy*). Major white varietals include Chardonnay (*almost everywhere in the world, but especially France and California*), Riesling (*Germany, France, and California*), Sauvignon Blanc (*France, California, and Italy*), and Gewurztraminer (*France, Germany, and California*). The finest wines of California usually are varietal wines, meaning that they bear the name of the grape that (by law) makes up at least 75 percent of their contents.

Varietal character refers to the total package of sensations—aroma, taste, feel—produced by a noble grape varietal. This remains to some degree the same in any wine made from the grape, but it can vary in intensity, and it can be manipulated by growing practices and techniques of vinification. Consequently, varietal character, varietal intensity, and fidelity to varietal become important considerations in professional evaluations of, for example, California Chardonnay and white Burgundy (made with Chardonnay).

In case you're wondering: yes, it is certainly conceivable that someone might find a wine pleasing to drink but a terrible version of the varietal, and vice versa.

Okay, now for the taste test.

First let's talk about fruit in these two wines. In the Beaujolais, you will probably taste a bit less fruit than the aroma led you to expect: most people react that way. The fruit is still ample, however, flavorful and round and definitely falling into that cherry/berry range (most tasters probably will call it strawberries).

The Zinfandel, on the other hand, has almost a superabundance of fruit: it strikes most people as full, soft, deep, and very fresh. And most tasters have no trouble pinning it down to a specific fruit: they taste a distinctly spicy blackberry flavor in the wine, accompanied by what you have to describe as a kind of pleasant scratching sensation on the tongue. Both these flavors are characteristic of these kinds of wine.

What you are perceiving here, in whatever terms you may be using to describe it, is both varietal flavor and varietal intensity. The basic difference in the tastes of these two wines is directly traceable to the grapes from which they are made, the Gamay and the Zinfandel. Varietal flavor is a constant in varietal wines: that Gamay flavor will persist in all well-made Beaujolais, just as the basic Zinfandel flavor will persist in all decently produced Zinfandel wines.

On the other hand, the differences between the freshness of this Beaujolais and the force of this Zinfandel show what is meant by their degree of varietal intensity, and that is a variable that can be affected dramatically by the conditions of the harvest and of the wine's vinification. You'll have to take my word for it, but the degree of varietal intensity a wine possesses can make a great deal of difference in your appreciation of it: a more intense Beaujolais (though that is hard to imagine, for this is a big one) and a less intense Zinfandel (much easier to imagine) might be very difficult for you to distinguish at this stage of your wine apprenticeship.

In fact, this whole distinction may not be as simple for you to perceive as I have been assuming, since in these two wines you don't taste the fruit by itself. It doesn't come to you in isolation, but rather is surrounded by other components of the wines that modify the intensity of the fruit and the way it strikes you. To talk about this at all, we've got to artificially select out elements one at a time and look at them in sequence, but when you actually taste the wine, you get them all at once.

One of the major elements in a wine that alters the way you taste its fruit is acid. There are, of course, all sorts of acids in the world, many of them not so pleasant. The ones that occur naturally in wine—and they are numerous—mostly tend to contribute to the liveliness of the wine. Acid makes a wine taste fresh, gives it a little lift, lets the fruit sing.

In the case of the two wines we're dealing with here, the Beaujolais has a lot of acid; that's why it tastes so bright. Fortunately, there is enough fruit there to sustain all that acid, so the wine doesn't taste thin or insubstantial. The only sign that the acid may be a little excessive is a slight tingling sensation, as if the wine were nearly *pétillant*. In all fairness, I have to say that many Beaujolais fans find that quality very attractive and not a defect.

If the Zinfandel is at all unbalanced, it is in the opposite direction: too much fruit for its acid to carry, which makes for a certain limpness or flabbiness in the wine. Again, this is my palate speaking. For many tasters, a lot of softness in a wine like this can be as big an attraction as an acid tingle in the Beaujolais. The sensation it creates on the tongue for them is soft but round and live.

Round in wine language means two similar things: the way a wine tastes and the way it feels on the tongue. In both cases, smoothness is the key: the wine doesn't feel sharp, no single flavor component sticks out. If other important qualities are also present, the overall impression a round wine makes is completeness and harmony—not necessarily richness or fullness, though those may be present also. If other key qualities are absent or insufficient, a round wine may taste merely bland or excessively soft.

Whether they like it or not, however, most tasters will agree that the Zinfandel's softness stands out, especially in comparison to the Beaujolais.

This is true despite the fact that the Zinfandel is what we call a heavy wine. Try it again; you'll see what I mean. The Zinfandel feels as if it weighs more on the tongue than does the Beaujolais. That is the effect of, among some other lesser elements, alcohol, and it is this sensation that is usually meant by the term *body*. So if you were going to convey some of the characteristics of these two wines succinctly and technically, you would describe the Beaujolais as fruity and acidic, with a medium body, and the Zinfandel as relatively full-bodied, soft, and markedly fruity.

A final word about body: even though the major component of body is alcohol, all of the other elements of the wine also contribute. A high-alcohol wine with little fruit and little acid would not strike you as a big, full-bodied wine; you would taste it as harsh and biting. It is for reasons like this that concepts like harmony and balance are so important in talking about fine wines—and they obviously become increasingly crucial as the wines you taste possess more and more elements that need to be harmonized.

You're coming along just fine, and you should take a minute here to think about what you've done so far. Already, in only our third pair of wines, you've gotten to the point where you've dealt at least once with fruit and acid and tannin and body and texture and finish, and I've just taken it for granted that you can taste dryness or sweetness. Even in wines as relatively simple and straightforward as this Beaujolais and this Zinfandel (and these are regarded as very simple wines, wines a professional would not ordinarily subject to the kind of close analysis you've just done) you've had to deal with the interplay of several of these components.

Your preference, in a pair of wines such as this, is going to depend on subjective factors—for example, whether the vivacity of the Beaujolais pleases your palate more than the bigger, more abundant fruit of the Zinfandel. That kind of information about yourself, as you gradually accumulate it through this series of tastings, is what is going to help you to define your own taste and select the kind of wines that are going to give you pleasure. It can also, if you let it, show you what the limits of your taste are at present so that you can expand them if you wish to. No one ever pitched at ninety-nine miles an hour the first time he or she threw a baseball; practice strengthens your palate just as surely as it does your arm.

If you found something lacking in both wines in this flight, that doesn't mean there's anything wrong with your taste; on the contrary. Taking a very hard-nosed view of them, both the Beaujolais and the Zinfandel, for all their pleasantness, are one-dimensional wines—fruit is really all there is to them. That's just about all you really should be looking for in wines of this class, but that doesn't mean that that is all wine has to offer, nor is it all you have to settle for. The world of wine offers a great variety of attractions, and the honest pleasures that these wines afford are a starting point from which you can move as far afield as you wish.

The important thing about these and all wines is not to criticize them for what they lack but to enjoy them for what they have to offer. These are simple, unpretentious wines to drink with simple, light foods; they are not wines to make a fuss about or use to show off your newfound expertise.

For your information and files, here are some data on these two kinds of wines.

Beaujolais is one of the most popular wines in the world. It is produced in south-central France, between the southern end of the Burgundy region of great wines and the city of Lyon. It is made from the Gamay grape, which is also grown in California.

Beaujolais is so widely enjoyed because it is a simple, straightforward wine, light, fresh, and modestly fruity. An even lighter version now enjoys great popularity (even though many red-wine drinkers—myself, alas, included—find it too soda-poppy for their taste): that is what is called Beaujolais *nouveau* or Beaujolais *primeur*, which is rushed to market with great fanfare every November. This is the first wine of that fall's harvest, and it is always very light and often distinctly *pétillant*—lightly fizzy. The house of Jadot is a major Burgundian *négociant* and one of the foremost shippers of quality Beaujolais.

Those latter two French terms are in wide use among wine people—*négociant* because there really isn't an English word that quite expresses the combination of wine-related activities a firm such as Jadot is involved in (they are growers and buyers of grapes, and makers, buyers, blenders, and sellers of wine), and *pétillant* because it sounds much more sophisticated than fizzy. Fizz is what kids' drinks do.

Zinfandel comes close to being a native American wine grape. Certainly the wine it produces is unique to California, and the grape's origins are obscure enough (current theory holds the vine is related to the Italian Primativo from Puglia) that it can be regarded as an American classic.

This is a hearty grape that makes all sorts of wine, from a simple, fruity, picnicky style up to the level of estate-bottled, complex wines for long aging. What we have here, as indicated by its simple California appellation, is a Zinfandel blended from grapes grown in several counties of California and showing only hints of the provocative varietal flavor that specimens from the best growing areas can achieve.

Paul Masson is one of several divisions of The Seagram Wine Company's wine interests. Masson makes California wines at several levels of distinction, from generics through popular varietals such as this one up to good limited-production varietals released under its Pinnacles Selections label. Generic wine is a term used to describe those American wines sold under European or pseudo-European names other than the names of grape varieties—for example, Burgundy and Chablis, which have nothing in common with the wines that come from the region of Burgundy or the town of Chablis.

Here, at last, ends our third red-wine-tasting session. Pour yourself a drink; you've worked hard. If you intend to follow the trail of your own preferences through this book, you'd be well advised at this point to go straight to Flight 4—the last training flight—and begin your preferring there. Nevertheless, there are several other ways for you to proceed from here.

Following the lead of your own preferences:

If you liked the first wine better, Jadot Beaujolais, go to Flight 7.

If you liked the second wine better, Masson Zinfandel, go to Flight 5.

Following the kind of grapes:

The first wine: go to Flight 7.

The second wine: go to Flight 17.

Following the wines of the country:

The first wine: go to Flight 4.

The second wine: go to Flight 5.

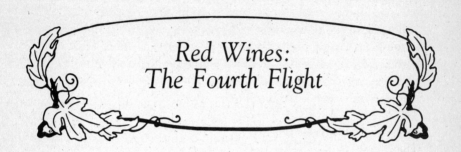

Red Wines:
The Fourth Flight

VALBON ROUGE NV
AND
RUFFINO CHIANTI CLASSICO 1983

One of the wines in this pair is a nonvintage bottling, the second such you will have had so far. If you have not finished the wines from previous tastings, you might learn something further by tasting the two together—Valbon Rouge from this pair and Villa Banfi Roman Red from the first.

Alternatively, you might try blind-tasting them and two of your vintage bottles to see if you can taste any difference among them. To do that, simply wrap each bottle tightly in a brown paper bag right up to the lip (or better yet, have somebody else do that), number the bags, pour, and taste. Don't unveil until each person has cast a ballot for each sampling. It can be fun, instructive, and often surprising, especially if you have exaggerated notions about vintage. But we'll talk more about that after you taste this pair.

Ready? Proceed through all of the "s's" as before, trying to remember and utilize everything we've said so far. Bear in mind those categories we've touched on: fruit, acid, tannin, alcohol, body, texture, and balance. Don't feel you have to mention—or even experience—every one of them with every wine, but have them ready as usable categories if you need them. Above all, concentrate on what is in your eyes and nose and mouth.

After as many of you as are tasting together have said your piece about these two wines, read on. (I hope by now you see the value of your talking out your own responses to these wines before you read what I have to say. It's too easy to be bullied by the printed word into thinking you tasted things you didn't. People need to develop greater skepticism about what they read. That *is* political advice.)

Appearance. In color the Valbon Rouge and the Ruffino Chianti Classico are very similar. Both are essentially a medium ruby, with the Chianti perhaps showing a few amber or tawny highlights.

Those amber highlights, by the way, are typical of many Italian wines, and in some of the best Chiantis and Barolos and similar wines the tawniness increases markedly with bottle-aging, so that it is often a good indication of maturity in those wines. In many French or California wines, on the other hand, a heavy amber tone often indicates that the wine is over the hill.

Aroma. Most tasters will get a definite scent of alcohol, almost a rush, from the Valbon. Some will say it smells warm, or hot: what they will in all probability be referring to is the alcohol. This doesn't mean that this is a particularly strong wine, simply that the other elements are sufficiently subdued that the alcohol shows strongly. The aroma is in any event a light one, with some slight "sweetish" (as most people describe them) elements and a subdued but definite scent of fruit. The Chianti, too, has a light aroma but a bit more intense and drier-smelling than the Valbon—many people find the Chianti's odor reminiscent of freshly cut stems and twigs. Some people may also detect slight suggestions of tobacco in it.

Taste. In flavor, the Valbon is what I would call a mannerly wine. It's not very assertive, and you taste it more as a blending of components than any single thing. There is some fruit, some tannin, some acid, and they all seem to get along quite nicely. The wine gives the impression that it was blended to fit unobtrusively into as many niches as possible, to accompany almost any kind of food. Smoothness and roundness are its major characteristics, and in that respect it is a distant echo of the great Burgundies that are its inspiration.

The Ruffino, too, offers itself in a rather understated way. It is nicely balanced, and it shows both a bit more fresh fruit than the Valbon (many people may even pick up a suggestion of cherries) and a bit more acid to bring the fruit to the fore—discreetly. You may feel on your tongue a slight prickly sensation; this usually results from an abundance of acid or tannin. The Valbon feels fuller and strikes the taster as a single flavor. This Chianti seems smaller-bodied but more complicated: you taste more different elements in its flavor. To differentiate it firmly from the Valbon, I would describe it as drier and more acid and brisk, not as full, and a touch more austere and more complex. In these respects it, too, echoes its nobler relatives the older Chianti Classico Riservas.

Valbon is made by Bouchard Père et Fils, a major Burgundian firm whose wines are distributed in the United States by The International Vintage Wine Company. The Ruffino firm makes a complete range of fine Chiantis as well as other wines. Schieffelin distributes its products in the United States.

With this pair of wines, you have embarked on a whole new path in this book. (Rotten trick, isn't it, just when you thought you were finding your way around?)

Up to this point, the pairs of wines I've been presenting to you were chosen for contrast, so that differences would stand out with some clarity. With this pair, you've begun to taste wines that possess some affinities to each other and a subtler range of differences that have to be talked about less in terms of stark contrasts (This wine has guts and that one's a wimp) and more in terms of degree (This wine has less fruit than that, but it is fuller and seems more balanced). It's less dramatic, and it means you're going to have to work harder—but you're also, from this point on, going to have increasingly more to work with. This does not mean I'm demeaning the wines you've tasted thus far—no one should ever condescend to a well-made wine, no matter how simple—but I am saying that the real fun is just beginning.

Before we go too far down this new garden path, however, we ought to talk a bit about vintage and what it means. The labels you are looking at illustrate the basic dichotomy, vintage-dated bottlings and nonvintage (almost always abbreviated nv). The Valbon Rouge is not vintage-dated. That means that it is probably blended from more than one vintage in much the same way as it is blended from grapes from

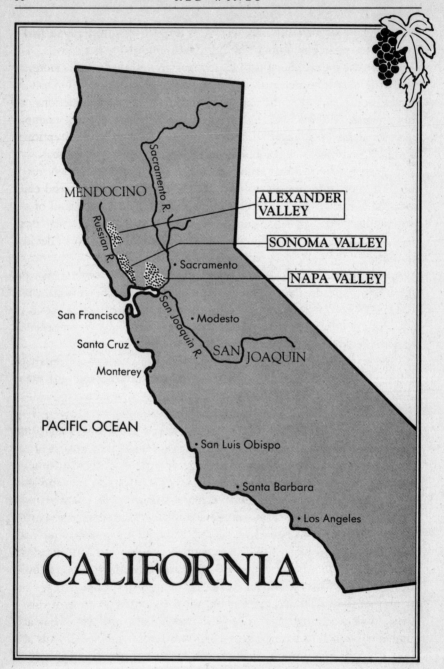

MENDOCINO

Sacramento R.

Russian R.

ALEXANDER VALLEY

SONOMA VALLEY

• Sacramento

NAPA VALLEY

San Joaquin R.

San Francisco

• Modesto

Santa Cruz

SAN JOAQUIN

Monterey

PACIFIC OCEAN

• San Luis Obispo

• Santa Barbara

• Los Angeles

CALIFORNIA

more than one growing area. At very least it means that the maker wanted to retain that option. Why? Lots of reasons.

Before the big wine boom in California, for instance, it was more the exception than the norm to vintage California wine, and old habits die hard. (Sometimes they don't die, but then we call them traditions and honor them without question.) In Champagne, as another example, nonvintage bottlings still are the norm and vintage dating the exception—and no one regards Champagne as any the less prestigious for that.

There are sound economic reasons not to vintage: you are then free to use one year's big crop to eke out another year's small one. And crops vary from year to year not only in size but also in quality in all of the world's fine-wine areas—even in California, despite the popular delusion that the sun always shines there. For the wine maker, it's a decided advantage to be able to prop up an ailing vintage with a hearty one.

And then there are the intangibles: things such as house style, and the sense of the market, and the desire to make accessible wines or affordable wines. This is the area where economics and family pride, a sense of public spirit and the long-range hope of developing a market go hand in hand.

California is the example closest to home. Many very reputable California wine firms adopted vintage dating reluctantly, and many continue to make nonvintage wine as well. Blending different vintages enables them to produce a wine—a house wine almost—that will be consistent in taste and style and quality bottle after bottle, year after year. It enables them to make a wine that could be the equivalent of the table wine you would have drunk almost every day had you grown up in that small town in a winegrowing country that we spoke of at the start of this book. And it enables them to make wine at an affordable price so you can drink it every day if you wish. Valbon and Roman Red are such wines, wines like those served in carafes in little restaurants all over France and Italy, wines about which you would never dream of asking the vintage. Even if you did, odds are the restaurateur, perhaps even the maker, wouldn't know for sure.

Obviously, the reason for making such a wine is not pure altruism: these firms are strongly hoping you *will* drink such wines every day and that it will teach you the custom of taking wine with all your meals and that you will in the long run turn into a regular customer not only of their simple wines but also of their more complex, more costly ones as well—in short, that you will become something between a fan and a connoisseur. (Heartless wretch that you are, you have probably never spared a single moment's thought for the hundreds of thousands of wine makers around the world who go to bed every night piously praying for your increased sophistication.)

So much for nonvintage; what, then, is the point of vintage dating? The answer is simple: uniqueness, and the variety that comes with it. Each vintage is different; this means you have to take your chances on some disasters, but your highs can be very, very high indeed.

Vintage, in fact, increases in importance according to the potential of the grape varieties you are dealing with and the capacity of the soil you are growing them on. Vintage matters most when you have a combination of noble grapes and great vineyard, and from there on down the scale it matters less and less as grapes and vineyards decline in quality. Naturally, a great harvest can make even normally mediocre wine very pleasant indeed, just as a miserable harvest can make normally superior wine very mediocre. But under average circumstances, vintage becomes a serious consideration only when you are dealing with a very limited number of fine grape varieties growing in a very limited number of environments: Napa, Sonoma, Monterey, and a few other choice locales in California, some spots in Washington and Oregon and New York, Bordeaux, Burgundy, Champagne, Alsace, and the Rhône in France, Piedmont and Tuscany and a few other areas in Italy, Rioja in Spain, the Rhine Valley in Germany; those are close to all the truly noble wine-growing zones in the world. With Central Valley Zinfandel and Algerian Cabernet, vintage is not a serious consideration.

From here on you will be dealing with wines of a caliber wherein vintage becomes an increasingly important factor. I have specified vintages throughout this book; wherever possible, try to get the exact vintage I name. I try in the Appendix to indicate reasonable substitutes (either alternate vintages or sometimes wholly different wines) that will approximate the package of qualities I'm trying to show you.

The vintages I select will not always be the top-ranked, 20-out-of-20 best: sometimes the typical is going to be more useful for us than the stratospheric. Sometimes I will have gotten cold feet about asking you to spend as much money as a really terrific vintage would cost. And sometimes we'll just have to work with what is available in the marketplace—there would be very little point in my talking about a wine none of you could find.

So you're going to be getting a very mixed bag of vintages in the wines that follow, and I wanted to let you know that so none of you thinks that the fact of a wine's appearance in this book automatically means it is superb. Some of them are, some of them aren't. Besides, if I told you they all were, or all the odd-numbered ones were, you'd then feel obliged to admire them whether you really liked them or not. Be prepared to hate some wines that the rest of the world calls great and to love some wines everybody else thinks very ordinary. Remember, you drink only with your own mouth.

This is the conclusion of our fourth red-wine-tasting session. There are several ways for you to proceed from here.

Following the lead of your own preferences:

If you liked the first wine better, Valbon Rouge, go to Flight 6.

If you liked the second wine better, Ruffino Chianti Classico, go to Flight 5.

Following the kind of grapes:

Wine 1: this is a very miscellaneous blend; try either Flight 7 or Flight 12.

Wine 2: go to Flight 14.

Following the wines of the country:

Wine 1: go to Flight 6.

Wine 2: go to Flight 9.

Excelsior.

KNIGHT'S GAMBIT

Red Wines:
The Fifth Flight

FEDERICO PATERNINA "BANDA AZUL" RIOJA 1981
AND
ALMADÉN SAN BENITO GAMAY BEAUJOLAIS 1982

Here is your chance to see what happens to a little French immigrant in California: the Gamay Beaujolais, whether or not it is the same grape from which the French Beaujolais is made, has at least been definitely identified as French in origin. Rioja is the name both of one of Spain's most important wine-producing regions and of the wine made there.

Once more into the breach, dear meanies: see, swirl, smell, sip, savor, spit, take notes, and talk it over. Remember to concentrate particularly on the aroma, since that is the sense function we normally exercise least: with practice you can wind up with an Arnold Schwarzenegger-class smelling apparatus.

Appearance. The Rioja shows a typical distinct ruby, perhaps a little pale, but very clean and bright. This is just about middle of the range for Rioja: you will see a few lighter or darker, and in this kind of wine at least those shadings of color usually will be good indications of the wine's body—that is, lighter color usually comes with lighter body in Rioja reds.

The Gamay is much paler, edging up to strawberry but not quite moving into the rosé range. This is a bit lighter than normal for wines of its type. You will find many California Gamays of a more pronounced ruby than this.

Aroma. The Rioja offers a good, strong, but not overpowering aroma. It gives a pronounced suggestion of earth and oak, a tannic scent that some tasters may liken to the smell of cold tea and others may describe as a mix of earth and pepper. Fruit, dry and ripe, emerges for most people well underneath those heavier scents. There is a warm alcoholic strand in the aroma, too, and some tasters may feel a slight alcohol tingle in their noses. Overall, this is a very representative set of Rioja characteristics. Most tasters respond very favorably to it. Those who don't like it usually call it too strong or rubbery-smelling.

A lot of the oaky, tannic odors derive from the wooden barrels the wine ages in. Barrel oak is most commonly perceived in a wine's bouquet as whiffs of caramel or vanilla; some tasters discern those scents in this wine, and some do not. Naturally, the longer the wine is aged in oak, and the smaller the barrels, the more effect the wood will have on both the aroma and the taste of the wine when it is finally bottled. We're going to have plenty of chance later to talk about wood and what it does to wine.

In comparison to the Rioja, the Gamay has a smaller aroma but a much fruitier one. Most people immediately spot acidic red fruit in it, and alcohol, and then far behind, a bunching of light floral or shrubby scents. This is not at all a big aroma, but it is distinctly fresh and clean. Some will describe it as sprightly and find it very attractive; others will call it cloying and describe it as smelling artificial, or smelling like soda pop.

However the aroma strikes you subjectively, it is objectively, even though a bit small, rather typical of the scent of California-grown Gamay. The degree of ripeness the grapes normally achieve there develops their sugars and their scents to what sometimes seems an exaggerated degree. For this reason, the aroma of this Gamay is simpler and more one-dimensional than that of the Rioja. Fruit really almost completely dominates it, and you either like that or you don't; there is little else to consider.

Taste. In this pair of wines, the lines drawn by their aromas hold true in their flavors as well: the Rioja is fuller and more complex, the Gamay lighter, simpler, and more immediately appealing.

Let's take the Rioja first. Just about everybody tastes it as a medium-bodied wine, dry, with a good feel in the mouth. It is neither soft and flabby nor overly acidic and biting, though it has a discernible touch of tannin, either from the grapes themselves or from the barrels. Most people can feel that along the insides of their cheeks or on the top of their tongue—a drying, slightly puckering sensation.

In addition, most people also taste a generous burst of fresh, sprightly fruit, more than the Rioja's aroma might lead them to expect. A good number of them will specify the fruit as tasting of black cherry or raspberry (some may even find this wine vaguely reminiscent of Zinfandel). Finally, the wine finishes long and dry, with a slightly bitter aftertaste in which some people will detect the barest suggestion of almonds and others will find woody/oaky traces, perhaps even an oversteeped-tea tang. With food all these elements plump up a little bit larger. Those who don't take pleasure in this flavor range may taste all these things as sour, or astringent, or unpleasantly bitter.

In the flavor of the Gamay as in its aroma, fruit overweighs almost everything else. The wine is soft and definitely lighter than the Rioja. Most tasters credit it with good, bright acid, both because of the liveliness of its fruit and because of the slightly spritzy sensation many of them feel on their tongues. Very few find any trace of tannin here. The fruit flavors fall definitely into the red fruit group in most tasters' reports: the majority tastes strawberries, a few taste black cherries, but neither is strongly distinguished. Some detect sufficient ripeness in the fruit that they experience it almost as a trace of sweetness, as if there were the merest trace of residual sugar left in the wine. Those who dislike it report that as a sort of soda-pop flavor.

This Gamay has a nice dry but short finish—that is, its flavor ends rather completely with the swallow. In a simple wine such as this, one intended to be drunk young and without fanfare, that is not a serious flaw, but for a mature claret or Burgundy or estate-bottled California Cabernet to finish so short would be a very grave defect indeed.

This pair of wines illustrates—or at least I mean them to illustrate—a fundamental and too-often-ignored wine distinction, the difference between a simple and a complex wine. This distinction is the Grand Canyon and the Continental Divide of the wine world. Between simple wines and complex wines there is a great gulf, and the gulf is not simply the prestige accorded one group and withheld from the other but a gulf of taste and temperament—and that can be the most unbridgeable depth of all.

In his play *Man and Superman*, George Bernard Shaw has Satan explain the abyss that separates Heaven and Hell as the incompatibility of the heavenly and hellish temperaments. Angels and demons would be bored to tears in each other's domain. In the world of wine, matters stand very like that. People who really love complex wines can tolerate and on the right occasions even enjoy simple wines, but most of the time they are bored by them. Vice versa, lovers of simple wine aren't palatally tone deaf: they appreciate what complex wines can offer, but it's just not what they want most of the time. Would you want always to dine on caviar and foie gras? Never eat any fruit but kiwis? Read only *War and Peace*? See only Antonioni movies? Ninety-nine percent of us would find that unbearable. So why should it be any different with wine?

Because, unfortunately, someone a long time ago impressed us all with the fact that some wines are *better* than others, and we, damn it, are not going to settle for anything less than the best. What's the point of being American if we do? Anything else we're willing to admit is a matter of taste—even of mood, of whim—and we'll fight to the death to maintain that our opinion is just as good as anyone else's. But with wine, somehow, an absolute ranking takes over and we become servile in the face of it. We all know—or think we know—that there are wines we *ought* to swoon over even if we don't know anything else about wine. So we feel embarrassed about liking simple wines. We apologize because we don't appreciate, or know about, or have any experience of, the prestigious classified growths and noble wines. It's hard to think of any other area of life in which Americans allow themselves to be bullied as thoroughly as they are about wine.

Well, it's time to make your own personal declaration of independence and own up to what you like. As an apprentice wine taster, your opinion about the different elements you can discern in a mouthful of 1945 La Tache doesn't amount to a hill of beans compared to what an Alexis Lichine or a Michael Broadbent can tell you about that wine. Informed opinion, opinion based on knowledge and experience and skill, is what matters there. But on the subject of your preferences, on the matters of your own tastes and your pleasures, no one is better informed than you. On the subject of what you like, you are the final authority: your opinion is absolutely incontrovertible.

All this amounts to saying that there is nothing wrong or stupid or embarrassing about preferring simple wines—especially if you have tried complex wines and found that they just don't suit you. The relevant factor here is *informed* opinion. No one need ever feel embarrassed for not knowing what he or she could not know—and that simple fact lets most of us off the hook about wine knowledge. Wine lore is simply something that was not readily available to us. Wine was not something we grew up with, like chopped-and-channeled Chevvies for one generation and the Beatles for another.

What you should be embarrassed about is knowledge available to you that you ignore. For that, shame on you. This book is your opportunity for that kind of wine knowledge. Even if you think you already know what you like, try a few more wines, explore a few more kinds, give new sensations a chance. You might find something you like. If you do, you're that much ahead of the game. If you don't, you've lost very little time and very little money, and those are good investments if the return makes you feel secure about your taste and free from qualms for the rest of your life. So sip on for a while.

All right then, what is this distinction between simple wines and complex wines that I'm making all this ridiculous fuss about? You've got a graphic example of it in the glasses in front of you now: two pleasing wines, but pleasing in different ways and for different reasons.

Simple and complex are the most honest and precise of all wine terms, because they mean exactly what they say. A simple wine is easy to deal with, easy to understand. It's not elaborate, not complicated. A complex wine, on the other hand, requires more attention: it has parts, components, facets. It rewards concentration by revealing more and more aspects of itself.

Our Gamay Beaujolais is an example of a simple wine: its fruitiness of aroma and flavor—what amounts to a mild varietal flavor, the taste of the Gamay grape—is its main and almost its exclusive feature. Other sorts of simple wines can be more intense or more subtle, more lively or more restrained, with greater or lesser depth of flavor, but they will share the essentially single thrust of this Gamay. This is in no sense a dismissal of this wine. It is an excellently made example of exactly what it was intended to be, a light, enjoyable Beaujolais-style wine.

The Rioja, on the other hand, offers us a medley of sensations, and the longer we linger over it, the greater the number of suggestions it makes to us. Many of them are muted, it is true, but the wine nevertheless presents differing facets and ideas to us, revealing different aspects of itself by its variety of parts—hints of vanilla and oak, scents of earth and wood and fruit. This is not because this Rioja is a great wine: objectively speaking, it is a well-made, sound, and typical young Rioja. But it is a wine whose vinification (the process by which its grapes were turned into wine) and whose grapes themselves (maybe) opened many possibilities of development. It is a wine that was made differently from the Gamay, in a manner that tamed the fullness of its fruit flavors somewhat to allow other elements present in the wine to express themselves.

The broadest goal of a vintner is always to make a drinkable wine: the more competent the wine maker, the more interesting and pleasing he will try to make it within the limits of the available material. Within this objective, these are two chief goals for which vintners can strive in handling grapes: to achieve the fullest possible expression of fruit, to the exclusion of other elements; or to create a harmony of fruit and other components.

Even so, the limits and the variables are myriad. First, the grape variety and its characteristics: some grapes achieve great sweetness. Some stay relatively tart. Some have a very pronounced and distinct flavor, readily identifiable. Others are much more subdued. Some naturally have a lot of tannin, which means that they have a greater potential for aging and development. Many of these characteristics are themselves not constant even within a grape variety but alter dramatically with the soil the vines are grown in, the sunlight or moisture they get, the stage of ripeness at which the grapes are picked.

Then there are the conditions of vinification, starting right with fermentation. Is it produced by naturally occurring yeasts or controlled introduction of selected yeasts? If the latter, which ones? Is the temperature controlled during fermentation? Is the fermentation long or short? In wood or steel or glass? How long are the skins of the grapes left in the liquid? How is the wine kept after fermentation?

There are even more variables. Just to give you a sense of the possibilities: if the wine is aged in wooden barrels, what capacity barrels? (because volume determines the actual degree of contact between wine and wood surface); what kind of wood? (it's usually oak, but there are variations from that); young or old? toasted (lightly charred) or raw?; and finally, for how long?

All these things alter the taste and style and heft of the finished wine. But don't be fooled if making wine begins to sound like the return of Dr. Frankenstein or Better Living Through Chemistry. For all the technical apparatus and scientific expertise, winemaking still remains more an art than a science; that's why there still are only a handful of really transcendent complex wines in the world. The most all that technical know-how can guarantee is that basic wine is sound, that good, simple wines can be made reliably and consistently and inexpensively. Beyond that level in winemaking and in wine enjoyment, there can never be any guarantees.

The Almadén Wine Company hardly needs an introduction. One of California's largest, it produces an almost bewildering array of wines, from simple jugs to good-quality, vintage-labeled varietals, all at very fair prices.

Paternina is a large and much-respected Rioja firm producing both the red and the white wines of that region. Its wines are imported to the United States by Monarch Wines. Those who are pleased by the style of the Rioja might want to try other examples of young Rioja from different makers. Marques de Murrieta, Privilegio, Gran Condal, Marques de Caceres, and Marques de Riscal all offer sound and interesting wines. Most of these firms also market older Riojas with longer barrel age and longer bottle age. These are frequently very fine wines of great complexity, and they are often—for wines of their quality—quite inexpensive.

This is the conclusion of our fifth red-wine-tasting session. There are several ways for you to proceed from here.

Following the lead of your own preferences:

If you liked the first wine better, Paternina Rioja, go to Flight 6 or Flight 14.

If you liked the second wine better, Almadén Gamay, go to Flight 7.

Following the kind of grapes:

There is really nothing else like this Rioja in our tastings.

Wine 2: go to Flight 7.

Following the wines of the country:

There are no other Spanish wines in the red-wine tastings.

Wine 2: go to Flight 6.

Red Wines:
The Sixth Flight

MOUTON CADET 1980
AND
CHRISTIAN BROTHERS NAPA VALLEY CABERNET SAUVIGNON NV

Here's a pair of wines to give your budding skills a chance to cope with complexity. Mouton Cadet is a very popular wine from France's famous Bordeaux district. Cabernet Sauvignon is the grape variety that constitutes the major component of the finest red wines of that area, and it is now intensively and very successfully cultivated in California's best wine districts.

Once again perform the ritual, concentrating especially on smelling the wine and remembering during tasting to let the wine run over the entire surface of your mouth and tongue. Take your notes, discuss the wines with other tasters, and then push on to the next paragraph of my purple prose. (That's the wine speaking.)

Appearance. These two wines show some kinship in their coloration. Both are an attractive deep ruby, the Cabernet slightly darker than the Mouton Cadet and possessing some tawny highlights. Most Cabernet-based wines display this color range when young; it lightens to the traditional claret color (traditional because claret is the collective name by which the great red wines of Bordeaux are known) as they age, acquiring a distinct tawny (some call it mahogany) rim when you tilt the glass in the proper light.

Aroma. In both wines, the aroma has developed several facets. Different tasters will emphasize different elements according to both their sensitivity to those elements and their ability to recognize and put names to them. In the Cadet, most people are likely to detect just a little fruit in the red range: they are likely to specify currants, if anything at all. Other vegetal aromas are more noticeable. Common descriptions might include peppery, herbaceous, grassy, mossy, and/or earthy. Some may pick up slight vanilla tones. Those tasters for whom this combination of aromas falls into an unpleasant range are likely to use such words as "chemical" or "cooked" to describe the odor they perceive.

For most people, the scent of growing things is prominent in the Cabernet as well: grass and fresh twigs or a medley of herbal smells. But in this Cabernet, fruit is important, too, and many tasters will remark on its aroma of ripeness. Again, those for whom that particular level of olfactory intensity is unpleasant will describe it as the smell of overripe or rotting fruit, or as artificial-smelling. Either group of tasters may detect alcohol in the aroma of this wine.

Taste. The differences between these two related wines continue to multiply and intensify as we progress from color and aroma to taste.

In tasting the Cadet, many people will experience prickly sensations at the tip and sides of their tongue or a feeling of astringency all through their mouth. These are, respectively, the results of acid and of tannin, which is also often felt as a puckering sensation on the cheeks. Unfortunately, for many tasters they so dominate this wine that little else is discernible in its taste. Many people report that only a bare minimum of fruit comes through, and it has no special characteristics and no particular force. The wine finishes very short and, for many people, somewhat bitterly. Most tasters find it drinkable and forgettable, a bland, inoffensive wine.

After tasting the Cabernet, many people will express a divided reaction—disappointment that the wine doesn't fully live up to the promise of its aroma, and pleasure that it gives more than the Cadet.

Once again, the relationship between the two wines makes itself felt: tasters will almost invariably find in the Cabernet the same elements they experienced in the Cadet. The difference here is the presence of a much larger amount of fruit to balance somewhat the still plentiful acids and tannin. That fruit unhappily lacks the distinctive ripeness the aroma possessed. The majority of tasters describe it as having at most a slight berrylike quality. Its finish is short but pleasing. The whole wine is usually described by tasters as like the Cadet but having more character: fuller, or rounder, or more interesting, or more assertive.

This pair of wines seems to me very instructive for what they can teach you about the importance of complexity and balance even at an unsophisticated level of wine. Both are well-made wines in the sense that there is nothing adulterated in either of them and no shortcuts have been taken in their vinification: they are the products of sound ingredients treated respectfully. The Mouton Cadet is undoubtedly a blend of Cabernet Sauvignon and some other grapes (probably Merlot and/or Cabernet Franc, as is traditional in Bordeaux). It seems a safe guess that there is a considerably higher percentage of Cabernet Sauvignon (it could even be 100 percent) in the Christian Brothers, though it is obviously a blending of two or more different vintages.

By itself, that higher percentage of Cabernet Sauvignon would not necessarily make the Christian Brothers the more balanced wine. Cabernet Sauvignon is a very tannic, very hard grape—hard in the sense that young wine from Cabernet grapes is often harsh and unpalatable. California sunshine has a lot to do with the balance of this wine: riper fruit has more sugar and more fully developed flavor, which in turn yields a bigger, more alcoholic wine with greater fruitiness surviving to balance the natural acids and tannins of the grape. On the other hand, the Mouton Cadet suffers because of the general dreadfulness of the 1980 vintage in Bordeaux. It was a bad year and it made thin, acidic wines. So the greater ripeness of California grapes generally and the advantage of blending two or more years' wine together give this Christian Brothers nonvintage Cabernet a decided edge in balance against this off-year specimen of Mouton Cadet. That small difference in balance amounts to a great difference in enjoyment.

Let's make no mistake about it: by the criteria of connoisseurship, these are still simple wines we're dealing with. Mouton Cadet lives by its name, whose associations with Château Mouton Rothschild, one of the world's most esteemed wines, lead many people to believe they are getting something like an estate-bottled claret when all they are actually getting is a shipper's Bordeaux Rouge, exactly like Prats' Maître d'Estournel or Eschenauer's Oliver de France, or any other red wine, with or without brand name, that simply bears the appellation *vin rouge de Bordeaux*. The Christian Brothers Cabernet Sauvignon we're tasting here is not vintage-dated but is a blend of at least two vintages, albeit all from the Napa Valley, which is a particularly prized California viticultural region. My point, however, is not to belittle these wines; this kind of wine offers decent value for price and a degree of consistency from bottle to bottle that more ambitious wines find it difficult to match. It offers security and reliability if you are content with an inoffensive wine and don't want to go to any trouble thinking about it.

But the thinking man's (and I emphatically mean woman's, too) palate can make trouble in paradise, because this class of wines is not uniform across the board. You *can* taste differences among them. You just did. The simple fact is that at every level of production, you can get better or worse wine, more pleasing or less pleasing wine, for about the same amount of cash—so it makes sense both in terms of your enjoyment and in economic terms to explore your palate and the wines it likes and to learn to make these sorts of distinctions.

In the cases we have before us in our glasses, we have a distinction drawn by the element of balance. One wine has it; the other doesn't. In one wine, acid and tannin dominate the fruit, so the overall flavor, while not displeasing, is slight, thin, and quickly passing. In the other, fruit and a bit more alcohol (take a look at the labels) turn the duet into a quartet, with the result that the total flavor is more interesting and more lasting. Ninety-nine percent of the time, drinking this Cabernet you wouldn't even think twice about its balance; but the fact that it is there enables you to enjoy this wine more than once.

Mouton Cadet is produced by Baron Philippe de Rothschild, the proprietor of Château Mouton Rothschild. Mouton Cadet is probably *the* largest-selling brand of red Bordeaux in the United States.

The Christian Brothers have been making wine in California for over a hundred years. They produce a reasonably full selection of California wines, mostly nonvintage, though more and more vintage bottlings are appearing. Their prices are always very fair for the quality of their wines.

So concludeth our first case of red wines. If you've made it this far, consider yourself a B.A., Bachelor of Alcohol. There are several ways for you to proceed from here.

Following the lead of your own preferences:

If you enjoyed either the first wine, Mouton Cadet, or the second wine, Christian Brothers Cabernet, go to Flight 10.

Following the kind of grapes:

Wine 1: go to Flight 10.

Wine 2: go to Flight 15.

Following the wines of the country:

Go to Flight 7.

CONTROLLING CENTER BOARD: SOME MEDIUM-BODIED REDS

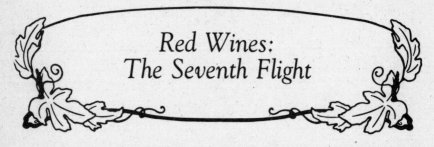

Red Wines: The Seventh Flight

PEDRONCELLI SONOMA COUNTY GAMAY BEAUJOLAIS 1982
AND
LATOUR BEAUJOLAIS VILLAGES 1983

A solid California wine firm and one of the most respected Burgundy *négociants* provide the wines for this flight. Beaujolais is the name of the district in France where the Gamay grape makes its most enjoyable wine, a fruity, lively wine meant to be drunk quite young. Despite the California wine's name, it is not made from the Gamay grape, though for many years this was thought to be the case. It is, however, intentionally cultivated and vinified to emulate the style of French Beaujolais, so in this tasting you will be making your first full-scale attempt to differentiate between the styles of similar wines.

Remember to perform the whole ritual of observations: note the color of the two wines; swirl them gently to release their aromas and then sniff; sip the wines and taste them all over your mouth before spitting them out. A little trick you may find helpful in tasting the wines is to put a little of it "in the hole." Let a little wine run down into the space below your tongue and behind your front teeth. Let it sit there for a few

The Name of the Gamay

There are in fact two grapes called Gamay in California, and neither of them is the Gamay grape cultivated in Beaujolais. The one known in California as Gamay Beaujolais has turned out to be a subvariety of Pinot Noir, which is the most important variety cultivated in Burgundy but so far has not been remarkably successful in California. The other variety, the Napa Gamay, appears to be no relation to Burgundian grapes. Because of long-standing practice, however, both are legally permitted to bear the name Gamay Beaujolais on their labels.

The wines of Beaujolais are bottled with several different types of regional designation on the label. The simplest, Beaujolais, designates a wine made from grapes drawn from all over the zone. Beaujolais Supérieur does not designate a better wine, but a wine with a slightly higher percentage of alcohol. The next regional class, Beaujolais Villages, indicates wine blended from grapes drawn only from a designated cluster of townships in the north of the zone.

The class above Beaujolais Villages is a single cru Beaujolais, one made exclusively from grapes from one of the nine named crus (classified growths) of the region—in other words, the nine villages with the best soils or climates for producing the wine. They are Brouilly, Chenas, Chiroubles, Côtes de Brouilly, Fleurie, Julienas, Morgon, Moulin-à-Vent, and Saint-Amour. The final classification of Beaujolais is cru Beaujolais with an estate designation, indicating that the wine is the product of a single vineyard. Normally only the very best vineyards find it economically worthwhile to bottle and sell their own wine under its unique designation. All of these classifications are covered by the French appellation d'origine controllée (AOC) laws, which legislate and police the accuracy of the regional designations.

seconds, then taste with the tip of your tongue: you should get the full effect of whatever sweetness and fruit the wine has, plus a generous sense of its acid and tannin. The technique is unnatural, but the effect is frequently worth it.

After you have untwisted your tongues and talked over your notes (remember: only after all have finished tasting, not while anyone is still reacting), go on to the descriptions of the wines.

Appearance. Both are attractive wines of a clear, bright ruby color, very lively-looking. The Latour Beaujolais Villages might be a slight shade lighter than the Pedroncelli Gamay.

You can expect the color in wines of this sort to vary a great deal from harvest to harvest. They can be anything from a slightly dark rose shade to purple as mimeograph ink, and often the color is a good indicator of just how much body or guts they're going to have. The colors you have in the glasses before you are almost textbook examples of what these two wines ought to look like in their best vintages: a pretty, translucent ruby, neither paling to pink nor darkening to purple.

Brick or orange tones in a Gamay wine this young would definitely not be good signs. They are usually manifestations of aging, and their premature appearance can warn about the condition of a particular vintage. Beaujolais and the whole class of red wines like it, wines whose claims to fame are youthful zest and fruit, should not be held for maturation, because the changes they undergo in the bottle do not improve the wine but rather kill it. The rule with Beaujolais-type wines is to drink them as young as possible.

But don't be too literal-minded about this. I don't mean you can't buy a case or two of Beaujolais for drinking over the course of a year—or even two years if it's a very good vintage—but that's the outer limit. Beaujolais is not a wine to cellar for five or ten or more years. Even the best vintages should be drunk before they are three years old; they gain nothing from bottle aging.

Aroma. Ideally, what you ought to smell in a Beaujolais is fresh fruit and not too much else. The aroma ought to be inviting in a kind of healthy, outdoorsy way—nothing subtle, just a direct, sensuous appeal. The better the vintage, the bigger the aroma and the stronger the appeal should be.

Happily, most tasters find exactly that kind of aroma in these two wines. There are differences, of course, from wine to wine and from taster to taster, but the vast majority describe both wines as first, aromatic; second, fruity; and third, alcoholic (sensed as a kind of warm or hot component in the aroma, sometimes even as a tingle in the nose).

Do you want particulars? Here goes.

Most people describe the California Gamay as strongly fruity and alcoholic, and they specifically sense very ripe fruit—usually they say strawberries, though a few may smell peaches. A very few find the scent too strong and call it overripe and off-putting. But most find the fruit aroma very pleasing. Some may also report a sort of mixed stemmy or woody or earthy undertone that builds up somewhat as the wine opens in the glass.

The Beaujolais Villages is similarly called very fruity, though usually it is said to be slightly more delicate, or in a higher register, than the aroma of the Gamay. People may describe this scent as spicy or slightly sweetish. It too is warm and alcoholic. Almost everybody agrees that strawberry is the fruit component they smell in it, and almost everybody likes it.

Vintage and age do make a real difference even in wines such as Beaujolais, whose attractions are simplicity and directness. The fresh, lively fruit smell in both these wines isn't always there with the clarity and vitality it has in this vintage. Sometimes acids will be more prominent, making the wine very bright and lively, but also thinning it a little, making it sharper and less easy on the nose, sometimes even acrid. Sometimes alcohol will dominate, and warmth will be the primary sensation. Try to remember the aromas you're smelling now; they make very usable standards for the breed.

Despite the many similarities between these two aromas, people still can be sharply divided on the question of like or dislike. Most will find both wines pleasing, but there will also be extreme parties about both—tasters who will call the Gamay too strong and cloying or the Beaujolais Villages too thin and soft-drink sweet.

Taste. Tasting will pretty much bear out what sight and scent have so far established. Most people find both wines as fresh and fruity as advertised, relatively simple, and quite pleasant drinking. The Latour Beaujolais even reveals some characteristics of what a person who knew French wines could identify as Latour's house style (a certain heft, a fleshy quality to the fruit). It's not possible to say anything like that of the Gamay because the Pedroncelli firm has not yet evolved a clearly identifiable house style.

House style in wine talk means simply the general way in which a vintner or winery or *négociant* handles wines so as to lend them all a set of distinctive characteristics. For instance, for the past few years the house style of the New York Yankees has been civil war; of the Los Angeles Dodgers, sentimentality. The style of Latour wines (he ships many different Burgundies) is marked within the context of French wine by bigness: you can reasonably expect one of his wines to have real impact. Beaulieu Vineyards make wines that, especially by California standards, are distinguished by great finesse, great elegance. You don't necessarily expect great power from them, but you do look for real complexity and balance.

What most people taste in the Gamay is pretty much what the aroma led them to expect: intense fruit, tasting initially as if it had to be sweet though it turns out not to be so. Most tasters call it cherry-flavored. Some find it very bright with acid and some rich and fat with alcohol and extracts. Some take the middle ground and call it balanced. Most people report a little tongue prickle from acid, though they divide on whether they consider that an attraction or a distraction.

The Beaujolais too gives many tasters an initial impression of sweetness, although it also proves to be completely dry. As with its aroma, this Beaujolais Villages' taste is slightly higher, its body slightly thinner than the Gamay's—though, paradoxically, many people will describe its fruit as being fleshier and more rounded. The flavor they most often name is strawberry, ripe and dry. It too seems fairly high in acidity.

Despite the fact that they may use much the same words to talk about these two wines, most tasters are quite aware of the very real distinctions between the two. These are very different styles of wine, and taken side by side like this they very nicely point up each other's real defining characteristics. The Beaujolais, for all its acidity, strikes the palate as all soft fruit and good manners, a pleasing, almost genteel light wine. The Sonoma Gamay seems by comparison a bit coarse but definitely bigger, harder, almost brambly in flavor and perhaps better structured. Even their fruit is different—and both are fruity wines. You can learn a lot about style in wine by just taking a few more sips of these two and reflecting a bit longer on the differences you can perceive in the nature of their respective fruitiness.

Pedroncelli is an old, reliable, and sizable California winery that markets only wines with a Sonoma County appellation. It offers good value for dollar throughout its line, from jug wines to prestige varietals.

The firm of Louis Latour is one of the most important of Burgundy's *négociants*. It deals in the whole line of Burgundian wines, from simple Bourgogne Rouge to the finest *Grands Crus* bottlings. Its wines are imported by Frederick Wildman.

This is the conclusion of our seventh red-wine-tasting session. There are several ways for you to proceed from here.

Following the lead of your own preferences:

If you liked the first wine better, Pedroncelli Gamay, go to Flight 9.

If you preferred the second wine, Latour Beaujolais Villages, go to Flight 8.

Following the kind of grapes:

Wine 1: there are no more California Gamays in the tastings. Try Flight 8.

Wine 2: go to Flight 8.

Following the wines of the country:

Wine 1: go to Flight 10.

Wine 2: go to Flight 8.

Red Wines:
The Eighth Flight

CHÂTEAU DE LA CHAIZE BROUILLY 1983
AND
JADOT MOULIN-À-VENT 1982

This pair matches one of the most esteemed single-estate Beaujolais against one from a highly regarded *cru* and an excellent shipper. The Jadot firm is one of the most important in Burgundy and one of the most reliable shippers of both Burgundies and Beaujolais to the United States. The purpose of pairing these wines is as much to test your discriminatory powers (since the wines will inevitably have many similarities) as to show the differing possibilities even within the confines of a single wine like Beaujolais.

Because of its inexpensiveness and abundance, Beaujolais allows us (over this flight and the preceding one) to sample the differences and degrees of refinement possible in three important geographical classes of the same wine—one drawn from the whole region (the simple AOC Beaujolais of Flight 7); one drawn from a single, highly rated township within the region (this flight's Moulin-à-Vent); and one drawn from a single estate within a named township and region (this flight's Château de La Chaize). Nevertheless, all are Beaujolais, and that means your tasting skill will be stretched here, so pay careful attention to the "infamous s's." And oh yes—don't forget to enjoy these wines, too. When you're finished, come back here.

Appearance. These two wines fall firmly into the true Beaujolais range. Both are a sound, attractive ruby, clear and bright, translucent and light-looking. The Moulin-à-Vent is perhaps a shade darker than the Brouilly. Both are attractive, lively-looking wines.

Aroma. The distinction between the two wines stands out pretty clearly for most tasters, though there is still a good deal of variety within the reactions to each wine. For instance, almost everybody says that the Château de La Chaize has a very marked fruity aroma, but there are many opinions as to its particulars: berries, some say, especially strawberries, while others say very ripe peaches. Some find the aroma heavy, with an almost caramel note in it; others find it lighter and absolutely unsugary. A few people even smell pepper in it. The Moulin-à-Vent also has only a small aroma, but it is more heavily floral, with undertones of things like fresh earth and mushrooms—a heavier, more pungent odor than that of the Brouilly. Both are for most people pleasant and unobtrusive, though a few tasters probably will find the scent of the Château de La Chaize too thin and that of the Moulin-à-Vent too heavy to be really pleasant.

Taste. Let's take the Château de La Chaize first. The range of responses to this wine tends to fall into two distinct camps: those who sense it as a rather full wine with a bit of muscle, and those who perceive it as light and elegant. Both camps remark, with varying emphases and degrees of pleasure, on its fruit and its acid, but it is almost always the fruit that strikes tasters first. It is usually described as fresh and clean and dry. The people in the full camp report it as smooth and well balanced, tasting in the strawberry-apricot range of flavors. The light people call it definitely strawberry, dry and soft and refined, with the acid initially very subdued but showing increasingly strongly with later sips.

Almost everybody feels an acid tingle in the wine. For some it's pleasant, for others excessive, but whatever the subjective reaction to it, it's the acidity that keeps this wine as lively and as pleasing as it is. Ideally, acid should be in balance with other parts of the wine (fruit and alcohol, for instance), neither dominating the wine nor disappearing and leaving a flabby corpse behind. The majority of tasters find that kind of balance in this Château de La Chaize, and because of it some may speak of it as possessing a degree of complexity unusual in Beaujolais. On the other hand, some of the tasters who describe the wine as light may think that fruit is all it really has.

Finally, almost everybody finds the wine's finish very pleasing—long and dry, so you still taste some of the best of the wine after it's gone. A very pleasant wine, quite easy to drink, and about as polished as Beaujolais is capable of becoming.

Like the Château de La Chaize, this Moulin-à-Vent seems to elicit a fairly uniform range of responses from tasters. Again, fruit is almost the first thing to be remarked upon, and again I urge you to try to taste past the fruit. The taste of the Moulin-à-Vent fruit is markedly different from that of the first wine. The Moulin-à-Vent fruit tastes fuller (there seems to be more of it and it seems to fill the mouth more). It is riper, a condition that some people describe as sweeter (though it is not sugar you are tasting but the condition of the fruit). And it is softer, that is, the textural sensation in your mouth is precisely softness (taste sips of the two wines sequentially again; you'll see what I mean).

Specific elements don't surface readily in the big, soft fruit of the Moulin-à-Vent's flavor. Most people will sense berries, and a few (particularly if they find the aroma and flavor too strong for their taste) may smell overripeness and taste something like banana there. Generally, tasters tend to find that this Moulin-à-Vent has more body and more power than the Château de la Chaize. Those who like that combination of elements describe this wine as having more character; those who don't, usually dislike some specific element sufficiently to isolate it for criticism.

Of course, tasting two wines comparatively as we are doing makes it easier for us to see the virtues and shortcomings of each; that's why we do it. Our Moulin-à-Vent is the bigger wine, but a taste of the Château de la Chaize will show us that for all its size, the Moulin-à-Vent is lacking acid, and it probably would be a much more admirable wine if its soft fruit were supported and enlivened by a good dose of that. After tasting the Moulin-à-Vent, on the other hand, it's easy to see that the Château de la Chaize, for all its pleasantness, is really a fairly thin wine and could very well use more body and fruit.

Remember that we are dealing here (with the Brouilly, at least) with just about the best that Beaujolais can do. The 1983 vintage was a glorious one for Beaujolais. There hadn't been one to compare with it for years before, and it may be a good many more years before we see its like again. That means that you are not here tasting the average for Beaujolais but the standard to which, in most vintages, it rather wistfully aspires. From the point of view of your wine knowledge, that's terrific, because you've really gotten to the heart of the Beaujolais game and can measure every other Beaujolais you'll ever taste by this very valid yardstick. Really to cement the lesson, it would be a great idea to rerun this test with the next vintage as soon as it becomes available.

Both in spite of and because of the excellence of the 1983 vintage, the differences you've been tasting between the Brouilly wine and the Moulin-à-Vent are right on target. Moulin-à-Vent is celebrated for being always the biggest and most tannic of Beaujolais, for being the only Beaujolais that really profits from any bottle age. In a very good vintage, the wines of Moulin-à-Vent may take two or three years to become ready, unlike most other Beaujolais, which are at their best at about a year old. And the characteristics you noted in the Château de La Chaize are those for which Brouilly wines are famed: freshness, lightness, balance, accessibility.

We were very lucky in our vintage with all these Beaujolais wines, but even an inferior vintage wouldn't necessarily have been a handicap, though it surely would have been less fun to taste. Even in off-years (as mediocre vintages are called, no doubt to give the totally untrue impression that they are unusual), carefully made wines will run true to their type. Their qualities may be diluted, but they will still be present. You may be able to judge something of the body from the shadow it throws—that is, you can extrapolate from an off-vintage what a good wine can do in a fine year. Use your taste first about the wine you've got in front of you, and then your imagination about the one you don't have.

Also (and this is in a sense a shopper's tip), it's often possible to buy off-vintages of very fine wines at a very reasonable price. If you're careful enough in your tasting of them and imaginative enough in your projection up the scale, you can make some pretty shrewd guesses from those inexpensive bottles about whether you really want to lay out the megabucks for their big brothers.

This is especially useful to keep in mind in restaurants, where off-vintages of normally expensive wines often can be the best bargains on the wine list. This is doubly true under restaurant circumstances because most restaurant wines are sold too young. Off-vintages tend to mature more quickly than their better-rated siblings, and you've consequently got at least a fighting chance of getting, at a decent price, a decent wine that's ready to drink.

Aren't you proud of yourself? You learned all that stuff today and you're going to save money, too. Go out and buy a case of wine to celebrate.

Château de La Chaize is imported to the United States by Château & Estate Wines Company. Jadot wines are imported to the United States by Kobrand.

This concludes our eighth red-wine-tasting flight. There are several ways for you to proceed from here.

Following the lead of your own preferences:

If you enjoyed either the first wine, Château de La Chaize Brouilly, or the second wine, Moulin-à-Vent, go to Flight 12.

Following the kind of grapes:

There are no more Gamay-based wines in the tastings (see preceding Flights 3, 5, and 7).

Following the wines of the country:

Go to Flight 10.

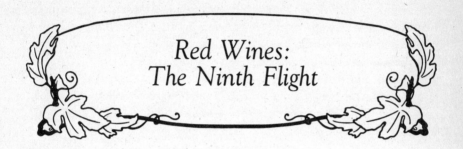

Red Wines:
The Ninth Flight

CORDERO DOLCETTO D'ALBA 1983 (MONFALLETTO)
AND
BERSANO BARBERA D'ASTI 1982

This flight introduces two different wines from a whole new (to this book's sequence) region, Italy's province of Piedmont, a subalpine region of rolling hills and foggy valleys. Dolcetto and Barbera are the names both of the two grapes and the wines made from them. Italy's DOC laws (legislation governing wine labeling, comparable to France's AOC laws) require specific geographical designations for these, as you see on these two labels: Barbera from Asti and Dolcetto from Alba, both sizable townships in south-central Piedmont.

Once again, you are dealing with wines normally characterized as fruity. In the area where they are made, most Dolcetto and much Barbera are consumed as young as possible—and as often as possible. Their local popularity is immense: probably half the wine production of the entire Piedmont is Barbera of one sort or another. Both wines accompany food well, and at elaborate dinners in the Piedmont they are served with the antipasto and pasta courses, giving way to the bigger Barbaresco and Barolo for the meat course.

Your mission, should you choose to accept it, is to taste these wines to try to determine how you can describe the differences in their fruit. I don't doubt you'll taste the difference readily enough, but putting that perception into words is the tricky part. This tasting is deliberately designed not only to introduce you to two delightful wines but especially to make you feel sympathy for a hardworking wine writer, me.

Oh, yes: one more little item for you to think about. Following the wine traditions of the Piedmont, each of these wines has been exposed to some wood, rather more than would be considered normal in other parts of the world for wines meant to be primarily fruity and to be drunk young. See if you can spot the effects—and the flavors—that arise from wood in these wines.

On your mark; get set; go. Appearance, aroma, taste. Expectorate and expatiate.

Let's talk about one wine at a time, starting with the Dolcetto.

Appearance. Its color is a deep, limpid ruby with what appear to be many purple highlights—very pretty and lively-looking.

Aroma. There should be near-unanimity about at least one element of this wine's aroma: just about everybody should smell fruit in abundance here, and most are likely to specify it as berries. But tasters will name other fruits as well, and some almost as prominently: cherry, plum, and apricot are all possibilities. Other elements that people are able to pick out in the aroma are alcohol; growing things (stems, and freshly cut grass, and sun-baked shrubs); sometimes spice; a slight bitter element that to some people is reminiscent of peach pits; and a heavier, almost *basso profundo* note that sometimes can be described as clay and some-times as very intense, very dry fruit. Both the bitter, peach-pit strain and the bass elements of this Dolcetto's aroma probably are traceable to a generous presence of tannin in this wine.

Taste. Tasting the wine will bear out and elaborate most of what has been discerned in the aroma. If there is any major difference between the two, it is that in the flavor of this Dolcetto, fruit is not as dominant for every taster as it is in its aroma. The fruit is very definitely present—lush and almost sweet—and some tasters will even identify it more specifically here as peaches and plum together, or even as raspberry. Many people will find earthy and woody flavors becoming stronger with subsequent tastes.

Also present in this Dolcetto are generous amounts of acid and tannin. Some tasters may find the acid too strong, though most will think it amply balanced by the full, dry fruit. The tannin especially may have the effect for many people of leaving their mouths a little puckered, a little dried-out or chalky-feeling. Others will merely discern a slight and pleasing underlying bitterness—often clearest in the finish—and an underlying, astringent dryness that seems to enhance the quasi-sweetness of the fruit. (I say quasi-sweetness because this is a completely dry wine, but—as often happens with wines of this and similar types—the intensity of the fruit creates in the mouth a sensation we are more used to associating with sweetness.)

Let me urge you to pay particular attention to this aspect of the Dolcetto: it is a pretty clear instance of a fairly tricky phenomenon, and it is well worth your while to be able to recognize the difference between sweetness and fruit. Put a bit of this wine "in the hole" as I instructed you before: let a few drops run down below your tongue and behind your front teeth. Let the wine sit for a few seconds to start drawing out saliva. Taste first with the tip of your tongue (which especially tastes sweetness) and then taste those drops all over your mouth. Was that sugar you tasted? Was that sweetness in any sense you're accustomed to? Not on your tintype; that was the fruit essence of this wine. All its sugar was long ago, in fermentation, converted into alcohol.

Many tasters find that this Dolcetto is not perfectly balanced; depending on their sensitivity, they may find it overly tannic or overly acidic. Nonetheless, it is hardly what you would call a harsh or biting wine. Rather, it has vivid character; lots of fruit; rather full body; and a pleasing, bitter finish. In the course of its vinification, a considerable amount of fruit of a fairly strong character has been brought into line with other elements that provide spine and structure to make a wine that almost goes beyond simple fruitiness into a different sort of interest, one built around a relation of parts to parts within the overall character of the wine.

That interest goes to the heart of what wine professionals mean by complexity in a wine and shows why they prize it. A complex wine, to put it directly, gives you a lot to taste. This Dolcetto carries the interest and the appeal of simple fruitiness just about as far as it can go in a wine. The Barbera with which it is paired goes one step beyond that.

Now let's turn to that Barbera.

Appearance. Its color is a deep, intense garnet, pure and clear. It looks heavier than the Dolcetto, though the Dolcetto looks livelier than it. These are quite classic colors for these two wines.

In the Piedmont, Barbera sometimes is allowed to age for a year or two (especially in good vintages) before sale. When slightly older, it may develop some tawny or amber highlights, which in Italian red wines generally and Piedmontese wines in particular are good indications of maturity.

They emphatically do not mean (as they sometimes do in French or California wines) that the wine is drying out—losing its fruit and often its life. In a wine like a Barbera, those tawny highlights indicate a wine past its first flush of youth but by no means over the hill. The expectations a color like that generates about the taste of the wine are that its youthful, intense fruitiness will now be subdued somewhat and that other elements should now be coming forward to create a more complicated total flavor. By those criteria, the Barbera you have in front of you is still a young wine.

Aroma. Like the Dolcetto, this Barbera has a fairly generous aroma. Some tasters will think it is like the Dolcetto also in the respect that the biggest component of its aroma is fruit—though they will more than likely describe this fruit as generalized and hard to pin down. If pressed to verbalize the difference, most people will say it is less grapey and less berrylike, more akin to plums. Some tasters will find this particular odor unpleasing and describe it as resiny or barrely.

Beyond fruit, the Barbera contains a whole range of important olfactory elements. Some tasters discern spice, some stems, some alcohol, and some herbal scents. It is also possible to pick out in the Barbera's aroma traces owing to the barrels in which it rested, particularly stray whiffs of vanilla, which is one of the characteristic odors imparted to wine by oak. By far most important, however, is a compound of scents that many tasters will detect but find very difficult to describe. Its most frequently mentioned components include tar, tobacco, chocolate, and pepper. Because of this, people who know Italian wine may describe this Barbera's aroma as being like a baby Barolo.

Generally speaking, most people will find that the overall character of the Barbera's aroma, in comparison with the Dolcetto's, is higher and a bit lighter—a tenor voice as opposed to a baritone. Both aromas, however, ought to be pleasing—intriguing, even—to the great majority of tasters.

Taste. For that same majority of tasters, this Barbera shows a pretty nice balance from the very first taste. There is a tannin presence here that is clearly discernible to most people; you may feel it as a slight puckering sensation in your mouth or taste it as a hint of vanilla, the barrels' gift to the grape. A few tasters may find this too strong and as a consequence lose track of the wine's fruit flavors and balance.

This Barbera has good acid, too, though not as prominent as its tannin. Its fruit is perceptible to most people as cherry, often specifically black cherry. Despite the clear presence and effect of acid and tannin, the majority of tasters feel the fruit as soft and fresh. As with its aroma, that compound of tar, tobacco, pepper, and chocolate flavors begins to emerge with the second or third taste and starts taking its place right alongside the fruit. Even with all these flavors present, however, most tasters describe the Barbera as round and harmonious.

In comparison with the Dolcetto, this Barbera clearly shows smaller fruit, lacking that intense freshness and concentrated flavor the Dolcetto has. It does not seem as big or as full a wine, nor as exuberant. On the other hand, the Barbera offers a kind of complexity and elegance the Dolcetto only hints at. This is a very composed wine, one that has reined in all its different parts so they cooperate to make an integrated whole. To put it briefly, this is what I would call a borderline noble wine, already crossing over the frontier from fruitiness into complexity.

Many people are not excited by this sort of wine. I most definitely am, and that is something you should know about my taste so you can put my raves and pans in proper perspective. Lots of other wine fans, professional and amateur alike, would unreservedly prefer the vitality of the Dolcetto to the restraint of the Barbera. But this is very much a question of personal preference. Some people associate the youthful exuberance of a wine like Dolcetto with soft drinks, and some think the more sophisticated style of the Barbera is simply dull. As the philosopher says, you pays your money and you takes your choice.

Just a reminder to you, lest you get a bit bored with all this, that you are now at a point in these tastings where you know a whole lot more about your own taste and why you like what you like than when you started way back there with the Mondavi Red and the Villa Banfi Roman Red. You've come a long way, baby—but you've still got a long way to go.

Right here, however, may be about as far as there is any point for us to travel on this particular road. You've now got enough basic information about fruity wines as a class to go out and do more extensive tasting on your own: different brands of Beaujolais, different Gamays, Beaujolais-style Zinfandels, the Loire red wines such as Chinon and Saumur, Chiantis from the hills of Siena or Primativo from the Italian South,

Merlots and Cabernets from the Italian North. The list is long, and there are plenty there to keep you happy for quite a while.

Most wine drinkers, no matter what more complicated wines they move on to, never really lose their fondness for these charmers. They are wines you can come back to endlessly for straightforward pleasures, renewed and varied every harvest. But there are many more pleasures in the world of wine than these, and where we go from here is out into the deeper vinous waters of the more complex wines—so keep paddling, and keep sipping, and keep on taking notes. Excelsior.

Cordero of Montezemolo, a family winery, makes this Dolcetto d'Alba from grapes grown on the slopes of Monfalletto. The same small winery also produces excellent Barolo from the same locale. Both are imported to the United States by Trebon Wine and Spirits Corporation, a firm that specializes in top-quality Italian wines.

Bersano is a large and highly regarded Piedmontese winery, producing the whole range of traditional Piedmontese wines. Its wines are imported to the United States by Browne Vintners, a division of The Seagram Wine Company.

Here ends our ninth red-wine-tasting session. There are several ways for you to proceed from here.

Following the lead of your own preferences:

If you liked the first wine better, Dolcetto, try Flight 12.

If you preferred the second wine, Barbera, try Flight 14.

Following the kind of grapes:

Neither Dolcetto nor Barbera figure in any more of our tastings. You will find other Piedmontese wines in Flight 18.

Following the wines of the country:

Go to Flight 14.

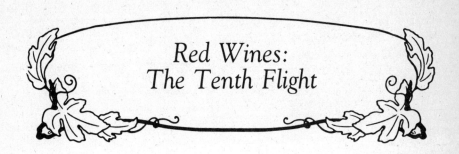

Red Wines:
The Tenth Flight

B & G ST.-ÉMILION 1981
AND
MARTINI NORTH COAST MERLOT 1980

This flight starts you on the taste trail of the Merlot grape. Extensively cultivated throughout Bordeaux, Merlot is used in the Médoc as a component in the blend of the best red wines, but in lesser percentage than the dominant grape, Cabernet Sauvignon. Across the Gironde River to the east, in St.-Émilion and Pomerol, the Merlot grape's contribution to the blend becomes much more important both in quantity and in the qualities it brings to the wine. In California, Merlot has so far been cultivated primarily to produce a varietal wine in its own right—to make a wine that contains at least 75 percent and in many cases 100 percent of the Merlot grape.

The first wine you have in front of you in this, your maiden attempt to grapple seriously with the phenomenon of varietal flavor in a noble *vinifera* strain, is a good shipper's St.-Émilion. The firm of Barton & Guestier have been wine merchants, specializing in Bordeaux, for over 200 years. Their wines are imported to the United States by

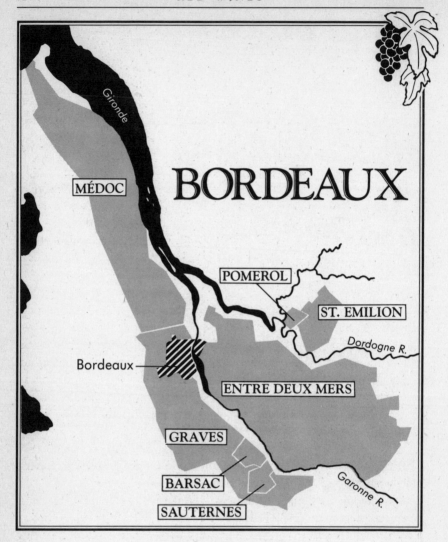

MÉDOC

Gironde

BORDEAUX

POMEROL

ST. EMILION

Dordogne R.

Bordeaux

ENTRE DEUX MERS

GRAVES

BARSAC

SAUTERNES

Garonne R.

Browne Vintners, a division of The Seagram Wine Company. The second wine of the pair is an important California firm's blended Merlot—that is, it's all made from Merlot grapes, but the grapes that went into it were grown in different parts of California.

The Martini family are wine old-timers by California standards—they've been making wine since before Prohibition, and the firm is responsible for some of the most important developments in California fine-wine production. The Martini firm was the first in California to market a 100 percent Merlot varietal wine.

Since this is your first real confrontation with varietal tasting (with a major varietal, that is; depending on how you got here, you may have tasted pairs of Gamay-based wines already), let me spell a few things out for you. It's reasonable to expect to find similarities between these wines, but don't be surprised if the similarities are swamped by the differences.

How can that be, if it's the same grape in both cases? Because of climate and soil, different agricultural techniques, even the way the vines are pruned—the whole package of things that add up to the growing conditions of the vines. These can change the nature of the wine completely. Add to them any differences in the techniques of vinification, and it is possible to transform the wine made from Merlot or any other grape into something altogether different from what it makes on its home turf. Vines behave differently in different circumstances, just as people do.

So what do you do now? You know perfectly well: the "infamous s's." You've got the tools to handle this job. Now use 'em. Check back here when you're done.

Appearance. Color is easily accounted for here: both wines are a medium ruby, with some amber or tawny highlights. Pleasing but not remarkable. The differences begin after this, so from here on I will talk about the two wines separately.

Aroma. Most tasters find the aroma of the St.-Émilion somewhat muffled. You can bring it up by swirling vigorously (careful! watch out for the rug), or even better by decanting the wine into a carafe or pitcher. The aroma will remain small and rather elusive, giving suggestions of grass and earth, what some people describe as a slight, pleasing tarry scent with floral overtones. Some tasters may find an unpleasant, oily scent in it.

Bordeaux Borders

Bordeaux is one of France's—and the world's—most important fine-wine districts. It is subdivided into several zones: Côtes de Blaye, Entre-Deux-Mers, Médoc, Graves, Sauternes, St.-Émilion, Pomerol, and Côtes de Bourg. Wines of every conceivable range of quality come from all of them, but the finest red wines—those that have been esteemed for centuries and that have influenced the growth and production of "serious" wines all over the world—come from the Médoc (a stretch of land on the west side of the Gironde and lying between it and the sea) and St.-Émilion and Pomerol (a plateau lying east of the Gironde). The Médoc is subdivided into several famous (at least in the wine world) communes or townships: from south to north, Graves (really separate from the Médoc but usually figured with it for red-wine purposes), Margaux, Pauillac, St.-Julien, and St.-Estephe. Subsidiary divisions of the other great red-wine zone are St.-Émilion, St.-Georges–St.-Émilion, Puisseguin–St.-Émilion, Lussac–St.-Émilion, Montagne–St.-Émilion, Pomerol, and Lalande de Pomerol.

Taste. The flavor of the St.-Émilion imparts more fruit than its aroma would lead you to expect; not a lot, but still a pleasant surprise. Most tasters detect as well a slight spiciness in its soft fruit, with both flavors enlivened by the wine's bright acidity. The wine is fully dry and medium-bodied, without much finish. But the overriding palatal sensation is tannin, whose puckery quality and prickly, astringent sensation almost every taster feels in this wine.

Aroma. The Merlot, on the other hand, has an aroma that, on first encounter, some people find objectionable because of its strength, a sort of cooked-vegetable or olive-oily quality that probably is due to the presence of some overripe grapes in the ferment. It is an exaggeration of the normal earthy and/or spicy and/or herbaceous smell of Merlot-based wines, which most people find very attractive.

Taste. Like the St.-Émilion, the Merlot's flavor surprises most tasters quite pleasantly by being less pronounced and more immediately enjoyable than its aroma. There is a nice, modest fruit presence in which some tasters will discern a hint of the overripeness more apparent in the aroma. People usually describe the Merlot's fruit as soft, but not as soft as the St.-Émilion. This Merlot has more acid and less tannin than that, though there is still (especially for people sensitive to tannin) a perceptible sourness and astringency in the Merlot.

Overall, preferences between these two wines should probably divide along the lines of complexity vs. fruit. The St.-Émilion, while not a very complicated wine and somewhat unbalanced by its heavy tannin, still offers more components and more structure than the Merlot (probably because of the presence of more Cabernet Sauvignon and perhaps Cabernet Franc in its blend).

The Merlot, on the other hand, gives you a much better idea of what its namesake grape is really all about, and its almost natural balance, owing to its more discreet tannin and soft fruit, are very characteristic of wines made from Merlot in any part of the world.

This is the conclusion of our tenth red-wine-tasting flight. From here you don't have many choices; all roads lead to Flight 11 and the continuation of your exploration of the Merlot grape.

Following the lead of your own preferences:

If you liked either the first wine, B & G St.-Émilion, or the second wine, Martini North Coast Merlot, go to Flight 11.

Wine Build

Structure is a very significant wine term and particularly important to understand when dealing with bigger, more complex wines. Think of it in terms of architecture: the façade of the building, the elements that hit the eye immediately, are like the flavor components of wine, the things that strike the palate right away. The internal structure of the building—the unseen parts, the beams and braces—are what hold that façade up and allow the building to stand in the first place. In the same way with wine, it is the interactions of the more submerged components, of acid and alcohol and tannin and fruit and extracts, that structure and support the flavor and make the wine viable. A wine wherein these different structural elements are harmoniously fused so that no one of them is more conspicuous than any other, is said to be well balanced. A wine wherein one of them immediately proclaims its presence or absence is unbalanced.

Note well, however, that balanced and unbalanced do not equal good and bad. A balanced wine can be boring, and an unbalanced one, if the right element dominates or surrenders, can be very enjoyable. To make a great wine, another balance is necessary: the quality of the grapes, the quality of the soil, and the artistry of the wine maker. Simple formulas never make superb wines.

Following the kind of grapes:
Go to Flight 11.
Following the wines of the country:
Go to Flight 11.

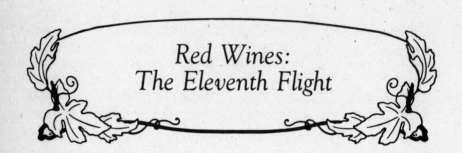

Red Wines: The Eleventh Flight

CHÂTEAU DE SALES POMEROL 1981
AND
GUNDLACH-BUNDSCHU MERLOT 1981

In this flight you are dealing with a very respectable Pomerol estate, planted about two thirds in Merlot vines (the remainder is about evenly divided between Cabernet Sauvignon and Cabernet Franc) and an equally respectable California vineyard with a continuous, more than one-hundred-year history of grapegrowing (Prohibition interrupted the winemaking). In addition to Merlot, Gundlach-Bundschu also produces a wide selection of other varietals, especially Cabernet, Chardonnay, and Gewurztraminer, plus a few special-label bottlings from its prized Batto Ranch site.

Even more than the wines in Flight 10, this pair of wines should demonstrate pretty clearly some of the major differences between French and California styles in winemaking. Also (and by no means to be overlooked), these wines will give you fair examples of the potential of the Merlot grape.

The ball is in your court; it's time for you to do your stuff. Pay particular attention here to the way these wines react to food. And make sure you look this time not just for color but for legs as well—little streamers formed by the wine flowing back down into the glass after you've swirled the wine.

Appearance. In color, these two wines are hard to distinguish. Both are a pretty, clear ruby, the Merlot perhaps a shade darker, moving toward garnet. And for what it's worth, both readily form lots of legs, quite distinct and persistent.

Aroma. When we come to their aromas, most tasters find it quite easy to make distinctions between these two wines, and the distinctions they most often make are essentially typical of the styles of French and California wines. I don't mean just of French and California Merlot-based wines, but of French and California fine wines generally.

First and broadest distinction: The majority of tasters, by a wide margin, senses the aroma of the Merlot as heavier than that of the Pomerol. Those who like it call it richer; those who don't call it coarser.

Second distinction: The same large percentage of tasters finds the Merlot's aroma the more deeply grapey and fruity of the two, the Pomerol's the more compound bouquet, less dominated by a single element.

Whether it results from California's techniques of vinification, which minimize blends of grapes and maximize single-varietal wines, or whether the California climate simply grows more intensely flavored grapes, California winemaking has until now been largely understandable through the idea of varietal intensity. Each wine seems to be striving to become the "perfect expression" of the grape variety from which it is (often exclusively) vinified. California wine makers used to get very mystical when they talked about it, as if there were a Platonic idea of Zinfandel or Chardonnay floating in the ether and waiting to be incarnated by some suitably reverent and devoted Grape Master.

More recently, some wine makers have begun experimenting with blends and modifications of varietal wines in the direction of balance, elegance, etc. This is not to say that those qualities are or have been missing in the best California wines. But even with a winery that strives for a kind of European style, as does Gundlach-Bundschu, California wine makers can't help making California wines, which are big, intense, and usually dominated by fruit or (in some cases) oak.

The kind of aroma you are getting in this Merlot (at least in its gross effects, as we've described them so far) is characteristically California:

Wine Legs

Legs, or tears, are the trails formed by the wine as it slips back down the sides of your glass after you have performed the ritual swirl-and-sniff. They have an ambiguous place in wine lore.

Supposedly they are an indication of richness and body in a wine, because wines higher in extract and glycerine, and theoretically therefore higher in viscosity, will form thicker, slower-moving, longer-lasting legs. Many wines, particularly light-bodied simple wines, make no legs at all when swirled: the wine simply flows back in an even and uniform thin sheet.

But after that, all bets are off. For one thing, there doesn't seem to be any real connection between glycerine and viscosity. For another, the formation of legs and in particular their thickness probably depend as much on the condition of your glasses as the condition of the wine. Finally, why use so hieroglyphic a sign to read the richness and body of a wine, when you can judge both much more directly and accurately by just tasting a mouthful?

Not too many years ago it was believed that some wonderful property of really fine wines caused them to create legs by a kind of bizarre capillary action, the wine actually creeping up the sides of the glass like some sci-fi attack of the killer caterpillars. That particular piece of pseudoscientific mumbo jumbo has quietly died, but the rest of leg lore still is with us and to my way of thinking is just as suspect.

Legs probably are a pure piece of wine-snob hokum—but they'll do as well as anything else to break the conversational ice at a cocktail party. At any rate, you're now armed either to start your own pretentious conversation (and I don't believe you'd do that) or to deflate the next pompous legman (or legwoman) you meet.

big, heavy, intensely grapey, with other elements emerging only slowly from behind that overpowering first rush. The first impression that a California wine typically makes upon you is power. Size. Strength. We're not necessarily talking about alcohol here, though alcoholic strength can and does play a part. Mostly it's just an impression of raw, physical bigness, like an overgrown kid who's been working out regularly and has developed a super body but still can't dance and maybe you wonder if he really can walk down the block without tripping over his own pectorals.

I told you wine tasting was very subjective.

All right, so what else is there to say about these wines? Plenty. We're not even done with the aromas yet.

When you do get past the initial impact of the Merlot, what do you smell? A mix of things, all more or less in minor keys: some woody, oaky aromas (some claim they can even smell charcoal there); some herbaceous and grassy scents, maybe even hay; and some earthy smells, particularly damp, freshly turned earth—all very nice.

The Pomerol, by contrast, presents its aroma as very much of a medley right from the start. Most tasters pick up the scent of fruit, but markedly lighter than in the Merlot. You feel as much as smell a sort of alcohol and tannin prickle in the nose. Maybe because of that sensation, some tasters describe the wine as smelling young and lively. After that, some tasters get a whole rush of scents: spice and pepper, earth and grass, wood odors such as vanilla and especially cedar. The cedar component even grows as the wine breathes in the glass. In its own very different way, this is all just as pleasing as the Merlot's aroma, but it's an entirely different creature, more restrained, more subtle, more provocative, a courtly old statesman hiding his power rather than flaunting it.

Taste. Everything that the aromas of these two wines have suggested to us is borne out by their flavors. Almost everybody reports that the Pomerol is soft, complex, medium-bodied, with a good tannic bite to it. The fruit tastes young, as if it were not yet fully developed. A good many tasters can pick out traces of cherry and of currants, nice dry fruit hints. It even has a little discernible grassiness and earthiness, and in the finish, though it is not long, some people find a definitely intriguing suggestion of licorice. You could never call this wine crisp, but it is attractive and round, a wine worth paying attention to, though it is too well bred ever to importune your attention.

The Merlot, on the other hand, grabs your lapels and not only introduces itself but also gives you its whole medical history to boot. As in its

Wine Lungs

Most fine red wines respond well to being allowed to breathe for a while, though just how long that while should be is one of the most arguable—and argued—questions in all of wine lore.

Breathing can take either of two forms: simply pulling the cork and letting the wine stand, opened, for whatever period of time you choose, or pouring the wine into a decanter. Once decanted, some serve it immediately; others let it stand and breathe for a while longer.

The point of either form is to allow the wine to open, to let its aroma and flavor develop, by exposing it to oxygen. Obviously if you decant it, you are exposing all the wine to oxygen in a short time, and a good rule of thumb is that decanting is roughly equivalent to about an hour's simple breathing. Generally speaking, Italian red wines such as Barolo and Brunello need several hours of breathing, California's best reds seem to do well with about one hour, and France's finest reds are best served by decanting just before serving. But that is very general advice as well as very subjective opinion. A lot depends on the stage at which you like to drink your wines, so conduct a few experiments of your own and taste a wine at fifteen- or twenty-minute intervals after you uncork it to see how it changes. Once you think it has opened sufficiently for your pleasure, you can simply push the cork back in if you are not ready to serve it immediately.

aroma, most tasters find that the prominent element in its flavor is fruit, a big, muscular, ripe, "sweetish" (in quotation marks because this still is a fully dry wine), perhaps berry taste. For most people, tannin is right behind the fruit, however, and very quickly discernible as a major component of this wine. Despite the fact that this Merlot still is clearly a medium-bodied wine, most tasters describe it as bigger in most respects than the Pomerol. This Merlot seems to have higher alcohol and definitely has more tannin. It even seems to have more fruit, even though the fruit is not now as clearly expressed (it's more muffled) as that of the Pomerol.

The two wines share some very important elements. In both there is that fine, pleasing, though brief licorice finish. And in both there is a flavor, very hard to describe, that many people discern mostly high in their mouths as a sort of overtaste, straight down the center of the tongue, a kind of high tenor fruit sweetness that in my mind at least is a characteristic of the Merlot grape. I've heard it described as reminding people of everything from currants to licorice to butterscotch. However you perceive it, if you perceive it where I've indicated, you are in all likelihood tasting an essential flavor of the Merlot grape, the basic affinity that links these otherwise oceans-apart wines.

A few final thoughts for you about these two and the sorts of wines you'll be going on to in the next section. You are here on the verge of full-bodied wines and already well launched on wines that improve with bottle age. These two bottles are, by any serious standards, very young wines, and you, thoughtless as ever, have just committed something very close to infanticide in opening them.

If a really knowledgeable drinker had been sipping along with us, he would have been surprised by only one thing: not that the Merlot was somewhat muffled, but that the Pomerol was so drinkable.

Why? Because in wines of this class, where tannin in particular is so important a contributor to both the wine's balance and its longevity, it is expected that for several years after bottling (these '81s were bottled only at the end of '83), the wine will be harsh, tannic, alcoholic, acidic, or all four. It takes time for all those elements to learn to lie down together peacefully: in a great vintage, it can take decades—and 1981, in Bordeaux and in California, was a very fine vintage year. So this particular Pomerol is what we call a very forward wine, one ready to drink unusually early. That does not mean it is now at its peak. Probably far from it, because wines of this sort commonly go on developing in the bottle for—in a good vintage—five to ten years before reaching a peak and an equilibrium, where they may remain, if properly stored, for another ten to twenty years.

No one really knows if California Merlot has that kind of potential for development and longevity because there just isn't enough of a track record for California wines. But this much is certain: This particular Merlot still is developing, and its real flavor has yet to emerge. It might be one year away or it might be ten, but this is a wine that will go through several changes before it reaches adulthood, so don't be surprised if you taste it again in a few months or a year and get an impression completely different from what you received today. That, too, is one of the fascinations and pleasures of wine, as well as being the main reason people put together wine cellars.

Since we are talking here about aging wines, and since you are already well engaged with wines that take well to aging, this is a good place to say a few words about a flavor that many connoisseurs regard as peculiar to the taste of quite mature wine. Some don't like it at all and call it the flavor of old and tired wine.

This flavor can be perceived by different individuals as anything from plum to raisin to resin. Usually it is simply called plummy, and it is regarded as more or less characteristic of many older wines. The "more or less," of course, depends on the grapes they are made from. And depending on the grapes and their vinification, the plummy flavor we are speaking of does not necessarily stand alone or even unmodified. Other fruit flavors may coexist with it, harmonies that were masked by an earlier heavy fruit or heavy tannin may become apparent, overbright acid may subside; any number of changes can go on during the bottle-aging of a fine wine. But all really mature wines show something of this plummy character, and the whole class of clarets does so particularly.

Because of the different grapes and the vinification techniques used, different wines mature at different ages. What is maturity for a Barbera and senility for a Beaujolais is scarcely adolescence for a Barolo or a Bordeaux. But that suggestion of plumminess, whenever you get a scent or taste of it in a wine, usually is a good clue that the wine is at or near its mature peak. That doesn't mean it's going to fall apart and decay in the next twenty-four hours, but it probably does mean it's not going to get significantly better than it is right now. So if, for instance, you happen to taste that telltale accent in a wine you've squirreled away two or three more bottles or cases of, you'd be wise to start drinking 'em up pretty soon. Some wines may persevere in exactly this condition for many years, and many of them can be very lovely indeed in this state of absolute maturity, but don't plan on keeping them long like that unless you really know the wine and its staying power, or unless you are content to risk the loss.

You should know also that many connoisseurs do not like wine in this condition. For them, this is already too old, and they prefer to drink their wines, whatever kind they may be, with a flush of youthful fruit still intact. This is, as are so many things to do with wine, purely a matter of personal taste.

Château de Sales is imported by Château & Estate Wine Company. Gundlach-Bundschu wines are distributed by the same firm.

Here ends our eleventh red-wine-tasting session and the section on medium-bodied red wines. From here you can:

Follow the lead of your own preferences:

If you liked the first wine better, Château de Sales Pomerol, go to Flight 14.

If you liked the second wine better, Gundlach-Bundschu Merlot, go to Flight 16.

Follow the kind of grapes:

This is the last predominantly Merlot flight. For wines with small admixtures of Merlot, go to Flight 15.

Follow the wines of the country:

Go to Flight 12.

CASTLING: FULL-BODIED RED WINES

You stand right now at the gateway to what is for me the most fascinating and pleasurable stretch of territory on the whole world wine map. The full-bodied red wines are the heavy hitters of wine's biggest league. As a class, these are the wines you select to accompany your best meals, to serve your best friends, and to comfort yourself with when everything else is going sour.

Because of their size—and I mean that in the metaphoric sense—these are wines that last, so they are the wines to buy young and relatively inexpensively to lay down until they mature.

These are the wines that I wish every would-be or might-be wine drinker could taste at least a mature mouthful of: they would skin your tongue back and teach you more in a few seconds about why people make a fuss about wine than everything I or anyone else could ever write.

What constitutes the excellence of these wines? What makes them big and full-bodied, and why does that make them capable of age? I'm glad you asked me that.

The answer cannot be given in one word. You have to start with the variety of grapes. Some few red varieties—Cabernet Sauvignon is the best example—seem to produce top-quality wine wherever they are planted. Some, such as Pinot Noir, make superb wine in one location (Burgundy) and in another (California) give only hints of what they might do. A grape that in one place yields an enormously powerful wine (the Grenache in the southern Rhône) elsewhere gives only a mild-mannered rosé (the Grenache in California). So at the start, it is a combination of vine and soil and climate that together create the possibility of a big red wine.

After that, a great deal depends on the skill and the methods of the wine maker, on the combination of tradition and innovation each individual brings to each harvest. Normally, for big red wines, wood-aging plays an important role in the wine's development. As the wine rests in the barrels, an intricate exchange between wine and wood takes place, the most marked effects of which are the addition to the wine of wood tannins (different from grape tannins both chemically and in flavor) and flavors from the barrels (new or used barrels can make a tremendous difference in this regard). Also, the wood permits a tightly controlled, indirect contact between wine and air, so a very gradual and limited oxidation goes forward, contributing further to the wine's maturation. Just how long a wine remains in wooden barrels varies incredibly from region to region, even from wine maker to wine maker.

In Burgundy, for instance, it used to be routine practice to allow the fresh-pressed juices to ferment on the skins—that is, in direct contact with the crushed grape skins and stems and seeds—for from two to four weeks. That made a wine high in extracts (dissolved solids), deep in color (leached from the skins—most grape juice is clear), and rich in tannin and acids (tannin particularly from skins, stems, and seeds). Because of the Burgundian climate, the Pinot Noir rarely ripens there to the degree it normally does in California, so in the past, young Burgundies were freshened with heartier wines from the South, which were naturally much higher in sugar: now, because of AOC laws, the addition of sugar to the ferment is the norm.

The practice of adding sugar to the fermenting juices is called Chaptalization, after Count Antoine Chaptal, an early nineteenth-century promoter of the virtues of beet sugar. The purpose of the addition is to turn sugar-deficient grapes into wines of adequate alcoholic strength, since during fermentation, sugar converts to alcohol.

Chaptalization probably is the simplest and most widely used chemical process in winemaking. It is frequently employed in Burgundy, where the grapes often fail to achieve full ripeness, and it is permitted (and seems to be used with increasing frequency) in Bordeaux. In Germany, it is allowed for wines up to the level of *Qualitatswein* without *pradikat*, but not above that. In Italy it is never permitted. In the

Wine Beds

Laying down wine, or cellaring, probably carries a greater freight of romance than any other aspect of wine lore. People inevitably think of cobwebbed racks containing vast numbers of bottles that have slept undisturbed for generations in the ancestral vaults of some decayed aristocrat. The reality is very different. If you've got 12 bottles of your favorite Zinfandel stashed away in the hall closet, you've started a wine cellar.

Anyone can keep wine till maturity if certain minimal conditions are met: darkness, because sunlight can destroy wine; tranquillity, because motion or vibration can destroy wine (that's why some wines "can't travel"); consistent moderate temperatures, no higher than 65 to 70 degrees Fahrenheit and no lower than 45, with only gradual alterations within that range, because temperatures too high rush the wine through its life cycle far too fast—cook it, in effect—and because sudden temperature changes can cause wines simply to fall apart. If it meets those conditions, a broom closet, a stairwell, or an ordinary basement can serve as a wine cellar.

Those are the minimal requirements. What are the optimum conditions for wine storage? Most experts agree on dark, tranquillity, a constant temperature of around 55 degrees, and a slight amount of humidity in the atmosphere. And check your corks every fifteen to twenty-five years or so; they might need replacement.

United States it is subject to state law, and therefore practices vary considerably. Chaptalization is not permitted in California.

Changes in vinification have made enormous differences in the finished wine. An old-style Burgundy, drunk young, could be harsh and ungiving, its fruit almost completely masked by tannin. Laid down for ten or more years, a good vintage would ripen into a wine that can only be called opulent: a big, generous wine that opened softly on the palate to reveal depth after depth of flavor. A new-style Burgundy is likely to be much more drinkable young, with more readily appreciable fruit, but it seems unlikely ever to develop the size and resonance those wines used to have. Changed vinification methods have completely changed the wine. They are still great wines, but they are different wines. (Unfortunately, they still command the same prices, among the highest of all wines. Burgundy may not hit as forcefully as it used to, but economically at least it is still playing in the major leagues.)

In Burgundy, in Bordeaux, in California, aging the fermented wine in small barrels (called *barriques*) is the normal procedure in setting out to make a fine wine. Sometimes in California the barrels are made of redwood, but most of the time oak is the preferred material, and French oak if it can be found. Even in areas such as the Piedmont in Italy, where aging in huge wooden vats has been the normal procedure for centuries, innovators are now finishing their wines in *barriques*. Why? Because the size of the *barrique* ensures optimum exposure of the wine to the wood and thereby the greatest possible interaction between the two. What the oak adds is, once again, tannin, plus some flavor elements: the vanilla or caramel strains in the aromas and tastes of some wines are directly traceable to new oak barrels.

All of these factors contribute ultimately to the longevity of the wine, since the two principal components that keep a wine going are tannin and alcohol.

The latter brings us full circle, back to the grapes again. You can always strengthen the tannin presence in your wine by the way you vinify and age it, but for good alcohol you need good sugar levels to start with. And if you want to end up with high alcohol and big tannin for longevity, you need to have something worth keeping alive, or else you wind up with a zombie wine, a walking corpse animated by alcohol and tannin but with no real spark. So you need a grape that makes a flavorful wine, a flavor capable of standing up to high alcohol and a lot of tannin, and you need good acid to keep that flavor bright and to prevent the wine from going flabby.

This is why the greatest red wines are normally the aged, full-bodied reds—they simply have more of what makes any wine good, have it in greater concentration, and have it more harmoniously. So what you will be tasting for in the flights that follow, aside from the newly introduced varietal flavor of a few sorts of wine you've not met before, is exactly what you've been tasting for all along. The difference is that here you should find all those elements you've been learning about present more abundantly, more precisely, and in better balance. Enjoy.

Red Wines:
The Twelfth Flight

PROSPER MAUFOUX CÔTE DE BEAUNE VILLAGES 1979
AND
ZACA MESA SANTA BARBARA COUNTY PINOT NOIR 1981

This and the next flight are devoted to exploring the nuances of the Pinot Noir grape, a variety that probably has broken more vintners' hearts than all the others combined.

In Burgundy, in that narrow stretch of vineyards known as the Côte d'Or (the Golden Slope), Pinot Noir can produce some of the most sinfully luxurious wines your palate will ever have the pleasure to be ravished by. I say "can produce" because even in Burgundy the Pinot Noir is a fickle grape and the climate is also tricky, so that for every sensational harvest you get three or four mediocre ones and one or two downright rotten ones. And even in the best harvests Pinot Noir yields are small, or should be, because a heavy growth of fruit on these vines means flabby, characterless wines. So really fine red Burgundy is scarce and very expensive. Almost certainly, these wines will be the costliest of any this book asks you to buy; Burgundies are pretty much the price leaders in the world of wine.

If the Pinot Noir grape is troublesome on its home turf, it is a complete sociopath everywhere else. In climates less demanding than Burgundy's it grows well and bears good crops and makes, on the whole, dull wine. Wine makers in California and Long Island and South Africa and Australia have tried every conceivable trick of cultivation and vinification, and the end result has been, overall, very forgettable. Only a few really fine bottlings from various makers in scattered vintages have given hints of what the grape might do outside Burgundy, if someone can ever find the magic formula.

The two wines you're going to taste in this flight are an example of a successful California Pinot Noir made outside the most favored zones of cultivation (Pinot Noir always seems to do its best as a wine grape in circumstances that are in agricultural terms adverse or at least difficult), and a wine blended from the produce of several of the communes of the Côte de Beaune, which is the southern half of the Golden Slope. Once again you are being asked to taste as much for similarities as for differences, to try to help you fix in your mind what Pinot Noir tastes like—that is, what is essential to its flavor and what in it can be altered by soil and climate and technology.

Wine apocrypha has it that some fabulous palates can identify in the flavor of a Pinot Noir the forest the barrels it aged in came from. You are free to doubt this.

Okay, go ahead and see, swirl, smell, sip, savor, and spit. Be bold, and tread on the aspirations of whole generations of wine makers.

Appearance. Both wines are clear ruby, though the Pinot Noir falls slightly more into the brownish/orange range than does the Beaune. Ideally, you would like to see a greater depth of color here—both are a little pale for the true Burgundy shade.

Aroma. Both are rather subdued immediately after pouring, but both open in the glass after a few minutes (long breathing doesn't seem to change these wines very much).

The range of comments people are likely to make about these two wines is large indeed, because both present very complex sets of scent, what are properly, in wine jargon, called bouquets rather than aromas. That is not a distinction without a difference, though the difference is a difficult one for many people to perceive. Aroma, technically speaking, means only those odors that originate from the grapes themselves, while bouquet denotes all those odors arising from the whole process of vinification and bottle-aging. The distinction is essentially a useless one for people who have never had the opportunity to smell freshly pressed Pinot Noir or Gamay or any other grape, and throughout this book, if I make any distinction at all between the words "aroma" and "bouquet," I tend to use them as I do here, employing aroma to mean simpler odors and bouquet more complex ones.

Individual tasters' descriptions of the Beaune's bouquet can run from full, balanced, and fruity on one hand to practically nonexistent on the other. The median position probably is as close to objective truth as we can get with wine: the aroma is of middling strength but persistent, and it shows good, fresh fruit with pleasing leafy and floral over- and undertones. Most people find it very composed, very balanced, strongly suggesting elegance in the wine to come. The fruit component they seem to find particularly intriguing, describing it as, among other things, rich and attractive and smelling of cherries or plums or currants or cassis.

Perceptions of the Pinot Noir's aroma can range from finding it sweeter, fuller, and more spicy than the Beaune's to smelling a sharpness and acridity in it. Again, about the middle of the spectrum seems closest to target. This Pinot seems to have an aroma somewhat bigger than the Beaune's and decidedly fruity, with herbaceous and floral notes in it and a tart or astringent bass tone underneath everything.

Taste. The polarities of opinion about the bouquets of these wines probably will continue into tasters' reactions to their flavor. Those lining up on the positive side about the Beaune probably will like best its clean, fresh fruit, which they will taste as soft, warm, and at least suggesting sweetness. Cherries and plums are the specifics most often mentioned. Tasters describe the wine as not exactly crisp, but bright and lively, with decent acid and plenty of tannin contributing to an overall impression of balance, roundness, and some softness. At least some will taste a small but persistent dry finish that ends the wine very nicely. Those who are negative about the Beaune will find it somewhat sour and astringent in the mouth and, in comparison to the Pinot Noir, rather bland.

Those positive for the Pinot Noir will describe it as similar to the Beaune wine but smoother, perhaps bigger, with more fruit or more enjoyable fruit and with a bigger finish. They may remark on some attractive quasi-syrupy, quasi-liquory undertones as well. Those feeling negative about this wine may at one extreme find it a bit thin and too acid, perhaps with an unpleasant touch of tartness or sourness or bitterness, and with a bitter finish. At the other extreme, they describe it as excessively fruity and flabby.

What is the objective truth about the two? Well, you should know by now that when it comes to wine, objective truth is a very elastic concept. If you pushed me to the wall, I'd say that both the Beaune and the Pinot Noir are clearly well-made wines and that they share many similarities, even many specific flavor elements, that derive directly from their common grape variety. Neither is really big in body; both are more like middleweights, and that is a real defect according to my personal ideal of what a Pinot Noir-based wine ought to be. I like them with more heft and more guts to them: these two are on the soft and charming side rather than the big and impressive side. Nevertheless, both are substantial wines and round in the mouth.

The big difference between them seems to me a perfect illustration of what I think of as the classic France/California split. The Pinot Noir has more fruit—so much more that sometimes it can seem unbalanced—and the Beaune has more breeding, more elegance—it is so harmonious and restrained that sometimes I wish it were more assertive, more aggressive. Those differences, I think, concisely illustrate what the norms and goals of winemaking are in the two areas at this time, and they are emphasized (some would say exaggerated) by the fact that there really do exist such things as California palates and European palates, tastes and taste buds that naturally lean toward one or the other of these sets of characteristics. A California palate relishes the big fruit in the Zaca Mesa wine and finds the Beaune too thin, too small, too unsubstantial. A European palate delights in the elegance of the Beaune and finds the Pinot Noir unbalanced, flabby, overstated.

Who is right and who is wrong? Both. Neither. By now you know as well as I do that the right wine is the wine right for you and right for the occasion (I wouldn't take either of these wines to the beach, but I could happily drink either of them in many other places). And by now you should also know enough about your own palate and about at least some kinds of wine to be able to choose the one you like without feeling embarrassed at not liking the other. So cast your ballot as you please.

Prosper Maufoux is a highly regarded Burgundian *négociant* handling the whole gamut of the region's wines. His wines are imported to the United States by The House of Burgundy. Zaca Mesa is one of the pioneers of quality winemaking in California's Santa Ynez Valley in Santa Barbara County. Zaca Mesa's wines are distributed by Frederick Wildman.

This is the conclusion of our twelfth red-wine-tasting session. There are several ways for you to proceed from here.

Following the lead of your own preferences:

If you liked the first wine better, Côte de Beaune Villages, go to Flight 13, where you'll taste some more of the Pinot Noir's French incarnations.

If you liked the second wine better, Zaca Mesa Pinot Noir, go either to Flight 13 or to Flight 14.

Following the kind of grapes:

Go to Flight 13. If you wish to explore further the adventures of American Pinot Noir, there are many other first-rate California vineyards also trying their hand at this difficult grape. Those in the Alexander Valley/Carneros Creek area seem to be having the most luck so far. Wineries in Washington and Oregon are also beginning to turn out quite interesting Pinot Noir. Here are the names of some you might want to try: Acacia Winery, Davis Bynum, Kenwood, Joseph Swan (if you can find any), or Carneros Creek, all in California; in the Pacific Northwest, Adelsheim Vineyard, The Eyrie Vineyards, Knudsen Erath Winery, and Tualatin Vineyards. You may have a hard hunt for some of these, because distribution still is a serious problem for many Pacific Northwest wine makers.

Following the wines of the country:

Wine 1: go to Flight 13.

Wine 2: go to Flight 16.

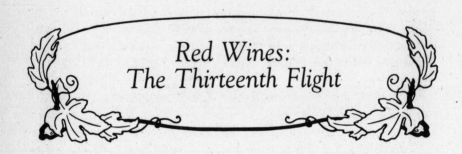

Red Wines:
The Thirteenth Flight

DOMAINE DUJAC MOREY ST.-DENIS 1980
AND
PROSPER MAUFOUX POMMARD 1981

Allow me at this point in our tasting together to extend to all of you fledgling Burgundy fans my sincerest condolences. You probably are embarking upon a passion that is going to leave you in financial jeopardy for the rest of your life. It is a real question whether in economic terms a fondness for Burgundy is more or less costly than playing the horses or playing the stock market. In any event, there is little question that you will drink well, and I'll be happy to come to dinner any time you ask.

Why is Burgundy so costly? For the usual reasons: high quality and low quantity. We've already talked about the balkiness of the Pinot Noir and the iffiness of the Burgundian climate. Multiply those erratic low yields by the fact that the entire Golden Slope is only about thirty miles long and averages only about half a mile wide. At some spots, a strong arm could throw a rock from its western to its eastern limit. That accounts amply for scarcity.

The quality comes from two sources: first, a tradition of cultivating

Pinot Noir (and Chardonnay, but that is for another section of this book) that runs back at least as far as the establishment of Cistercian monasteries in the Middle Ages, and second, accidents of soil and sun that have made a few precious plots the *ne plus ultra* vineyards of the wine world. For devoted oenophiles, La Tache, Romanée Conti, Clos de Vougeot, Clos de Bèze, Le Corton—these are names to conjure with, great red wines that will, sadly, dye your bankbook that color, too.

Despite the small size of the Côte d'Or, its topography and output are quite varied. It is conventionally divided into the Côte de Nuits and the Côte de Beaune. Its northern division, the Côte de Nuits, runs southward from the edge of Dijon to a few miles north of Beaune. The Côte de Beaune continues from that point all the way south to Santenay. The Côte de Nuits is famous for its red wines and the Côte de Beaune for its whites, but the southern division also produces some lovely reds, as you will soon see.

Within these two big divisions exists a series of small townships, some of which are used as official AOC designations and therefore pretty carefully regulated, and some of which are not. In addition, wines may bear the name of individual estates or vineyards, some of which may be shared by several owners, any or all of whom may bottle their wine separately. And to top that, there is a classification of *crus* in which *Premier Cru* (First Growth) is actually the second rank and *Grand Cru* (Great Growth) is the first. So the label situation for the consumer is very confusing until you learn exactly what to look for.

Where the AOC is attached is one of the crucial items to keep your eye on: in order of refinement, a wine can be AOC Bourgogne (Burgundy), or AOC village name, or AOC vineyard name. AOC vineyard name applies only to *Grands Crus*, which are the only wines so labeled. So great is their prestige, in fact, that in many cases the village that contains these *Grands Crus* has added their name to its own. For instance, the *Grand Cru* is Le Corton; the village is Aloxe, but on wine labels you will see Aloxe-Corton—and you will pay for the extra two syllables.

That's enough prologue. If you're not already completely confused and discouraged (it's really not as puzzling as it looks at first), get ready to discriminate between the wine of one of the least-known villages of the Côte de Nuits, Morey St.-Denis, and what probably is the best-known red wine of the Côte de Beaune, Pommard. Okay, let's do it. See, swirl, smell, sip, savor. Expectorate and expatiate.

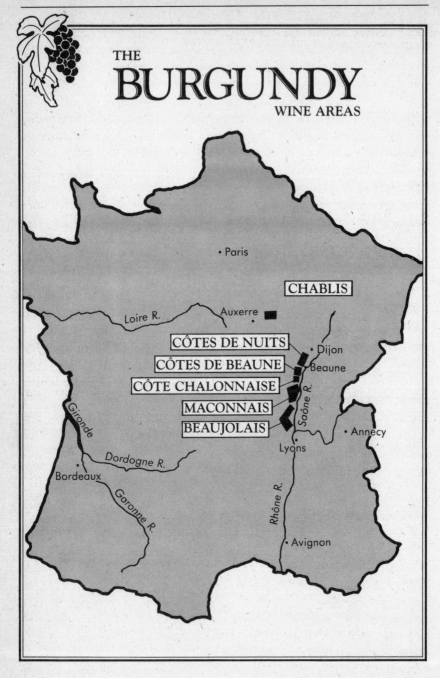

THE BURGUNDY WINE AREAS

CHABLIS

CÔTES DE NUITS

CÔTES DE BEAUNE

CÔTE CHALONNAISE

MACONNAIS

BEAUJOLAIS

• Paris

Auxerre

Loire R.

• Dijon

Beaune

Saône R.

Gironde

• Annecy

Lyons

Dordogne R.

Bordeaux

Garonne R.

Rhône R.

• Avignon

Appearance. Both wines are ruby, showing some tawny highlights. If you tilt the wines in the glass you should see in both a faint purple edge, very thin, succeeded by a narrow band of brownish amber, which is exactly what you ought to see in good young Burgundies like these.

Aroma. Neither wine seems yet to have developed a very big aroma, though there is every possibility that it will come for both with time in the bottle.

The scent of the Morey St.-Denis will strike most people first with its alcohol and acid—a little peppery prickle in the nose, a sense of warmth—and then with its fruit and some odors related to its vinification. You can pick out herbal scents and fresh wood as well as good, clean earth odors and just the faintest hint of truffle, with a pleasing, generalized fruitiness under everything. Even though this is not a large or particularly strong bouquet, it conveys the impression of a heavier, sturdier wine than its appearance suggests. Most tasters find little to dislike here; even if they are not partisans of Burgundy, they rarely say anything more negative than "it smells too acidic."

Responses to the aroma of the Pommard are likely to be more varied. Some will find it fuller, others thinner, than that of the Morey St.-Denis. Most will find the Pommard both slightly smaller and slightly more complex, with its fruit elements discernible as fresh, cool, bright, perhaps even apple-y, and backed up by suggestions of mint and flowers. There are some very slight undertones of earth and stems; the overall impression is smoothness, restraint, a sort of cool, woodsy, moss-on-stones scent. Again, few people find anything to dislike here; at worst they find it too faint, too insubstantial.

Taste. There will no doubt be more diversity of opinion about the taste of these wines than about their aromas. Some tasters tend to be thrown off by the acid of the Morey St.-Denis and consequently perceive it as a lighter and less substantial wine than it is. This may also be due to the fact that it does seem to need a bit more tannin to structure it. It's very important to taste this wine carefully all over your mouth to sort out these niceties of balance, because they can tell you a lot about the possible longevity or long-term pleasure potential of the wine.

In any event, most tasters probably will respond very favorably to the fruit of the Morey: it's soft, with definite berry and currant flavors in it, and completely dry. Some will taste a flavor hard to describe but most like the wininess of a good Winesap apple: whatever you call it, it is a positive attraction of this wine's taste. Overall, the Morey strikes most tasters as round, soft, with good acid and a nice, astringent finish.

Most tasters will also respond very favorably to the Pommard; if there are reservations or negatives, they will probably center on the wine's tannin, which for some palates will mask or at least partially obscure the wine's other components. But tannin to the degree this Pommard has it is only to be expected in a young Burgundy, and it bodes well for the wine's future.

Those not bothered by the tannin will find the Pommard smooth and weighty on the tongue, clean and full, as if it were delivering simply more of whatever it has than did the Morey. The Pommard shows a remarkable balance for so young a wine, and its various components— acid, fruit, tannin, alcohol—and flavor elements are already so inter- twined that it is very difficult for most people to separate them even verbally. The impression the wine creates in the mouth is at once more uniform and more complicated than that of the Morey, a kind of robustness wrapped up with elegance. Most tasters discern a rather nice finish as well.

Looked at from the point of view of an ideal red Burgundy (or at least my ideal red Burgundy), the worst thing I can find to say about these wines is that they are about twenty years too young. I'd love to open a bottle of each on New Year's Eve in 1999 to see how they've grown up. Both are very forward for Burgundies, but of course more and more of them are now being vinified precisely for that, to become drinkable sooner. Whether that affects their ability to age remains an open question— another reason I'm curious to try one of these again at the turn of the century.

By the way, and just for the record: The relatively greater body and robustness of the Pommard completely upsets one piece of conventional wine wisdom, that the reds of the Côte de Nuits are bigger and gutsier than those of the Côte de Beaune. So much for wine wisdom.

A final word about these wines: If you are going to begin seriously exploring Burgundies, try to find a knowledgeable wine dealer to help you out. Everybody needs guidance with these wines, especially because of their cost. My general advice is: Until you know your way around, stick with wines from reputable shippers—Prosper Maufoux, Bouchard Père et Fils, Louis Latour, Drouhin, Jadot, Bouchard Ainé, Faiveley, etc. And good luck.

Domaine Dujac is one of the most prestigious of Burgundy's smaller growers. Its wines are imported by Frederick Wildman. The wines of Prosper Maufoux are imported by The House of Burgundy.

This is the conclusion of our thirteenth red-wine flight. There are several ways for you to proceed from here.

Following the lead of your own preferences:

If you liked either the first wine, Morey St.-Denis, or the second wine, Pommard, go to Flight 18.

Following the kind of grapes:

These are the last Pinot Noirs in the tastings.

Following the wines of the country:

Go to Flight 15.

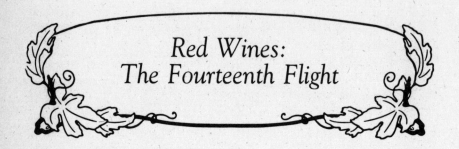

Red Wines:
The Fourteenth Flight

VILLA ANTINORI CHIANTI CLASSICO RISERVA 1979
AND
BRUSCO DEI BARBI 1979

In this flight you are tasting wines made from different clones of the Sangiovese grape, one of Italy's two or three most important red-wine varieties. Both clones are cultivated in Tuscany, but in different geographical areas. Although not far apart as the crow flies, these districts are quite distinct from each other, since the topography of Tuscany is so broken that every kilometer north or south, east or west, uphill or downhill can mean a new soil composition and a separate microclimate. Add to that the variations in vinification sanctioned by Tuscan tradition and you wind up with a major viticultural region where even neighboring wineries can turn out radically differing wines.

You may be surprised to find a Chianti among the full-bodied wines. The common stereotype of Chianti as a light-bodied spaghetti red in a wicker flask has been outdated for some time, but this is one of those classic cases where perception lags reality—which creates some nice bargains for you, since it has caused Chianti prices to trail well behind their real worth as well.

The basic grape in all Chiantis (yes, Virginia, there is more than one kind of Chianti) is the Sangiovese: it comprises 60 percent and upward of any wine bearing the Chianti name. The remaining 40 percent (often much less) is made up of another red grape, the Canaiolo, and, in the traditional formula, two white grapes, Trebbiano and Malvasia. In Chianti destined to be aged for *riserva*, these last two grapes figure less and less importantly.

Chianti is labeled for the zone in which it is grown as well as for the aging it receives. The zones are Colli Aretini (the hills near Arezzo), Colli Fiorentini (the hills north of Florence), Colline Pisane (the hills around Pisa), Colli Senesi (the hills south of Siena), Montalbano (northeastern Tuscany), Rufina (farther east), and Classico (the traditional heart of Chianti, lying between Florence and Siena). The age designations are *vecchia* and *riserva*, indicating two and three years respectively, of barrel- and bottle-aging. Wines from any zone may be made into *riserva*, but it is most commonly and most successfully done in the Classico.

A Chianti becomes a *riserva* by receiving its education in wood: it must be aged in barrel and in bottle for three years before it can be labeled *riserva*. That, at least, is the legal requirement, but most Chianti makers first exercise a rigorous selection process, starting with the grapes at harvest time, to set aside only the very best of their wines for *riserva*. So for all practical purposes the *riserva* designation indicates not only barrel-aging but quality control as well.

It also indicates an important difference in the handling of the young wine. Chiantis intended to be drunk young—non-*riserva* Chiantis—often are treated with the *governo Toscano*, the introduction to already fermented wine of new musts from reserved, partially raisined grapes. This brings on a second fermentation, which raises the alcohol level, deepens color, intensifies fruit, and sometimes leaves the wine lightly fizzy— what Italians call *frizzante*. It may also leave the wine somewhat unstable, with too much volatile acidity, and therefore unsuitable for any lengthy keeping. But it makes, par excellence, a fresh, fruity wine for immediate drinking, which is the appropriate fate of most simple Chiantis. Chiantis earmarked for *riserva* status never undergo the *governo Toscano* but instead are vinified and aged in the conventional manner of all fine wines.

Antinori is among the oldest and most respected family firms in the Chianti Classico, active in the Tuscan wine trade for six hundred years.

They make several different Chiantis and other Tuscan wines. Their wines are imported to the United States by Buckingham Wile.

Vintners in the area around the hill town of Montalcino, south of the Chianti Classico district, cultivate a special clone of the Sangiovese known as the Sangiovese Grosso or the Brunello. In this very restricted zone and under very rigorously controlled conditions of viticulture and vinification, these unblended grapes yield what is perhaps Italy's finest and certainly its most expensive wine, Brunello di Montalcino. It is also one of Italy's newer wines, with a history of little more than a hundred years. The Barbi firm, one of the most important producers in the area, takes grapes from its young vines—too young for use in a great Brunello— and subjects them to the *governo Toscano* to make its proprietary wine, Brusco dei Barbi. In its mode of vinification, this wine resembles non-*riserva* Chiantis, designed to be drunk young and fresh, while its single grape links it with the austere and long-lived Brunello. Barbi's wines are imported to the United States by P. L. Importers, Inc.

So you are now about to taste the Sangiovese in its two forms and treated by two different methods. Be prepared to pay attention both to similarities and to differences; what you taste in these two wines can be a complete capsule education in the variables of winemaking.

All right, swirl away, and read on when you're ready.

Appearance. An easy one: both wines are a deep ruby with tawny or amber highlights. The latter, in Italian wines, do not necessarily indicate complete maturity, though they do show a wine that is, as both these ought to be, past its first youth. Generally speaking, fine Italian red wines show more amber/orangey highlighting at every stage of their development than do French or California wines of comparable age and quality.

Aroma. Depending on how long these wines have been uncorked, their aromas will be more or less pronounced. Not, as you might expect, that they will dissipate after uncorking, but rather that their aromas will grow over a substantial period of time. Both of these wines—and this is true of fine Italian wines generally—would benefit greatly from being allowed to breathe for about an hour before they are served. If you have uncorked them just a few minutes ago, arrange to leave them on the table for a while if you can; they will change and open even in the glass. Or decant them to provide a little instant aeration. Alternatively, leave a little wine in your glasses, taste them again in half an hour, and match the notes you take then with those you've already taken. I can promise you the differences will be very instructive: the wine really improves—literally seems to open up—with breathing.

Back to work. To most tasters, the Chianti Classico smells vinous in the best sense of the word: a satisfying, winey aroma in which you can identify an alcohol warmth and fruit-sweet scents, with other, smaller elements occasionally surfacing (a little salt-air tang, a bit of grass, perhaps a hint of vanilla). Most people agree that the Brusco dei Barbi has a slightly bigger aroma, dominated mostly by a soft fruit scent (berries, perhaps?) and an alcoholic tingle, with earthy undertones and some freshly sawed wood notes. Those who don't like this sort of wine are likely to find either or both aromas too alcoholic on one hand or too insubstantial on the other, but most tasters seem to find them quite pleasing.

Taste. The first impression the Chianti Classico creates on most people's palates is a combined sensation of roundness, warmth, and fruit-and-tannin together. Even if you find the tannin initially a little too strong and perhaps masking the fruit (the tannin will soften in the glass and the fruit will come forward in a short while), you should nevertheless be able to discern this ensemble of characteristics because the wine presents itself complexly from the outset.

If you are really having trouble picking out the fruit, put a little wine "in the hole" behind your front teeth and under your tongue as I explained earlier. After a few seconds, the tip of your tongue ought to be able to pick up a distinct sweetish, grapey flavor there. The feel of the wine in your mouth is smooth and slightly chewy. To many tasters it gives the impression of a substantial presence, even though this particular vintage strikes me as inclining more toward medium rather than full body. It also has a very attractive bitterness that is particularly discernible in its finish. Overall, the impression it leaves is a compound of complexity (from the various elements of flavor) and elegance (primarily from what you feel in the texture and finish of the wine). I piously trust that by this stage of the game you can see just how far this is from what you used to think Chianti was.

The Brusco dei Barbi usually strikes tasters as an altogether bolder and less subtle wine. Its most prominent feature is very soft, sweet fruit—nut-sweet—with a small, underlying tannic bitterness. This wine seems bigger than the Chianti, fruitier and more full-bodied, but also less live and less balanced. While some tasters may find this Brusco dei Barbi too big and alcoholic for their pleasure, most will enjoy the pronounced character of its soft fruit and drink it happily with the simple foods for which it cries.

It is a fact of life that almost any wine will bloom when you match it with the right food, but one of the great advantages of many Italian wines is that they partner so well with such a diverse range of foods, often revealing flavors and nuances hidden before. This is particularly true of Sangiovese-based wines such as these. The Brusco dei Barbi and the simpler Chiantis, which, like it, have undergone the *governo Toscano*, respond very well to simpler foods such as plainly broiled chops, omelettes, cheeses, and charcuterie. The Chianti Classico Riserva and other wines of its kind—particularly older specimens—marry quite well with roast meats or elaborately sauced meats and fowl or excellent cheeses. Really fine vintages would wonderfully accompany game.

If this range of wines pleases you, there are many more examples of it to try, both from Antinori and Barbi as well as other fine Tuscan wine houses. If you like the style of the Antinori, look into the same firm's Riserva Marchese as well as the Chianti Classico Riserva from such houses as Ruffino, Brolio, Frescobaldi, and Fossi, as well as smaller estates like Monsanto, Monte Vertine, Badia a Coltibuono, Villa Cerna, and Spalletti. And don't forget Chianti's kissing cousin, Vino Nobile di Montepulciano, a very elegant wine in the same style as the Chianti Classico Riserva you've just liked.

On the other hand, if you prefer what you tasted in the Brusco dei Barbi, then try some of the other Montalcino wines, starting with a simple Brunello and working your way palatally and fiscally up to the most highly esteemed Brunello di Montalcino Riserva, that of Biondi-Santi, which family created the wine in the last century. Be warned, however: a real Brunello can be very, very hard in its youth, and it can take a long time to come around. A decent vintage normally will not be drinkable until it is at least ten years old, and as a class these wines are famous for their longevity. They are supreme examples of wines worth buying young—and relatively inexpensively—and laying down for the days of their fabulous maturity. Chianti Classico Riserva also rewards such treatment, though to a lesser degree than Brunello.

Here ends our fourteenth red-wine-tasting session. There are several ways for you to proceed from here.

Following the lead of your own preferences:

If you liked the first wine better, Chianti Classico Riserva, go to Flight 15.

If you preferred the second wine, Brusco dei Barbi, go to Flight 16 or Flight 17.

Following the kind of grapes:

These are the last Sangiovese wines in our tastings (an earlier example was in Flight 4).

Following the wines of the country:

Go to Flight 18.

Red Wines:
The Fifteenth Flight

CHÂTEAU DE PEZ 1978 (ST.-ESTÈPHE)
AND
CHÂTEAU SMITH HAUT LAFITTE 1979 (GRAVES)

You are about to embark on what might for some of you turn out to be a lifelong journey of exploration among the thickets, forests, and peaks of Cabernet Sauvignon. Right now Cabernet is probably *the* international glamor varietal, but don't hold that against it. Despite all its current swank, it makes great wine, and it does so in a wide variety of soils and climates. For centuries it has been the basic constituent of claret, a lovely red wine in which, according to Bordelais tradition, it blends with varying amounts of Merlot and/or Cabernet Franc. Now it also makes fine straight varietal wine (that is, 100 percent Cabernet) in California and Long Island and South America and Australia and is beginning to respond well in experimental plantings in Italy and Spain.

Cabernet possesses one of the most readily identifiable aromas and flavors of any great varietal grape. Once you have tasted a few good specimens, you should be able to recognize its characteristics even when you come across them diluted or subdued. So here is your chance to add an important volume to your palatal library. This flight matches two clarets from different communes of Bordeaux, and the next will expose you to two different styles and regions of California Cabernet. This is, by general consent, the most important and perhaps the most rewarding red grape varietal in the world, so taste very, very carefully.

Ready? Okay, see, swirl, smell, sip, etc.

Appearance. The Château de Pez shows the classic color of a young claret: a clear, pretty garnet. The Smith Haut Lafitte is slightly lighter, what I would call dark ruby, with some amber lights. Generally in clarets this is regarded as a color typical of a more mature wine. It would be surprising here, since the Graves is a year younger than the St.-Estèphe, except that 1979 was a lighter vintage than 1978 and more forward. Clarets of 1978 are generally regarded as real *vins de garde*—perfect wines for cellaring until they mature fully, whenever that may be.

Aroma. You will probably find that the Château de Pez seems to have a distinctly big, two-stage aroma. The first thing that strikes most tasters is a composite of wood and fruit and growing things. You can get quite a range of descriptions for this—grassy, sunny, a warm orchard scent, flowers—but generally speaking, we can call it pleasing growing things. The de Pez's big, tannic, alcoholic aroma opens farther in the glass— some will say deepens or intensifies—to climax in a scent of cedar that many connoisseurs regard as a hallmark of Cabernet Sauvignon.

Most tasters will describe the Smith Haut Lafitte as smelling very like the de Pez, but smaller, less emphatic, less alcoholic. Tannin is a bit more prominent in its odor, and the cedar comes out sooner, accompanied by a pepper and spice aroma that many experts also consider characteristic of Cabernet. Both wines are giving a pretty good show of the range of typical Cabernet Sauvignon scents.

Taste. On the palate, the de Pez usually makes a very clear impression, first of fruit—fine, sweet, intense fruit—followed by wood. The fruit is berryish and only suggests sweetness because it is fully dry. The wood flavors have a definite tang that suggests fresh oak to most people. Most tasters are also aware of a lot of tannin—you can feel it especially on your cheeks—but it does not mask the fruit, probably because there is so much of it. The sensations on the tongue are likely to be of weight and richness: this is a complex, full-bodied wine that seems to fill the entire mouth. It ends with a long, elegant finish in which some people will

Clearing Up Claret

Claret is the traditional—though completely unofficial—name for the fine red wines of Bordeaux and especially, if not exclusively, those of the region called the Médoc, along the Gironde north of the city of Bordeaux. The Médoc is divided into communes: Margaux, St.-Julien, Pauillac, and St.-Estèphe. Although Graves and Sauternes lie south of the city of Bordeaux and are not part of the Médoc, their wines are of as high a quality, and they are often placed in the same category with them.

The wines from all these communes have long been prized by connoisseurs. Their most prestigious productions are always the wines of single estates or châteaux. In 1855 the various châteaux were ranked into five growths or crus. This ranking, although in many particulars now inaccurate, still greatly influences the prestige and prices of Bordeaux wines. The most famous—and expensive—of Bordeaux's wines are the handful of premiers crus: Château Lafite, Château Latour, Château Mouton Rothschild, Château Margaux, and Château Haut Brion.

perceive the flavor of currants, yet another hallmark (so expert opinion has it) of the Cabernet grape.

The flavor of the Smith Haut Lafitte, most people will find, parallels that of the de Pez in many respects. These similarities are where you should look to learn the essential nature of red Bordeaux: the quality of freshness of the fruit and its special accents, the particular interplay of tannin and acid and alcohol with that fruit, and the wood or oak elements overlaid on it. Those are really the keys to understanding and appreciating any claret, and these two wines are doing a lovely job of laying them out before you.

Most tasters will locate the differences between the Smith Haut Lafitte and the de Pez primarily in two areas: body, and the relation of tannin and fruit. Most people find the Graves the less full, slightly thinner wine of the two, and they will describe its fruit as softer, less intense (some will say less sweet), with the taste of tannin more prominent, perhaps muffling the fruit a little. Most of the flavors we spoke of in the de Pez also can be found in this Graves, but a bit more muted. There are also in this Graves hints of licorice or tobacco, and some people describe this wine as more vinous and more mellow than the St.-Estèphe. The Smith Haut Lafitte also has a long finish, pleasing and astringent.

These are both lovely wines, and some of the differences between them are attributable to their different vintages. I would say that the greater fullness of the St.-Estèphe and the more prominent tannin of the Graves result from the differences of their harvests and not from the geography of their communes. On the other hand, that slightly licorice suggestion and the vinosity of the Smith Haut Lafitte seem to me definitely characteristic of the red wines of the Graves, while the whole attack of the de Pez, its opulence of bouquet and flavor and abundance of tannin and fruit, seem to me representative of the best qualities of the wines of St.-Estèphe. (That, by the way, is a distinction many wine professionals might argue with.) Both wines share an elegance that distinguishes them from the style of California Cabernet, which you will be tasting in the next flight.

Although Château de Pez is not a classified growth, most connoisseurs rate it in that league. It is imported to the United States by Peartree Imports. Château Smith Haut Lafitte is a well-esteemed classified growth, the property of the Eschenauer firm. It is imported to the United States by Heublein's International Vintage Wine Company.

This is the conclusion of our fifteenth red-wine-tasting session. There are a few ways for you to proceed from here.

Following the lead of your own preferences:

If you enjoyed either the first wine, Château de Pez, or the second wine, Château Smith Haut Lafitte, go to Flight 16.

Following the kind of grapes:

Go to Flight 16.

Following the wines of the country:

Go to Flight 19.

Red Wines:
The Sixteenth Flight

SIMI ALEXANDER VALLEY CABERNET SAUVIGNON 1979
AND
RIDGE YORK CREEK CABERNET SAUVIGNON 1981

What you are confronting in this flight should be two excellent examples of the California approach to Cabernet Sauvignon. Both are from prime Cabernet country. York Creek is in Napa, which has effectively set the pace for Cabernet cultivation and vinification in California. Alexander Valley is right behind it, and some would say abreast or ahead. Simi Winery and its winemaker Zelma Long are consciously emulating a French style in their Cabernet. Ridge and its winemaker Paul Draper, although they have tamed their wines considerably from the exuberance of some of their first bottlings, are still producing what many think of as the true California style in Cabernet—big, robust, and muscular wines.

Once more you will be tasting for a number of things: the similarities and differences in the styles of the wines as well as for yet more information about the essence of Cabernet Sauvignon. In the previous pair of wines, if you paid close attention, you should have been able to taste the character of French Cabernet. Here, if you work just as hard and enjoy just as thoroughly, you should be able to pick out the character of California Cabernet.

Okay, enough prologue: hop to it. Seeswirlsmellsipsavorspit!

Appearance. We have clearly distinguishable differences in color here. These are among the darkest wines, and the densest in appearance, that we have dealt with. The Simi is the lighter of the two, a very deep ruby to the Ridge's emphatic garnet. If you tilt your glass to about a 45-degree angle and hold it against a white background, you should be able to see very clearly that both wines still show the purple rim that indicates their youth. Both probably still have a lot of maturing to do.

Aroma. Both these wines have big aromas, though the Ridge seems much more assertive, and for that reason you'd better have finished your sniffing of the Simi before you even put your nose to the Ridge: its aroma can pretty much make anything else seem wishy-washy.

Almost every taster is struck by the Simi's young, powerful fruit, a deeply grapey smell carried by alcohol and tannin. Some people may describe the latter as a slight oakiness or perceive it as an astringent quality in the aroma. Behind that initial fruit wallop comes what are usually sensed as a battery of peppery, herbaceous odors. Descriptions of these can vary considerably, but most experts consider scents in this range typical of California Cabernet.

A few people respond to the tannin in the Ridge Cabernet's aroma before anything else, and indeed sometimes find that almost everything is masked for them by the tannin. Most, however, find that the Ridge's aroma jumps out of the glass at them, and if they find themselves overwhelmed, it is by fruit and flowers. Some even identify the specific scent of raspberries here. Most will describe the aroma as heady because of its high alcohol. And most will discern grassy, tannic elements as well as herbal notes, with pronounced smells of pepper and cedar following after (cedar, too, is thought of as typical for the aroma of California Cabernet).

Taste. For most people, the Simi presents three successive waves of flavor. The first impression it makes is of a soft fruitiness, which some describe as grapey and others berrylike. The second occurs when the tannin and acids bite in, creating for some people an unpleasing sort of scrubbing sensation on the tongue; most perceive it as a dry, austere, tannic follow-through from the initial flavor. The third stage is the wine's true finish, a strong, lingering aftertaste that mixes fruit and tannin in about equal quantities, though different palates probably will perceive it as inclining to one side or the other.

With the Ridge Cabernet, a few people again are going to be over-whelmed by the tannin and simply not taste anything else; they'll have to wait until the wine is a few years older before they are able to appreciate this or any other Californians in this style. Most tasters are going to be surprised, however, by how much of the fruit they can enjoy despite all the tannin they discerned in the aroma. The tannin is still there—many will taste it right behind the fruit—but the fruit itself is very forward, soft, and deep. To many tasters it recalls the flavor of currants. Some even taste in it a specifically flowery quality, almost a delicate honey taste. Behind or underneath all these overt sensations lurk what are sensed at this stage as more than suggestions but less than full-fledged presences: pepper and licorice and tobacco and chocolate and other deep tones are among the possibilities you may taste. Most people find the wine has an exceptionally big, dry finish.

These two provide marvelous illustrations of the California way with Cabernet. If you are able to taste them right along with or immediately after the two Bordeaux, you will see that by comparison the Simi looks big and very, very fruity and the Ridge simply massive. By the same token, the two clarets taste incredibly elegant and polished alongside the muscular and bumptious Californians. By themselves, the Ridge seems the bigger, more robust wine, the Simi the more polished. Both seem to have a long and quite interesting bottle life in front of them: you can look forward to their tannins mellowing and their fruit maturing and a lot of those just-perceptible undertones emerging into promi-nence. These too would not be a bad pair of wines to sample again on New Year's Eve in 1999, if you can manage to keep yourself from drinking them that long. In fact, these two will be very interesting to try again in just a few years—and surely you can restrain your impatience that long?

If you have enjoyed either or both of these wines, you've really got the whole state of California and its now over five hundred (I think) wineries before you, since most of them make a Cabernet, and many of them make several (usually labeled for different locations). Best bets? Try some of the more highly reputed ones, such as Mondavi, or Heitz, Beaulieu, Stag's Leap, Burgess, Martini, Château Montelena—the list could go on and on. And don't forget some of the bigger makers, such as

Almadén, who can produce a surprisingly good Cabernet at a surprisingly reasonable price. Happy hunting.

Simi wines are distributed by Schieffelin & Company. Ridge wines are distributed by Frederick Wildman.

This is the conclusion of our sixteenth red-wine-tasting session. Paths are beginning to converge.

Following the lead of your own preferences:

If you liked either the first wine, the Simi Cabernet, or the second wine, the Ridge Cabernet, go to Flight 17 or back to Flights 6, 10, 11, 14, and 15 if you have missed any of those.

Following the kind of grapes:

These are the last Cabernet Sauvignon wines in the tasting.

Earlier Cabernet flights are 6 and 15.

Following the wines of the country:

Go to Flight 17.

Red Wines:
The Seventeenth Flight

CLOS DU VAL NAPA VALLEY ZINFANDEL 1981
AND
MONTEVINA AMADOR COUNTY ZINFANDEL 1980

If there is any such thing as California's very own grape, the Zinfandel is it. Like the Etruscans and the hula hoop, its origins are shrouded in mystery. The latest theory has it that it is a clone of the Italian Primativo, a robust and early ripening vine from Puglia, that was brought to California in the nineteenth century by the near-legendary Agoston Haraszthy, who is blamed or credited for almost everything in California viticulture. Dissidents from this theory claim to be able to prove that Zinfandel was already being cultivated on Long Island in the eighteenth century.

Whatever its secret identity may be, Zinfandel in California is Supervine, producing three distinct types of wine. The best known is the style you've already tasted in Flight 3, a fresh, relatively light, and definitely fruity wine. Usually this is loosely referred to as a Beaujolais-style Zinfandel.

At the other extreme, Zinfandel yields an enormous wine of 15 or 16 (and occasionally more) degrees of alcohol and some residual sweetness.

This is the late-harvest style, vinified from extremely ripe grapes that have produced very high concentrations of sugar. In the fermentation of such a wine, the yeasts that convert sugar into alcohol are themselves often killed by the concentrations of alcohol they have made before they completely convert all the sugar. It's a thankless job, being a yeast. But what their heroic little deaths produce, in this case, is a powerhouse wine that blows away the competition at juried tastings. Unfortunately, it's also a useless wine if you normally take your wine with food, because its sweetness and alcohol won't let you taste anything else. You have to treat a late-harvest Zinfandel as if it were a port or a similar fortified dessert wine.

Between these two extremes, Zinfandel also produces a more claretlike wine that preserves some of the live fruit of the Beaujolais style and borrows some of the body and authority of the late-harvest style. For many wine drinkers this is the most interesting and rewarding of Zinfandel's incarnations. There is no orthodoxy about this kind of Zinfandel, so you get different emphases from different growers, ranging from a stress on freshness and vitality to a concentration on strength and power to an accent on elegance and breeding. This variety is one of Zinfandel's attractions. Within this claretlike style, all the variations show some aging potential and a real capacity to accompany the kind of meal that Dr. Johnson thought you could ask a man to. The wines you have in front of you are examples of this middle-style Zinfandel.

Okay, perform your ritual. Sniff as you have never sniffed before, because there should be more than ever for you to recognize here. And remember to taste the wine both with and without a bite of cheese or some such, to see how food does or doesn't change it. Then talk the wines over among yourselves and read on.

Appearance. There is a fairly marked difference to see here. The Clos du Val is dark ruby in color, bordering on garnet, translucent and brilliant. The Montevina, although it is a year older, shows a younger Zinfandel coloration—a very dark ruby or garnet, almost opaque, heavy-looking, with some very youthful purple highlights. Both are sound shades for Zinfandel of this type and usually indicate two different stages of development.

Aroma. Once again, there are readily observable differences between these two wines. Almost every taster will describe both aromas as strong, distinctive, and marked by fruit scents, but after that, consensus ends.

Most people like the scent of the Clos du Val, though they also frequently describe it as complex and difficult to pin down. They often say it has a fresh quality, but not like the fresh fruit of a Beaujolais-style Zinfandel—more balanced than that, and containing lots of individual odors simultaneously. The specific things they most often name are plums and alcohol and tannin (especially a strong-tea scent that develops as the wine opens), then a composite of rich scents such as berries and peaches and chocolate and fresh wood or cedar. That cedar scent, by the way, is one I strongly associate with maturing California wine, Cabernet as well as Zinfandel.

Just about every taster uses the word "intense" to describe the Montevina's aroma. To most people it smells deeply of very dry fruit; some people will even say prunes. This fruit smells different from the Clos du Val's, however. It does not seem as fresh; in fact, to many people it suggests thick, heavy, fruit jam. Most people mean by that to compliment the wine, though a few find that scent simply too strong for comfort. Like the Clos du Val, this wine, too, has a medley of specific odors merged in its bouquet—herbaceous scents and chocolate and tobacco and a kind of forest-floor scent as well as cedar. Many people find that a rather strong tannic odor, a blend of tobacco and strong tea, comes up as the wine sits.

Those who don't like this style of wine often find either the earth/tannin odor elements too strong (in which case they probably call the aroma musty) or the fruit/alcohol odor too powerful (in which case they are likely to talk about an acetone or overripe banana scent).

Neither this Clos du Val nor this Montevina Zinfandel is yet what you could call a fully mature wine. A more developed nose would in all likelihood show considerably less tannin than either of these wines do right now, and its fruit would be of a different quality and timbre, plummier, more rounded. By and large, however, these are pretty fair representatives of the aromas characteristic of this claret style of Zinfandel at this age.

Just for the record, "developed nose" is a legitimate piece of wine jargon, no matter how grotesque the image it conjures up. Try very hard not to think of a bottle with a proboscis like an elephant's trunk. "Nose" simply is a bit of professional shorthand (now there's an image) for the whole olfactory attack of a wine, aroma and bouquet altogether. "Developed" means only that the scents have evolved from a youthful condition toward what connoisseurs consider a more mature state. After you smell a few older wines, you'll as readily identify the characteristics of a mature bouquet as you now spot those telltale tawny highlights that reveal maturity in a wine's color.

Taste. Most people are surprised by how claretlike the Clos du Val tastes to them: they tend to use words such as "smooth," "soft," and "balanced" to express the quality of restraint they sense in it. Most describe the fruit as light, fresh, and dry and tasting of plums and berries. A very few may call the fruit bland, especially by comparison with the Montevina's, but most find it well in scale with the wine's unobtrusive acid, alcohol, and tannin. Many people report a lingering dry finish that they find very attractive. Some will call that finish chocolatey, while others will find it tannic. Overall, most tasters will tend to evaluate this wine as rather elegant, especially for their expectations (if they had any) of a Zinfandel.

The Montevina strikes most people as much more like what they anticipated in Zinfandel. This 1980 vintage is possibly still a little muffled (do *not* think of little children wrapped up for winter in their down coats), but the essential elements are all in place and need only a bit more bottle age to bring them out very clearly. The first thing almost everyone tastes in this wine is good fruit, fat and almost sweet, a full, berrylike fruit that for some people specifically recalls blackberries. This flavor is almost the hallmark of Zinfandel; it is as close as you can come to pinning down a varietal flavor in a single word. Sometimes you'll see it referred to as "brambly" as well as blackberry, but this still is the flavor that's meant. In this particular wine it arrives packaged with other flavors as well. Different tasters may name tar, chocolate, tobacco, spice (even camphor), tannin, acid, or alcohol as part or parts of what they discern here.

Along with that batch of flavors, and definitely contributing to the "brambly" quality, comes a nice tannic bite on the top of the tongue and on the cheeks. The sensation may feel as if your tongue were getting a good, vigorous scratching. The wine finishes quite pleasingly, with a long, dry, fruity aftertaste.

Put side by side like this, these two wines give you what is practically a paradigm of the styles available in Zinfandel. The Montevina is big and burly and intense. The Clos du Val, while not Little Lord Fauntleroy by any means, is more restrained, less vivid, but more complex and more seductive. Though the younger wine, it seems the more mature. Both wines, however, have years yet to grow and round out, to judge by the quality of their fruit, the quantity of their alcohol and acid, and the vigor of their tannins. It would be very interesting and instructive (and no small bit of fun as well) to clock the development of these two baby Paul Bunyans over the next five or ten years. You could roast a lot of ducks and nibble a lot of goat cheese very happily with either of these as accompaniment.

Clos du Val is a smallish Napa Valley enterprise with a French wine maker (if you thought you spotted a continental hand in that Zinfandel, you were right). Clos du Val makes Cabernet, Chardonnay, and Merlot as well as Zinfandel.

Montevina is also not a huge winery. Located in Amador County, Montevina has had its greatest success with Zinfandels in all three styles, which it distinguishes clearly on its labels. It also produces Cabernet Sauvignon and Sauvignon Blanc.

If you enjoy the Zinfandel flavor, you've got lots of territory to explore—hardly a wine maker in California doesn't make at least one Zinfandel. Many issue several different Zins, either vinified in different styles or made from grapes grown in special locations that lend a particular character to their wine. A good many Zinfandels, especially those in the more intensely colored and flavored styles, profit from five or more years of bottle age. And, of course, nobody knows just how long a well-made Zinfandel of a great year will last.

If you like the grape, you might want to think about a long-term experiment to see which expires first, you or your pet Zinfandels. After all, everybody should have a goal in life, and that one at least will keep you out of trouble. Besides, there is strong empirical evidence that people with the patience to wait for their wines to mature are not very likely, in the meantime, to bomb other people for disagreeing with them. Wine helps you take the long view.

This concludes our seventeenth red-wine flight. There are only a few ways for you to proceed from here.

Following the lead of your own preferences:

If you enjoyed either the first wine, the Clos du Val Zinfandel, or the second wine, the Montevina Zinfandel, go to Flight 18.

Following the kind of grapes:

This is the last Zinfandel tasting. There was an earlier Zinfandel in Flight 3.

Following the wines of the country:

This is the last flight of California wines. Go back to any of Flights 1, 3, 5, 6, 7, 10, 11, 12, or 16 you may have missed.

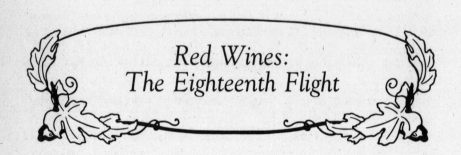

Red Wines:
The Eighteenth Flight

PRUNOTTO BARBARESCO RISERVA
MONTESTEFANO 1978
AND
PIO CESARE BAROLO RISERVA 1978

Among Italy's wine-growing provinces—and that means all of them—
Piedmont is perhaps the most esteemed for the quality of its red wines.
Like its great rival Tuscany, Piedmont builds its finest reds around a
single noble grape variety. In this case it is the Nebbiolo, which in
Piedmont produces three related but different wines: Nebbiolo, Barbaresco,
and Barolo. They are all 100 percent Nebbiolo wines—that is, unblended varietal wines—and all are made in a series of interlocking DOC
zones in southern Piedmont around the town of Alba.

The major differences among Nebbiolo wines arise from the soils in
which and the altitudes at which they are cultivated and from the
amount of barrel-aging they receive before bottling. Wines labeled Nebbiolo
are generally grown on lower and less desirable fields than either Barbaresco
or Barolo and receive the least barrel age of all three wines. Barbaresco
is grown on soils similar to and at the same altitude as Barolo, but it
receives a year less barrel-aging.

Nebbiolo is invariably the lightest wine of the three, but this doesn't mean it's a weakling—not by a long shot. Most Nebbiolo should be drunk within five or six years of harvest, but some very fine vintages produce a wine that stays alive and muscular for up to ten years. With Barbaresco and Barolo, your normal expectation should be to start drinking them about ten years from harvest. Except in very light vintages, these two wines are hard and tannic for a few years after bottling and start rounding out to show their true character at about six years of age. A first-class Barbaresco or Barolo from a first-class vintage is capable of developing in the bottle for ten to fifteen years and then remaining healthy and enjoyable for another ten to fifteen years.

In the Piedmont they distinguish between these two wines in terms of classic sexual stereotypes: Barolo is big, assertive, robust, masculine, while Barbaresco is soft, more elegant, more polished, feminine. Fortunately or unfortunately, the stereotypes are as inaccurate about the wines as they are about people, and in some vintages not even the wine makers can distinguish the two, so if you were starting to think of them as brother and sister wines you're going to have to accept them as occasional transsexuals as well.

Both these very big, austere red wines are appropriate accompaniments to the most important dinners, particularly to what are called in Italy *carni nobili* (the great roasts and furred game).

Okay, get to it—sniff, savor, etc., and file your report. Then read on.

Appearance. Once again, an easy question to answer. Both these wines are the classic garnet with amber highlights that together are almost the hallmark of a maturing Nebbiolo-based wine.

Aroma. This pair of wines will dramatically show the importance of allowing Italian wines to breathe. You should draw their corks at least a half hour before you plan to use them; a full hour would be better. (You can also always decant them if you prefer.) Even with that breathing time, they will continue to change and open in your glasses. They can progress from an initial condition that is almost mute to the olfactory equivalent of eloquence.

Although the aroma of the Barbaresco is nowhere near as big as it will be when the wine is mature, it nevertheless is already displaying on its smaller scale most of the components that connoisseurs identify as characteristic of the Nebbiolo grape. If you've really been exercising your nose as you ought up to this point, you should be able to pick out,

What's Up DOC?

Italy's DOC (Denominazione d'Origine Controllata) *laws corre-spond roughly to France's AOC laws—they control labeling, geographic designations, grape varieties, and other related matters. Italy is now introducing a new category, DOCG, which so far has been granted to only five wines: Brunello, Vino Nobile di Montepulciano, Barbaresco, Barolo, and Chianti. The G stands for "guaranteed," and what the Italian government is trying to guarantee is quality. The wines so designated must be tasted—each vintage, at several stages—by a panel of experts who certify that they are sufficiently fine to be called by their prestigious names. Any wine not measuring up is supposed to be declassified and then can be sold only as a simple red table wine. If it works, this will be a great protection for consumers. If it doesn't, it will be ranked as one of wine's most high-minded experiments.*

in the bouquet of this wine, at least traces of some of these: delicate fruit, alcohol, a general herby scent, fennel or licorice, and tobacco (sometimes described as a pleasing cigar-box aroma). In a fully mature Barbaresco, some of those elements would be very powerful; with this young wine you may have to hunt to find them, but they should all be there.

The aroma of this Barolo is similar to that of the Barbaresco (no surprise there) but more forthright (again no surprise). That is as it should be with these two wines. The Barolo's scent seems particularly marked at this stage of its maturation by alcohol, a warm, heady overtone that in effect colors the whole bouquet. Fruit and spice also seem more to the fore than in the Barbaresco: berries, spearmint, or peppermint, a salt or even saltwater tang, some suggestions of tobacco—you could detect any or all of those within the general framework of this Barolo's rich, vinous, almost pruney bouquet. You'll have to take my word for it that this, too, is still essentially a small aroma compared to what a properly aged and properly aerated Barolo will hit you with.

Taste. The taste of the Barbaresco at this stage doesn't really live up to the promises made by its provocative aroma. The fruit is present, and you can even pick hints of berries and especially cherries from it, but it is nevertheless somewhat muffled: the wine is still "closed"—its various components are still masking each other rather than supporting and revealing each other.

In this particular case, the tannin is disguising the other components; you can really feel its presence in this wine's big, chewy texture. In fact, tasters with a particular sensitivity to tannin may very well find that it almost completely hides the fruit from them and they perceive only a bland, somewhat astringent flavor. Given the youth of this Barbaresco, that is not surprising; the surprise is that the wine is this drinkable already.

Listen up now, because this is important and difficult. I've got you drinking immature wines for two very important reasons: money and availability (this whole discussion, by the way, applies as much to the previous half-dozen flights as it does to this one). If you could get a mature Barbaresco or Barolo it would cost you considerably more than these infants did—and that's the real rub. Presuming I were hardhearted enough to make you pawn your progeny to buy a really mature wine, and presuming you were by now sufficiently hooked on the joy of wine to be willing to part even with the dog and the parakeet if necessary to taste some really good stuff—even with all that, you might not be able to buy a mature bottle.

The facts of business being what they are (costs of overhead, storage, problems of cash flow) and the facts of agriculture being what they are (supply of any wine, but especially a fine one, is very, very limited), wines just don't stay in the shops for the length of time it takes them to mature. If they do, you—understandably from the maker's and the retailer's point of view—have to pay a hefty premium not simply for the years and years of storage but also for the money each of them has tied up in that bottle. It's an investment that pays no dividends and no interest until you decide you want them.

If I could be sure you all had access to older wines, I wouldn't hesitate to send you out to get them. After all, what's money? Especially when it's yours we're spending. If you had the older wines in front of you now, your tasting task would be simple and my writing chore a breeze—in fact, I'd probably have to spend more time restraining your enthusiasm than instructing you what to taste for. But alas! What you have to do with these two and the other big wines we are tasting is extrapolate— imagine what you taste here in bits and pieces and traces magnified and harmonized. You have to intensify intellectually your experience of these wines along the lines I suggest to you: the tannin diminishing its direct impact, the fruit coming forward and its flavor maturing, growing a bit liquory, the whole of the flavor and the aroma, too, expanding so that when you pull the cork, people halfway across the room know it by scent alone.

If you do ever have the opportunity to taste any one of these wines at its maturity, by all means grab it and render all this prose superfluous. If you don't have that opportunity but already like what you're tasting in these young wines, by all means buy some now and keep them for a few years. There are no better rewards for patience that I know of.

Enough of this long digression: we haven't yet talked about the taste of the Barolo. And after all that talk about young wines and mature wines, an irony—this Barolo, of the same age as our Barbaresco, is very forward and come-toish. It quite kindly makes itself available to you in a way that young Barolos most often do not. It is, first of all, extraordinarily well balanced for its age, quite complex and rich already. There is a big, concentrated fruit flavor right up front in the wine, hardly obscured at all by tannin even though there is plenty of that still in evidence; most tasters get distinct suggestions of plums and berries and currants all through it. The finish is long, with an almost licorice tang, and the overall palatal impression for most people is velvety and live. Comparatively speaking, in addition to being more advanced than the Barbaresco (which is definitely uncharacteristic), this Barolo is bigger, with more powerful fruit (which is what the clichés about these wines predict). It gives you a genuine and very useful preview of the way these wines normally develop. And remember, this one's got years to go yet.

I can conceive of the possibility that some people somewhere might dislike these wines, but I'd rather not know about them, thank you. It would destroy my faith in the human race.

If you are interested in the further adventures of the Nebbiolo grape, there is a whole world for you to explore. Other fine makers of Barolo and Barbaresco range from big firms such as Fontanafredda and Granduca, which make a whole line of Piedmontese wines, to smaller producers such as Gaja and Ceretto, Ratti and Macarini, Conterno and Giacosa and Vietti. In addition, in a different DOC zone in northeastern Piedmont, the Nebbiolo is vinified into another group of wines, generally lighter in body and sometimes more elegant than the two you've just tried: Gattinara (from Antoniolo and Monsecco) and Spanna (from Vallana) are particularly fine, but also look for Carema, Ghemme, and Boca.

The firm of Alfredo Prunotto is one of the most prestigious makers of traditional Piedmontese wines. Its wines are handled through Neil Empson and imported to the United States by Trebon. Pio Cesare is another equally estimable and equally traditional Piedmontese wine maker. The firm's wines are imported to the United States by Paterno Imports.

This is the conclusion of our eighteenth red-wine-tasting session. There is only one way for you to proceed from here.

Following the lead of your own preferences:

If you enjoyed either the Barbaresco or the Barolo, go to Flight 19.

Following the kind of grapes:

This is the only Nebbiolo flight among our tastings.

Following the wines of the country:

Go to Flight 19.

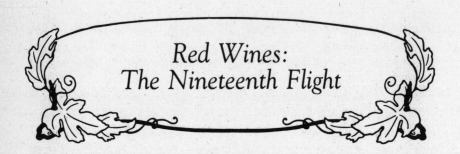

Red Wines:
The Nineteenth Flight

CHÂTEAU FORTIA CHÂTEAUNEUF DU PAPE 1979
AND
MASI AMARONE 1977

This final pair of red wines (yes, you've made it that far—graduation is at hand!) is distinctive in several respects. It's the only pair among these advanced red wine flights that doesn't share the same grape as its base, or the same method of vinification, or even the same country of origin.

So what have these wines got in common that justifies lumping them together, you ask, half expecting I can't answer that?

Hah, I say: size.

Size? Size.

These are among the biggest fully dry dinner wines in captivity. They have high alcohol (13½ percent is about as low as they ever get), high tannin, high acid, and often enormous fruit—big, mouth-filling wines with great, flavorful intensity. In the most literal sense, they stand in a class by themselves—which is why I have put them in a class by themselves.

Châteauneuf du Pape is produced near the city of Avignon on the banks of the Rhône in southern France. It is perhaps the finest hot-climate wine made anywhere. Contrary to what you probably think, the best wines do not come from those climes where the grapes grow most prolifically. Usually the opposite is true; in wine lore a hot climate usually equates with flabby, unstructured wines, too high in sugar and/or alcohol to make anything other than picnic wines at best. At worst, you can use them in your car's radiator.

To make even decent table wine in a really hot climate requires great care in growing and harvesting the grapes and great skill and control in their vinification. In Sicily, for instance, the production of light white wines pleasing to modern tastes required unlearning two thousand years of viticultural techniques plus wholesale importation of a brand-new technology: stainless-steel tanks, reduced-temperature fermentation, glass-lined holding tanks (also temperature-controlled), and anoxygenic bottling. In Châteauneuf du Pape and other locations on the Rhône (notably Hermitage), the skills of French vintners go well beyond that to create a wine not merely drinkable but outstanding by any criteria.

Amarone is another case entirely. The product of a far more benign climate, Amarone derives from grapes grown on the tranquil hillsides near Verona, not far from Lake Garda in Italy. Except for Amarone, Veronese vines do not produce big wines but rather light, smiling ones such as the popular white Soave, the red Valpolicella (see Flight 2), and Bardolino. In fact, the real surprise I have been saving up for you—if you will be good enough to cast your mind all the way back to that second tasting—is that the huge wine you are about to taste, Amarone, is made from exactly the same grapes grown in exactly the same fields as the pleasant light Valpolicella you drank then. Its full name is Recioto di Valpolicella Amarone—Amarone for short, though that is the only thing short about this wine.

I will explain all in a little while. For now, see, swirl, sniff, sip, savor, spit—especially spit, given the alcoholic strength of these two musclemen; I want you sober enough to be able to follow my golden prose right to the end.

Appearance. No problem. Château Fortia is a lovely clear garnet, and Masi Amarone is the same garnet with some tawny or amber highlights, which, I remind you for the last time, is a sign of a maturing Italian wine (though as Amarone runs, this one is quite an infant yet).

Aroma. Like the Nebbiolo-based wines, these two demand a bit of breathing time—about a week, someone at my last tasting suggested. Both wines have very deep aromas that will increase and complicate with age, and both wines, because of their concentrations of alcohol and tannin, are not easily harmed by oxidation. In fact, I have left half-empty bottles of Amarone standing for a week with the cork only loosely reinserted (and obviously half the bottle filled with air), and they have at the end of that time not only been perfectly drinkable but a few of them had even improved. I don't recommend that as a way to treat wines, not even wines like these, but it certainly does tell you something about them.

The first element of the Châteauneuf's aroma to strike you is likely to be its alcohol, a warm, heady rush that bears the rest of the scents on its back. There are many of those. Most people usually detect fruit first—a rich, plummy scent that some will think smacks of overripeness, though to my mind that is the characteristic sun-baked smell of southern grapes. After that they tend to pick up a cluster of perfumes—violets, cinnamon, stems and grass, a truffly/earthy smell. The overall impression is of strength, of graceful power.

The Amarone is not utterly different from that. The big, richly plummy alcoholic rush is present in it, too, though some tasters can discern a pleasing, almost apple scent as well. Flowery perfumes are present, too, though they are harder to identify specifically here than in the Châteauneuf. Many people also pick up what they identify as a smell of yeast or bread dough—a fresh, live scent that might be attributable either to an unfinished malolactic fermentation (unlikely but possible, and a small defect if present), or to the presence of *Botrytis* on the grapes (less unlikely and more possible, and a big plus for the wine if present).

For most tasters, however, the predominant sensation here is a very characteristic Amarone bouquet, a kind of heady compound of resin and raisin that, in a way very different from the Châteauneuf, nevertheless calls up images of sun on the vines and bright, hot afternoons. If the overall impression created by the aroma of the Châteauneuf du Pape is graceful power, Amarone creates a sense of powerful grace—and I am not just playing with words here; where the emphasis falls makes a very big difference in the wine.

Taste. Almost every taster describes both these wines as presenting truly complex tastes. The structural elements (tannin, acids, alcohol, fruit) and a whole range of flavor elements intertwine quite differently in each, though the overall effect of both is remarkably similar.

Some people are going to find both of these wines just too much and be put off by everything about them, describing them as too sweet, too strong, too astringent, too assertive, too sour. But if you have really been bitten by the red-wine bug (and you'd have to be a supreme masochist to travel this far with me if you haven't been), you should thoroughly enjoy the smoothness and authority, the iron-fist-in-the-velvet-glove character of these two wines.

The Châteauneuf fills your mouth with soft, "sweet" fruit. Various people taste in it berries and plums and nuts as well as herbal flavors. There is strong tannin discernible, too, as well as some vanilla notes contributed (no doubt) by the barrels, all of which makes for a pleasing, slightly bitter (some find a definite taste of almond) finish. With its high alcohol and abundance of acid added to these flavor elements, this wine makes a total impression of richness and variety that borders on opulence. Considering that this is a mere babe in arms as the fine Rhône wines go, I would say that the prognosis for its future health and long life are excellent. I would also say that I wouldn't at all mind being around for its twenty-first-birthday party.

Not that the Amarone is any slouch, either. It, too, is very smooth and balanced, with deep flavor and velvety texture. It, too, tastes of plums, but there are other fruit and herb suggestions as well—anise and peaches, for instance, and apples and raisins (the last particularly noticeable in the finish). The Châteauneuf du Pape probably is a fractionally bigger wine (on the scale of two such wines as these, small differences are hard to gauge) and the Amarone a better-balanced, more elegant wine. Rather than do anything as commonplace as leave you with an overall impression, it lingers with you. Its finish is remarkably long and full, so the ghost of the wine continues to haunt your mouth after you've emptied your glass. Smell the empty glass to see how persistent the bouquet is. This is a very complete wine—and once again, it is little more than an infant. Can you imagine what this lady will be like when she makes her debut?

For all their overt differences, the Châteauneuf du Pape and the Amarone make remarkably compatible partners. They share one striking similarity in their origins as well, and it makes the wonder of their bigness and grace all the more remarkable: Both are made from grapes that, grown in other places and treated in other ways, yield only ordinary wines at best. The grape that makes up almost 75 percent of this

Tech Talk

Two technical terms here deserve special attention: *malolactic fermentation* and *Botrytis*. They are very different from each other. Malolactic fermentation is a second, smaller fermentation that occurs (or should occur) in most red wines. Botrytis is the name of a mold that forms on ripe grapes. It rarely has any role in the making of red wines.

Immediately after the crushing of the grapes, all wines, red or white, go through what is called a violent or tumultuous fermentation. During this fermentation the grapes' sugars are converted to alcohol by the action of yeasts. Malolactic fermentation is a smaller, less violent fermentation caused by naturally occurring bacteria. This fermentation will happen naturally in most wines unless it is deliberately forestalled. It usually comes hard on the heels of the first fermentation, and it converts malic acid to milder lactic acid. Its effect on a red wine usually is to smooth it and advance its maturation. Consequently, almost all red wines undergo malolactic fermentation, but very few whites are allowed to go through it. This is because malic acid conveys a greater sensation of live acidity to the tongue than does lactic acid, and in most white wines it contributes importantly to your tasting a fresh fruit flavor that would be lost or seriously diminished by malolactic fermentation.

Wine jargon often shortens the phrase malolactic fermentation to simple malo.

Botrytis (in full, Botrytis cinerea) is a mold that causes grapes to lose water, shrivel slightly, and concentrate their sugars. It also imparts a distinctive, honeyed flavor of its own that with practice you can learn to identify in white wines made with grapes that have been visited by Botrytis cinerea. Any kind of mold usually is a disaster in the vineyard, but Botrytis at harvest time can be a blessing. The French call it the pourriture noble (noble rot). It is responsible for the magnificent sweetness of some of the world's most famous dessert wines—France's Sauternes and Barsac; Germany's Auslese, Beerenauslese, and Trockenbeerenauslese; and the Hungarian Tokay.

In the Verona area, sweet dessert wines are made with grapes partially affected by Botrytis; the wines are called simply Recioto di Valpolicella or di Soave, depending on the zone. Recioto di Valpolicella is already unusual in being a red wine made from such grapes; the word Amarone added to that name indicates the same sort of grapes vinified to full dryness—a very, very unusual condition. Grapes affected by Botrytis give a dry wine an intense fruitiness that is absolutely necessary to balance the very high alcohol resulting from the conversion of all those concentrated sugars.

Château Fortia is the Grenache, which outside of the Châteauneuf du Pape zone gives little better than a pusillanimous rosé. It is only one of thirteen generally undistinguished grapes (the Syrah is the only exception, and it is not often a large component) that may be blended into Châteauneuf. Amarone is made with those world-famous vines, the Corvina, the Rondinella, the Molinara, and the Negrara, which otherwise produce only the light and relatively low-alcohol Valpolicella.

So what turns Châteauneuf and Amarone into great wines?

In the case of Châteauneuf, it appears to be the peculiar combination of soil and climate along the southern Rhône that works the magic. If so, there is hope that many other regions may yet stumble on the vine that in their particular conditions will make a wine as good and as special.

In the case of Amarone, the magic seems to lie more in the skills of the wine maker and the unusual process of vinification that Amarone undergoes. If that is the case, there is hope that craftspeople will yet happen on the special techniques that will enable them to transform still more ordinary wines into causes for celebration.

Amarone is made by a process akin to that which normally yields dessert wines. Selective picking of very ripe bunches and parts of bunches begins the process. Then those grapes are arranged on straw mats or on special frames in bright, airy conditions and allowed to dry about halfway to raisinhood before being pressed. Their fermentation is very slow—it may continue most of the winter—and, unlike the fermentation of most sweet wines, it takes place in contact with the skins, so in addition to concentrated fruit and high alcohol, the wine also draws all of the available tannin and extracts from its grapes. And again unlike most sweet wines, the fermentation is never interrupted until all of the grape sugars have been converted to alcohol, leaving a fully dry wine.

If the style of either of these wines appeals to you, there is ample room to explore ahead of you. Other good makers of Châteauneuf are Château de Beaucastel, Domaine de Mont-Redon, and Domaine du Vieux Télégraphe. There are also the scarcer and more expensive northern Rhône wines, from Hermitage and the Côte Roti. Other good producers of Amarone are Bertani, Bolla, Santa Sophia, Tommasi, and Quintarelli (a smaller maker; his wines are hard to find).

Masi is a long-established Veronese firm, a quality producer of all the traditional wines of the region. Its wines are imported to the United States by Almadén Imports.

Château Fortia is one of the most prized estates of the Châteauneuf du Pape region. Its wines are imported to the United States by Villa Banfi.

This concludes the red-wine tastings. You made it. Congratulations! You now know all about a better red. If you're up for it, you might look back over the flights containing Italian wines (1, 2, 4, 9, 14, and 18) and those containing French wines (2, 3, 4, 6, 7, 8, 10, 11, 12, 13, and 15) and taste any of them you may have missed on your way here. After that, you can tackle the white wines. And then the rosés. And then the sparkling wines, including Champagnes. Meanwhile, I'll be working on the sequel to this book, *Son of Mastering Wine Entertains Count Dracula*. Look for it wherever books are sold.

WHITE WINES

BISHOPS AND
PAWNS

White wine is the chameleon of the wine world: it comes in every conceivable degree of dryness and sweetness, in every style from completely still through *frizzante* and *pétillant* and crackling to fully sparkling, and in every shade of color from the palest straw to almost deep amber. In fact, if you lump together rosé wine with white (as for all practical purposes you can), white wine comes in just about every color except white—a moral I leave the world to reflect on in its own time.

The uses of white wine vary as much as its guises. It's drunk as a light refresher, as a cocktail, as an appetite teaser or palate cleanser before dinner, as an accompaniment to dinner, as a partner to dessert, or as dessert itself. There's no mystery to its popularity; the only real question to be asked about the current white-wine boom is why it was so long in coming.

For all its popularity, however, white wine remains for most people at least as great an unknown as red. Maybe greater. My hunch is that a high percentage of the folks who simply order a glass of white wine in a bar or restaurant do so for one of several reasons:

• They can't be more exact because they don't know the names of specific white wines.

- They do know some names but can't remember whether they remember because they love them or because they hate them.
- They think all white wines taste alike.
- All the white wines they have so far tried do taste alike.
- They have been told that past the most basic level, white wine gets very expensive.
- It's all been just too much trouble to learn about, and besides, why take a chance embarrassing yourself with a mistake?

If any of those describes your state, let me assure you right off the bat that white wine is a much less complicated subject than red wine. White wines are a lot easier to sort out, and once you've grasped a small handful of key distinctions, there is a considerably smaller field of variations to keep in mind.

So, shrewd observer that you are, you are now asking yourself, "What, then, is this madman doing placing white wines after red wines in this supposedly logical book? What kind of sense does that make? Let's see him get out of this one."

Easy. Not only easy, but once again proof that I have nothing but your best interests at heart, that nothing but concern for your ease and pleasure guides my writing, and you'd have to be a churl and a scoundrel to doubt that after all we've been through together.

The fact is (or at least the fact as I see it is) that white wines are *intellectually* easier to learn than red wines but palatally more difficult.

Why? Because white wines are more similar to each other than are red wines. The flavor differences among white wines are more subtle, more delicate, and often more fleeting than those that divide reds. The gradations of intensity, of sweetness and dryness, shade more imperceptibly into each other. Even the noblest white-grape varieties are so subject to the influences of soil and climate and vinification that they can and do produce everything from the most frivolous quaffing wine right across the spectrum to the most serious dinner wine. No white grape is so austere and so distinct that, like the red Cabernet Sauvignon, it is essentially unusable for light wines.

So while white wines as a class are fairly easily understandable, and while generally speaking white wines are readily pleasing and palatable (accessible in that sense and to that degree), forming a knowing taste for white wines is, I think, a more difficult process than developing a knowledgeable palate for reds because the distinctions from wine to wine are so much finer. That is why I have positioned the white wines here, after red wines, so you will approach them after you've had some pretty vigorous practice tasting and distinguishing tastes. So limber up your nose and taste buds, because they are really in for a workout.

The basic equipment you need to taste white wines is exactly the same as you used for tasting reds. The only change you might want to consider is trading in your piece of cheese (I sincerely hope it hasn't been the same one throughout) for some toasted almonds or a simple unsalted cracker; those flavors are a bit more congenial with white wine for most people, though heaven knows, the right cheese and the right white wine make a lovely combination, too.

Tasting procedures are exactly the same; the ritual of the "infamous s's" remains intact. (If you're being a stubbornly independent soul and are beginning your wine tasting here, please take a look back at pages (16–22 for the basic tasting technique). The variation I'd counsel here is to urge you to concentrate even more on sniffing out the nuances of aroma, not only because they are more delicate in white wines, but also because they are so large a component of the pleasure of white wines and so often an accurate indicator of the flavors to follow. I guess this amounts to saying that aroma in white wine relates to flavor and to overall pleasure just as it does in red wine, only more so.

One note: Most white wines are best served chilled, not icy. There are exceptions to this in both directions, and I will try to call your attention to them at appropriate times. However, if you should encounter a wine that is giving you nothing—no scent, no taste—try letting it sit in the glass for a while to warm before retasting it. Overchilling can completely smother a wine and cause it to go absolutely mute, and different wines overchill at different points. If it is only overchilling that's wrong, the wine will relax and release scent and flavor as it warms. If you take it all the way up to room temperature and you still don't smell or taste anything, first make sure it's not just you coming down with a cold, and then return the bottle to your wine dealer. White-wine sensations may be delicate, but they shouldn't be invisible.

One last piece of what should be welcome news to you. At the level with which we begin these tastings—the level of simple, everyday table wine—the quality and accessibility of white wines is a good jump higher than that of red wines of comparable cost. This probably arises from the major innovations that have been introduced into the making of white wines over the past two decades or so; technology has taken hold there to such an extent that even a mediocre harvest usually can be made to yield palatable light and fruity wines. Why the same or related technology hasn't yet had the same effect on inexpensive red wine I don't know, but there seems to be more badly made red *vin ordinaire* than white. So rejoice! You're starting off at a very respectable level of winemaking here.

As with the red wines, each tasting session of whites concludes with a set of alternative paths for you to follow. Just as with the reds, I once again strongly urge you to taste straight through the first four flights before you start branching out—there is basic information in those first four pairs that will stand you in good stead through all the subsequent tastings.

I think you will find that white wines pretty readily offer themselves for your understanding in varietal clusters. At any rate, the number of paths and options available to the white-wine taster are fewer than those through reds, and you will find that a fair number of the tastings that follow are going to involve you in a straightforward sequence of flights built around the same grape. This is especially true with Riesling, Sauvignon Blanc, and Chardonnay, and it is part of the reason why white wines are so easy to come to terms with intellectually and often so difficult to distinguish palatally.

Happy hunting!

White Wines:
The First Flight

SICHEL BLUE NUN (LIEBFRAUMILCH) 1983
AND
THE MONTEREY VINEYARD CHENIN BLANC
(MONTEREY COUNTY) 1983

If you have no sweet tooth, be warned about these two wines.

If you do have a weakness for sweets, you probably already know these wines or others like them, since wines of this and greater degrees of sweetness comprise one of the largest-selling groups of wine on the U.S. market. They are here at the beginning of your plunge into white wines because for many people they form the bridge from what they have been drinking, be it soft drinks or pop wine or mixed drinks, to the world of drier dinner wines.

Even if you already have a dry palate, it's still worth your while to taste these wines carefully, because the flavor components we're going to be talking about in them will be basic to most white wines. Whereas in red wine the interplay of fruit and tannin became the basic building block on which you built your knowledge and preferences, in white wine you'll find the interplay of acid and sugar forming much the same base.

Acid and sugar will condition your perception of a wine's fruit, its liveliness, and its body. Their proportions relative to each other in a wine will determine whether you taste that wine as sweet or dry, fruity or austere, flabby or thin. It is quite possible, for instance, that wine A will taste to you sweeter than wine B, which may have more sugar in it. How can that be? Wine B could have either much more pronounced flavor and fruit to mask the sugar, or much higher acid to balance it, or a combination of both factors.

Certain levels of sugar are commonly regarded as above or below the perceptible level, which is usually estimated to be 1 percent sugar by weight. That figure should be taken only as a very loose average, subject to variation by the presence and absence of other elements in a wine and subject also to the varying sensitivity of individual palates. Some people seem able to taste even minuscule traces of sugar, while others are relatively unconscious of amounts that are well above that so-called threshold level.

Of course, the same is true of other elements in wine (notably tannin), but with white wines sugar is generally the first flavor factor to be dealt with. By the way, the presence of tannin in a wine seems to raise the sugar threshold—that is, in the presence of tannin, more sugar is needed for a taster to perceive sweetness. Because of the way most white wines are vinified, however—with little or no contact between musts and skins—they are normally quite low in tannin, so that is a complication you won't often encounter.

Some wines have so much sugar (many pop wines are in this class) that no natural flavor is perceptible other than sugar. These are wines that there is no point talking about because there can only be one thing to say about them—how sweet they are. A wine like that is unsuitable for use at a meal because all that sugar masks every other flavor; you cannot taste foods, and you certainly cannot taste other wines, after a sugary drink. As far as I am concerned, a wine that you can't drink with food is unfit for human consumption.

Many people who have become used to such wines find it very hard to retrain their palates to accommodate dry wines (which is one reason I'm trying to break you in gradually with moderately sweet wines in this first flight). I don't know whether it is scientific fact or not, but sugar seems to be an addictive substance; at least it can be as hard to kick the sugar habit as any other. The one reward I can hold out to you is that once you do make the effort to dry out your palate, you'll discover a

Sweet Talk

The name Liebfraumilch designates a German white wine, always semisweet, from the growing areas along the Rhine. Riesling (one of the truly great grapes), Sylvaner, and Muller-Thurgau grapes may go into it, and normally it is blended from the produce of several (if not many) vineyards. Connoisseurs tend to sneer at Liebfraumilch, but it has retained its international popularity for many years.

Chenin Blanc is a grape varietal that keeps threatening nobility. In France, along the middle Loire, it is a staple white-wine grape and makes wines that range in sweetness from fully dry to luscious and in style from the charming Vouvray to the impressive Savennières. In California it is mostly vinified with light sweetness, though every year a few interesting fully dry Chenin Blanc wines appear on the market.

whole range of wonderful flavors you never imagined before—and that is as true of foods as it is of wines.

In most circumstances, a wine's label or back label will give sufficient though sometimes coded information about its approximate degree of sweetness. If either label uses the word "sweet," you can be sure it's good and sweet. "Luscious" and similar words mean very sweet; wines so labeled properly belong with or as dessert. The euphemisms by which more modestly sweet wines present themselves are words such as "semi-sweet," which always means sweet; "semidry," which still means sweet; and "soft," which usually means sweet.

Got all that straight? Then get ready to taste two moderately sweet wines, one a Liebfraumilch and one of the most popular German wines in the United States, the other a California wine vinified from a grape varietal that produces both dry and sweet wines. They are paired here because both are commonly described as soft, fruity, lightly sweet wines. They are that, and yet there are striking differences between them. You can see you've got your work cut out for you; once again, you're going to be tasting to see if you can discern sameness and difference.

Perform the full operation, as directed at the beginning of this book: see, swirl, smell, sip/slurp, savor/slosh, and spit. Just in case you don't remember what all that is shorthand for, here are the directions in full.

See: Note the color of the wine, paying particular attention to its clarity or lack of it, its brilliance or dullness, its precise shade of color.

Swirl: Gently rotate the wine in the glass to aerate it slightly and free more of its aroma. "Gently" is the key word here.

Smell: Try to identify what you are sensing in the aroma of the wine, being as specific as possible about fruit, or flower, or mineral, or chemical scents. Trust your first impressions, no matter how bizarre they may seem, and remember, you are never wrong here; what you smell is what you smell, and that is all there is to it.

Sip/slurp and savor/slosh: Taking in as much air as possible, taste a small mouthful of the wine, making sure to bring it in contact with all the surfaces of your mouth and tongue, paying attention also to its persistence or disappearance after you swallow or spit it. Be as specific as possible in your description of what you taste. For example: If you taste fruit, what kind? Even by class will do: Red fruit or white fruit? Red like berries or red like prunes? White fruit like apples or white fruit like bananas? Citrus flavors like lime or like grapefruit? Mineral flavors like chalk or like clay? Leafy flavors like mint or like grass?

Spit: The idea is to prevent any buildup of alcohol in your system during the tasting, because it will inevitably affect your judgment. This is not so important if you are tasting only one pair of wines, but it can become quite serious if you are going to taste through several flights at one sitting. You will absorb some alcohol directly through your mucous membranes anyhow, so don't be surprised if you or someone tasting with you begins to show the effects of wine even without having drunk any; over a prolonged tasting, that often happens. If you are otherwise having trouble tasting a wine's finish, you might try swallowing a small amount. The quest for knowledge can make harsh demands.

All right, go to it. Take good notes, and if there are several of you tasting together, talk over your reactions when you are finished tasting but before you read any more about these wines. Just for the record, it's better for you to taste first and read later because it is much too easy to be coerced by the printed word. What matters in these tastings is not what I say but what you sense. The descriptions are given as grids against which you can match your own perceptions and your own taste. Ideally they should serve as a sort of double check for you, to prompt you to react with

"Hey, I didn't taste that at all: let me go back and taste that one again"

or

"I see what he means by that"

or

"I think he's describing the same thing we tasted but he's calling it something different than we did"

or

"Well, I've tasted this wine a couple of times now and I still think he's crazy."

That's a whole lot of prologue, I realize, but I'm stuck inside this bottle and have no way of knowing how long you've been gone since the red-wine sessions ended, or whether you're starting out with the white wines first and need all the preliminary instructions. My apologies if you've been bored. Drink on.

Appearance. Neither of these wines should present any difficulty as far as appearance is concerned. Both ought to be clear, pale-straw-colored, very clean-looking—almost textbook cases of a color that is characteristic of a whole class of young, fresh white wines. There may be the slightest degree of difference in shading between these two wines—the Chenin Blanc could be the tiniest bit darker than the Blue Nun—but it should be very slight. A bright lemony or brassy or urine color (it does happen) in wines like this is ninety-nine times out of a hundred an indication that the wine is too old. But pay attention to that phrase "wines like this," because there are some wines where a bright golden shade is perfectly normal.

Aroma. Most people are going to perceive the aromas of these two wines as having areas both of similarity and of distinction. The balance between likeness and difference for an individual taster is going to tilt in the direction of his or her individual sensitivities. Let's take the Blue Nun first.

Most people are struck right away by a sweet scent, which they describe as a sweet fruit scent or a flowery aroma. Some will also pick out citrus smells and leafy or herbal elements: often mint is named. Some profess to find the specific smell of dried apricots in the aroma of this particular wine. Those who don't like this style of wine will describe all these same things as excessive, cloying, sickly-sweet; those who like it will call it delicate and pleasant.

Whichever side of that taste divide you fall on, you ought to know that this is very close to a classic German wine aroma. Indeed, many of the elements you are smelling here (again, whether they please you or not) are directly traceable to the Riesling grape, which is responsible for Germany's greatest wines. Those flowery, sweet-fruit notes in the aroma (the latter often are spoken of as "honeyed"), the leafy elements, and the overall clean and lively character of the aroma: all these you will find, too, in the Riesling grape, whether it is vinified in Germany or New York, France or Italy, Washington or California. What percentage of this wine actually is Riesling would be difficult to say; nevertheless, Riesling certainly is present in its bouquet.

By contrast, the aroma of the Chenin Blanc will strike most people as drier—that is, there is a less marked sweet-fruit aroma, though fruit of one sort or another is still prominent. Like the Blue Nun, the Chenin Blanc's aroma is clean and refreshing, though most people perceive it as a bit coarser—the fruit seems wilder, the herbal elements less delicate (woodruff is one sometimes named). Many people discern one dominant sweet-fruit tone (melon is what most call it) balanced by a sharper, more acidic element such as lime or pineapple. Once again, the question of whether you like this or hate it, whether you find these aromas pleasing or repellent, is purely a matter of personal taste. For the record, however, you should note that this is a very typical aroma for Chenin Blanc; allowing for variations in vinification, this is more or less what Chenin Blanc ought to smell like all the time.

Okay, you're working on two new grapes for your repertoire in your first tasting of white wines. They're rather disproportionate: the Chenin Blanc only rarely reaches greatness, while the Riesling is regarded by most connoisseurs as one of the two noblest white grapes in the world. Nevertheless, both are capable of making accessible wines in a style that pleases multitudes of nonconnoisseurs.

On to their flavors, then.

Taste. It's fair to say that 99 percent of the people tasting these two wines are going to find their flavors absolutely consistent with their aromas, whether those individuals liked the aromas or not.

The Blue Nun is sweet, of course, though some tasters are surprised to find that it is not as sweet as they feared. The reason for that is twofold.

First, this Liebfraumilch possesses a very definite fruitiness that is perceptible by everybody except those whose sugar threshold is so low that every other flavor is masked for them. (If you are one of those, you are probably not going to find much to please you in German wine, though you may respond better to other nations' versions of the Riesling grape.) Some will perceive this fruitiness only as a generalized fresh flavor, others will describe touches of pineapple or peach, and some will even find a slight tartness lurking deep in the wine. In any event, the presence of this good fruit works to domesticate, as it were, a certain quantity of the wine's sugars: our palates incorporate them into those fruit flavors where they seem natural and appropriate.

Second, the Riesling grape naturally possesses a great deal of acidity, and the presence of that acidity in the wine works somewhat to hold the sugar in balance, or at least partially to restrain it. Most people taste the acidity in several ways—most specifically, perhaps, in that touch of tartness in the wine or in those bright and biting pineapple flavors, but most importantly in the general liveliness, freshness, and vitality of the wine. Without sufficient acid, this wine would be limp, flabby, dead—a sucrose corpse.

The acid animates it, and in that respect this wine reinforces a very valuable lesson at the start of these white-wine sessions. The trinity of fruit and sugar and acid is the key to understanding most white wines. Acid and fruit and sugar don't explain everything about white wine by a long shot—but you can use them as reference points to triangulate where your own taste lies, and you can use them to chart your own path through white wines. What the interplay of tannin and acid and fruit were to your understanding of red wines, the relation of sugar and acid and fruit can be to your grasp of whites.

Compared to the Liebfraumilch, the Chenin Blanc seems to most people simultaneously drier, fuller, and less vivid. It feels a bit bigger and weightier in the mouth but less lively, so that some tasters perceive it as a bit flabby. Others will find that its lesser sweetness, greater roundness, and the more subdued taste of its fruit (tasters frequently discern a slightly tart apple flavor) make it for them a better-structured, more satisfying wine, especially with food.

You can learn a lot about your own palate from this wine in this particular tasting. In this setting (that is, tasted after the Blue Nun), did this Chenin Blanc strike you as an essentially sweet or an essentially dry wine?

Mind now, I'm talking about the flavor in the mouth as separate from the aroma; if you're in doubt, take a little taste of the Blue Nun, wait a minute or two, then taste the Chenin again. Ask some of your friends to make the same test; I think you'll find the results very interesting. Perceptions will run from totally sweet to totally dry, with a lot of mixed reports about sweet starts and dry finishes and vice versa. By paying very close attention to your own reactions to this Chenin Blanc, you can learn a lot about just how much sugar you can tolerate, how much you enjoy, how much or how little sugar masks other flavors for you, and how well you are able to discern other flavors despite the presence of sugar. Unlikely as it may seem, the two wines of this flight can constitute a full-scale seminar in tasting if you give them the proper time and attention.

Blue Nun is the largest-selling German wine in the United States. It is produced by Sichel, a major dealer in quality German wines, and imported to the United States by Schieffelin & Company.

The Monterey Vineyard is a very large, very modern winemaking firm now owned by the Seagram interests. It makes large quantities of impressive quality wine from a full range of California's best varietals, and it sells them at quite reasonable prices.

This is the conclusion of the first tasting session. It would be very useful to you to go straight through the next three flights, but if you wish, there are several other ways for you to proceed from here.

Following the lead of your own preferences:

Whether you liked the first wine better, Blue Nun, or the second wine, Chenin Blanc, go to Flight 5.

Following the kind of grapes:

Wine 1: go to Flight 5.

Wine 2: there are no other Chenin Blanc tastings; try Flight 7.

Following the wines of the country:

Wine 1: go to Flight 5.

Wine 2: go to Flight 2.

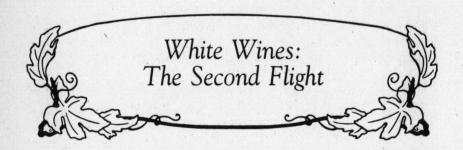

White Wines:
The Second Flight

MOREAU BLANC NV
AND
ROBERT MONDAVI TABLE WHITE 1983

If you are proceeding directly from the first pair of white wines to this tasting, make sure you take at least a bite of cracker and a large drink of water to wipe the sweetness from your mouth. Better yet, get up and walk around for five or ten minutes to let your palate clear so you can give these next two wines a fair trial. We're the victims of the logic of our program here: in moving from simple and accessible wines to more complex ones, we've been forced to start white wines with a fair dose of sugar, which runs dead counter to the logic of a tasting sequence. Normal tasting sequence places white wines before red wines, young wines before old, light wines before full-bodied, and dry wines before sweet. That is the usual pattern for serving wines at dinner, too. So try to scrape off as much of the sweetness as you can before you start sampling the next wines.

Ready? This pair of wines matches two very popular dry whites, one a French import, the other a Californian. Both are blends of several grapes from diverse but respectable growing areas. The Moreau Blanc is not vintage dated, so it is relatively important to try to buy this wine from a shop that handles it regularly. White wines of this type are not built for bottle-aging, and you don't want to get stuck with one that has been sitting on somebody's shelf with its cork drying out for two years.

Presuming you've done your shopping well, you should be ready now to pour the wines—well chilled but not icy cold—and subject them to your ritual eye, nose, and throat examination. So go to it, and check back here after you've registered all your comments.

Appearance. If you have by any chance gotten a bottle of either of these wines that is either too old or has been badly stored, the color should give you the first clue. Both the Moreau and the Mondavi should be pale straw in color, the Mondavi Table White perhaps a slight bit deeper in color than the Moreau Blanc. Any deeper shade of yellow—especially anything edging into bright yellow, brassy, or golden—will almost certainly mean that the wine has oxidized and will have no flavor left.

I know I've told you this before, but it is important. If you ask for a young white wine in a restaurant and it comes out of the bottle lemon yellow, don't even bother tasting unless it is a sweet wine like Sauternes; just send it back. If one of the two in front of you now is a color like that, taste it only if you are curious to know what oxidized wine tastes like; otherwise just bring it back to your dealer and get a fresher bottle.

Remember: Pale straw and slight variations from it are going to be the normal colors for the great majority of the white wines we'll be tasting together.

Aroma. Well, you may have had to work pretty hard here, because no one ever accused either of these wines of being intensely aromatic. Many people have trouble picking out any aroma at all, a condition that can result from everything from bottle variation in the wine to bad sinuses in the wine taster. If your wines are even a fraction too cold, the aroma of the Moreau Blanc particularly may disappear, so if you didn't get any scent initially, warm the glass in your hands a little—cradle it as you would a brandy glass—and swirl and sniff once more. But don't expect a whole lot.

What most tasters report they smell in the Moreau Blanc is a slight, clean aroma, dry and refreshing. Specific scents are difficult to isolate because the overall impression is faint, but some people do detect a bit

Through a Glass Brightly

As you cup that wine glass to warm its contents, you are present-ing yourself with a perfect illustration of the logic of wine-glass shapes. Why do all the experts insist on stemware for wine glasses? Precisely to keep hands away from the wine.

Every quality a wine glass should have relates to a quality of wine. You want to be able to see it clearly; hence, uncolored glass and crystal. You want to keep its temperature as constant as possible; hence, stems to keep hands from heating it. You want to be able to release the aroma; hence, wide bowls. But you don't want to dissipate that aroma; hence, in-curving rims or tulip shapes. The bigger aromas of red wines indicate that larger glasses are in order for them, just as Champagne's attractive bubbles want a tall, narrow glass to show them off best.

of generalized fruit, or acidity, or a delicate wheatlike scent. Don't worry if you didn't smell any of that; the aroma is small at best. Besides, let me remind you once again that this is not a test, and you are not graded—nor should you grade yourself—by how closely what you smelled matches what's on the page. I'm just trying to give you a range of typical responses, and if you smelled something completely different, it may mean that my range doesn't go far enough. What you smell is what you smell, and the important thing is for you to try to remember the scent and the wine and just how much they pleased or displeased you. In case you've forgotten, your taste is what counts.

The Mondavi White makes life a little (but not much) easier for your poor, overworked sniffer. Its aroma is stronger than that of the Moreau Blanc, though it is still small by any objective standards. Smelling it right after the Moreau seems to lead to two opposite responses in tasters. One group reports a dominant aroma of damp earth and wet straw; the other, a complex of slightly sweetish, fruity aromas—anything from honey and simple fruit to pears, pineapple, even canned grapefruit. And a taster familiar with white wines might be able to pick out a hint of one of the aromatic grapes—a vague suggestion of the floral, minty aromas associated with Riesling, for instance.

Once again, however, we are not dealing with a big aroma here, and these are not blockbuster, attention-grabbing scents but very slight, fleeting impressions, so don't give up on white wine if these scents are not coming through to you. I told you at the start, white wines are difficult precisely because they're so often delicate and their impressions subtle, so stick with them and keep tasting.

Taste. This leads us logically to the taste of these two whites. If you are tasting with others, you may be surprised by how much disagreement there can be about the flavors of what are, in the final analysis, two very simple table wines. People can perceive these wines as polar opposites— which is surprising enough—and different tasters may very well reverse each other's poles and find fruity what the other found sour, pleasing what the other found blah, and so on. I wish I could tell you why this is, but nothing I know about these wines explains that extreme range of opinion. If I didn't know it were so, I'd say it couldn't happen. At any rate, it means I can't really give you a majority opinion on either of these wines, so I'll just let you have the perimeters and some of the high and low points of each range of response, and you can see if your reaction falls anywhere on this map or if you're charting your own Northwest Passage to connoisseurship.

Of the Moreau Blanc, opinions run from sour and flabby up through soft and inoffensive all the way to pleasant and crisp and a little fruity with a nice touch of tartness. Everybody agrees that it is dry and light. Even those who don't think much of it agree that it makes a decent quaffing wine; as one taster put it, fine for outside on a warm day. The things that you clearly won't taste in this wine are big, full body and pronounced flavors. The tastes you will find fall into a broad range of delicate suggestions and nuances that you like or dislike according to your own sensitivity in discerning them—exactly as it was with the Moreau Blanc's aroma. This is a consistent wine, made to a small, but to many people very pleasing, scale.

Of the Mondavi White, opinions run from discerning in it an artificial, aggressive fruit taste, through finding it a little too fruity, all the way to tasting in it soft, very light fruit. Again, everybody agrees that it has a bit more body than the Moreau (though it is still light) and that it is dry. They agree, too, that the flavor doesn't really follow through on the various hints and suggestions of the aroma, that the wine doesn't seem to have any of the complexity its nose half-promised. And again, the general consensus is that this is acceptable quaffing wine, which is exactly what it's designed to be.

Pretty obviously, the average wine drinker is going to respond to these wines as the simple, straightforward wines they are, and our scrutinizing them as we've just done may look like putting a private on the rack for information only a general can provide. But these two whites, and many others like them, are drunk with pleasure every day in America. They appear on home tables with dinner. They're poured as house wines in restaurants and bars. They're probably even slugged from the bottle at picnics and ball parks. If by pushing them as hard as we've just done you can begin to recognize and isolate what you like and don't like in them, then you can use them for the starting gate they should be rather than the dead end they too often are.

Once they get you off and running, the makers of these two wines can also accompany you a good way down the track. Moreau is one of France's largest dealers in the white wines of Chablis, and he handles just about every conceivable gradation of Burgundian white wine. Moreau wines are distributed in the United States by Frederick Wildman.

Robert Mondavi is Robert Mondavi, a one-man wine industry: his pioneering winemaking and his equally brilliant publicizing were major forces in bringing California wines to the fore in quality and in the world's awareness of their quality. He makes almost the whole range of California wines, most of them very well indeed.

Here then ends the second white-wine tasting. You would do well to go straight on through Flights 3 and 4, but there are alternatives.

Following the lead of your own preferences:

Whether you liked the first wine better, Moreau Blanc, or the second wine, Mondavi White, go to Flight 3.

Following the kind of grapes:

Wine 1: go to Flight 12.

Wine 2: this is a very miscellaneous blend; try Flight 9.

Following the wines of the country:

Wine 1: go to Flight 3.

Wine 2: go to Flight 7.

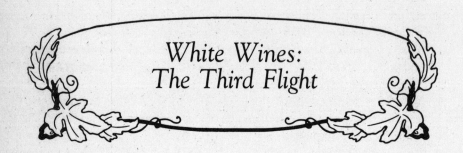

White Wines:
The Third Flight

SOAVE BOLLA 1983
AND
OLIVER DE FRANCE 1983

If there is a universally known imported wine in the United States that is *not* Lambrusco, it must be Soave, and if it's Soave, in most people's minds it must be Soave Bolla. The Bolla firm, maker of the classic wines of Verona (Soave for white; Bardolino, Valpolicella, and Amarone for red), has so successfully identified its name with the wine that many people seem to think it's one word—which is perfectly okay, since Bolla's is a good, representative Soave. Its wines are imported to the United States by The Jos. Garneau Co.

The other half of this pairing is an equally sound and representative white Bordeaux (*appellation controllée Bordeaux Blanc*) from the house of Eschenauer. Eschenauer is a long-established Bordeaux *négociant* handling a rather complete line of traditional Bordeaux wines from simple reds and whites such as this one (which bears the firm's proprietary name) up to classified *châteaux* from Pauillac and Graves and St.-Émilion. Its wines are imported by the International Vintage Wine Company.

All you really need know by way of preliminary beyond that is that at the level of production you are about to taste, both these firms can be relied on for a sound, well-made wine that will be reasonably consistent in flavor and style from year to year.

Now the ball is in your court: see, swirl, smell, sip, savor, and spit. Talk the wines over if you're tasting in a group, and then check back here for explanations, consolations, and advice to the winelorn.

Appearance. Once again the colors of these wines present no problems. Both are (or should be) pale straw, clear and clean. They are almost identical in shading: perhaps if you strain a bit you could see that the Soave is a hint paler than the Bordeaux Blanc, but the difference falls somewhere between negligible and invisible.

Aroma. Their aromas, however, probably will strike most people as markedly different.

For one thing, this particular vintage of Soave offers very little in the way of bouquet. Most people will find its aroma insignificant, almost nonexistent. Some, by dint of real effort and perhaps a lot of imagination, will catch faint whiffs of fruit and of light floral, herbaceous scents. Regard such absence of aroma as a real defect in the wine. It's obviously not serious enough to ruin your enjoyment of it, but it does deprive you of one of the wine's attractions. Soave should have a delicate—not hallucinatory—aroma that mixes fruit and flower and herb. It should definitely smell clean and fresh. This particular vintage doesn't smell unclean; it has scarcely any scent at all.

Comparatively speaking, the Bordeaux Blanc appears to have the more forceful and distinctive aroma. It may seem sharper, and to some people, perhaps because of their remembrances of dinners with wines of this type, to have a kind of salt-air tang, like the clean, fresh aroma that comes from a plate of freshly shucked clams or oysters. That's imaginative, of course, but why not? It points you in a right direction for the use of wines like these. By the way, it also means that people who dislike clams and oysters and whose associations with salt-air tang are low tide in Newark Bay may very well find the aroma of the Oliver de France unpleasant. For them its comparatively greater presence is not a plus but a minus.

More conventionally, however, most people tend to describe the scent of the Bordeaux Blanc as a composite of grassy, herby, fruity, and/or earthy tones. That covers a lot of ground, and few tasters seem to find anything more specific to put a label to. That is probably because

most Bordeaux Blanc is a blend, the most important parts of which are
two distinctly different grapes, Semillon and Sauvignon Blanc. Generally speaking, the grassy, herbaceous elements in Bordeaux Blanc probably are traceable to Sauvignon Blanc, the earthy, fruity components to
Semillon. In wines of this caliber those two grapes may well be blended
with several others of less note, but their aromas and flavors still should
be pronounced in the final harmony.

Taste. You should be able to distinguish the flavors of the Soave and
the Bordeaux Blanc equally clearly.

For most people, the Bolla moves: it seems sprightly, lively. This is
because of the relatively high acidity of this Soave, which some people
taste directly as a kind of bright tingling on the tongue. Those less
tolerant of acidity may find the flavor veering into the sour range, even
to the extent of outright unpleasantness. The majority of tasters, however, probably are going to find Soave Bolla pleasingly light, tart, and
acidic, with a fruit component in its flavor that suggests citrus to some
and apples to others. Among those who like this wine, a great number
discern a small but pleasing aftertaste they describe variously as tart,
nicely bitter, or almondy. Such a finish usually is thought of as a
hallmark of a well-made Soave.

The Oliver de France distinguishes itself from the Soave in most key
respects. Almost everybody feels it in the mouth as a less lively, slightly
more weighty wine: fuller but less sprightly. At its worst, this apparently
lower acidity in the Bordeaux can be sensed as not simply softness but
flabbiness, though that is likely to be a minority opinion. For most
people, the wine shows round and soft. On first taste it releases a little
burst of fruit sweetness (distinctly not sugariness) and then follows it
with what some people describe as a pleasing citric fruit flavor: most
simply taste fruit, period. The wine has a small but nice dry finish.

Both are well-made wines it is not unfair to think of as having been
carefully designed to respond to two slightly different tastes in white
wines. Neither is it unfair to think of them as good examples of differing
national styles in making white wines.

The Soave and Italian white wines generally (with some conspicuous
exceptions) favor the bright, light, acidic style. Most of them, particularly the varietal white wines from the hyphenated Italian areas of
Trentino-Alto Adige and Friuli-Venezia Giulia, display more fruitiness,
more clear taste of the grape variety, than Soave does, but they tend to

be every bit as acidic and lively. Because of that, they are preeminently wines for drinking chilled and young—within a year or two of harvest.

The Bordeaux Blanc and other French wines from the most esteemed growing areas—Bordeaux, Burgundy, Alsace, parts of the Loire Valley— predominantly favor the fuller style, with lower acid levels and more complex fruit flavors. Their greater body permits them to develop over time in the bottle, so they are characteristically (once you have moved beyond the simple shipper's wines such as the Oliver de France we have just tasted) wines for drinking at a few years of age and only lightly chilled in order to reveal their best bouquet and flavor.

There is, obviously, no good or bad at issue here. As always, it is at bottom a question of which style pleases you more—or, even better, which style pleases you more under what circumstances or with what food. You can have a lot of fun and absorb a lot of calories working out a complete answer to that one.

Here ends the third white-wine tasting. It would be best if you went right to Flight 4, but if you wish alternatives, there are several ways for you to proceed from here.

Following the lead of your own preferences:

If you liked the first wine better, Soave Bolla, go to Flight 5.

If you preferred the second wine, Oliver de France, go to Flight 9.

Following the kind of grapes:

Wine 1: there are no other grapes like this in our tastings.

Wine 2: go to Flight 9.

Following the wines of the country:

Go to Flight 4.

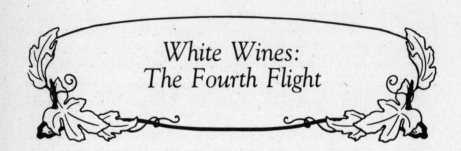

White Wines:
The Fourth Flight

CAVIT PINOT GRIGIO 1984
AND
BARRÉ MUSCADET 1983

These two kinds of wine normally both have pretty high acid levels coupled with complete dryness, which makes them very versatile dinner wines with uncomplicated foods. Italians would use a wine like Pinot Grigio to accompany antipasto, while the French think of Muscadet as a classic wine with fresh shellfish, especially oysters. Within their basic structural similarities, you should be tasting for differing kinds and styles of fruitiness, body, and balance. I don't think that anyone who has tasted several of these wines would ever, even in a blind tasting, mistake a Muscadet for a Pinot Grigio. What you should be looking for in this tasting is the reason why that is so.

Good luck: swirl away.

Finished already? Made all your notes and talked everything over? Tasted everything with and without a little nibble? Then let's get on with it.

Appearance. Yet once more, pale straw. The Muscadet may very well be the palest wine you've yet seen. That's not unusual for Muscadets;

they can be darker than this, but there is nothing at all abnormal about this degree of paleness. The Pinot Grigio's shade is absolutely typical.

Aroma. Here the differences start showing themselves. Though neither wine has a big aroma, each is distinctive.

The Cavit is fruity and fresh. You may pick up a sort of leafy scent and suggestions of mint in it. You will sometimes come across more forceful versions of it, but this aroma gives you a very faithful rendition of the scent of the Pinot Grigio grape (in French, *Pinot gris*—the gray Pinot).

The Muscadet smells crisp and clean. Some people sense a kind of tartness and acidity in it, a scent like crisp apples. It may give the impression of being drier—less sweet—than the Pinot Grigio's aroma. It, too, is a single-grape scent, though the Muscadet usually is much less intense in aroma than the Pinot Grigio. Neither is considered an aromatic grape.

The great majority of tasters find the bouquet of both wines lively, or pleasing, or refreshing, and they tend to summarize the differences between them by describing the Pinot Grigio as more delicate, the Muscadet as more complex, or the Pinot Grigio as having more fruit and the Muscadet more personality. That last word is vague; what people seem to mean by it is some combination of complexity and charm.

Taste. First of all, the Pinot Grigio strikes the tongue as lively, nervous, sometimes even a bit *frizzante* (fizzy). Sometimes it can be felt as a little prickly; that's the good, bright acid at work, animating the fruit.

Different people taste that combination of fruit and acid in markedly different ways. At one extreme, a taster may describe it as sharp, or bitter. Most are likely to be at the other end of the spectrum and taste it as fruit and spice—a nice, white-grape flavor, perhaps mixed with some suggestions of apple or of citrus or of clove, maybe even a hint of sweetness (if people taste that at all, it's usually right at the start, before the acid really asserts itself). The acid persists into the finish, which (depending on whether they like it or not) people will call everything from pleasantly astringent to sharp, sour, bitter. Overall, however, most tasters find this Pinot Grigio bright, crisp, and very pleasing.

Responses to the Muscadet can be very paradoxical. Objectively speaking, the wine seems to have both less acid and less fruit than the Pinot Grigio, but that dual reduction hits individual palates quite differently. Some can really feel the absence of the fruit and as a consequence find the wine too acid, almost sour. Some sense the lower acid and find the wine softer and blander than the Cavit. The great majority of tasters, however, seem to fall in the middle range. They describe a wine that is slightly fuller in body, a little less crisp, and a little less acidic than the Pinot Grigio, a wine that is very dry—almost austere—with interesting but subdued fruit and a completely dry finish. Most people take that greater fullness and total dryness to indicate that this is a great wine with seafood, and experience almost always shows they are right.

There you have it: very different wines, though because of the limits of our language for sensory description, the words and phrases we have to use to talk about them are uncomfortably similar.

Accounting for their differences is no easy task, either. Sure, the basic flavor of their grapes differs—the Muscadet is normally a more neutral grape—but what makes the fruit so much more prominent in the Cavit than in the Barré? I don't know for certain, but I'll risk a guess. There may be more residual sugar—naturally occurring unfermented grape sugar—in the Pinot Grigio than in the Muscadet.

In the course of fermentation, sugar is normally converted into alcohol by the yeasts on the grapes. Dry wines are the result of converting all the available sugar to alcohol. Sweet wines are produced when the fermentation either naturally halts before all the sugar is converted, or when the fermentation is stopped by raising or lowering the temperature to kill the yeast. Preserving a small trace of sugar in a wine of high acidity would help to reinforce the strength of its fruit and bring it more to the fore, perhaps even make it more full.

Because of the high acid in these two wines, you really wouldn't taste a trace amount of sugar as sweetness, but it would contribute toward fleshing out the fruit flavors and raising them up a notch or two on the flavor scale. If I'm right, these two wines make a fine illustration of just what an impact small adjustments in our trinity of sugar and acid and fruit can have on the final taste of a wine.

And that, class, concludes your lesson for today, and with it our fourth white-wine-tasting session. There are several ways for you to proceed from here.

Following the lead of your own preferences:

If you liked the first wine better, Cavit Pinot Grigio, go to Flight 5.

If you preferred the second wine, Barré Muscadet, go to Flight 9.

Following the kind of grapes:

This is the only tasting of either of these kinds of grapes.

Following the wines of the country:

Wine 1: go to Flight 5.

Wine 2: go to Flight 7.

White Wines:
The Fifth Flight

LIVIO FELLUGA TOCAI FRIULANO 1982
AND
SICHEL BEREICH BERNKASTEL (MOSEL QUALITATSWEIN) 1982

Your mission, should you choose to accept it, is to taste these two wines, decide which you like, and then figure out why.

Here are a few of the key elements that could play a part in your preference. First of all, one of these wines is markedly less alcoholic than the other. There should be differences in body between the two wines. Their grapes are different and ought to taste markedly distinct. Aromas, too—one is usually called spicy, the other floral. And there are differences in dryness and sweetness to be taken into account here. Finally, there should be a very perceptible stylistic difference between them, a distinction in what you could call their whole attack.

Other items may strike you as well: this is not meant to be an exhaustive list, just a set of reminders of what you can try to be aware of while you are performing your ritual sighting, swirling, sniffing, sipping, savoring, and spitting. So go to it, and take good notes. And just in case you've forgotten again, this is not like an examination in school.

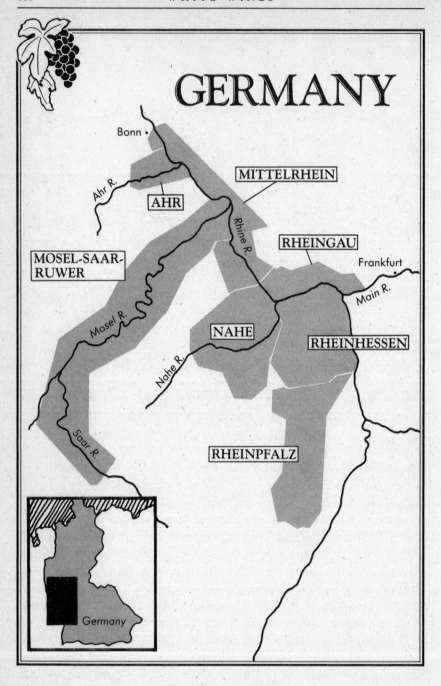

GERMANY

Bonn

MITTELRHEIN

Ahr R.

AHR

Rhine R.

RHEINGAU

Frankfurt

MOSEL-SAAR-RUWER

Main R.

Mosel R.

NAHE

RHEINHESSEN

Nahe R.

Saar R.

RHEINPFALZ

Germany

There are no wrong answers, unless you're really perverse and lie to yourself about what you like, or let yourself be bullied into something you think you ought to like. Even then, that's wrong only because it's wrong for you, not because there is anything objectively wrong with any choice you make.

Got that? Okay, stop that nauseating display of gratitude and go taste.

All right, let's talk about these wines one at a time, taking the second first because you've had a wine somewhat similar to this before—Blue Nun, in the first flight of white wines. Bereich Bernkastel is, as the name and the shape of the bottle indicate, a German wine. Bereich simply means district or area and is a word in common use on German wine labels. Bernkastel is the name of the particular winemaking district, in this case a very large and famous one on the Mosel River. *Qualitatswein* indicates approximately the middle level of the German wine-ranking system. So this wine is a cousin of the Liebfraumilch of your first flight, which is also a *Qualitatswein*, though that wine originated from a much larger viticultural area or group of areas, along the banks of the Rhine.

Appearance. In appearance, this Bernkastel looks very like the Blue Nun of the first white wine pair. It has the same light, pale straw color with just a suggestion of a few greenish highlights that is the hallmark of young Riesling-based wines. If your wine is showing darker than that, it is possibly too old to drink, in which case it should taste rather flat and tired—something akin to stale ginger ale.

Aroma. If all is well with your wine, however, the odds are very strong that most of you found its aroma very pleasant. Different tasters will report different degrees of intensity, of course, ranging from very faint to strong, but most use similar words to describe what they are smelling. Flowery and floral head the list, usually followed by fruity or sweet. Some tasters may discern more specific scents: peach, mango, and citrus are not unusual candidates among the fruits, and cinnamon, mint, and even camphor appear among the spices.

Normally a minority dislikes the aroma of this wine (though in any random group it might well be a majority). Those who find it unpleasing frequently describe it as smelling musty, or smelling of wet woolens. What they seem to object to is the fruit odor, which they find overpowering or cloying.

German Wine Geography

German wine labels can be very confusing to the uninstructed eye, and they aren't helped much in clarity by the abundance of Gothic script that squiggles across and around and up and down them. Under all that baroque camouflage, however, there is a wealth of very exact information.

Vintage, of course, is prominently and unambiguously displayed. After that, look for the level of the wine: Tafelwein, which is rightly not often exported; Qualitatswein, often abbreviated QbA; and Qualitatswein mit Pradikat (QmP). Under German wine law, the wines of the first two classifications may be fermented with added sugar (chaptalization), but Qualitatswein mit Pradikat can be made only with the grape's own natural sugars.

After that, look for the large geographical region from which the wine comes: Ahr, Hessische Bergstrasse, Mittelrhein, Nahe, Rheingau, Rheinhessen, Rheinpfalz, Mosel-Saar-Ruwer, Franken, Wurttemberg, and Baden. The most important on the American market are Mosel-Saar-Ruwer (usually just called Mosel and often spelled the French way, Moselle) and the three Rhine areas, Rheingau, Rheinhessen, and Rheinpfalz.

Finally, look for more precise geographical or vineyard information: a town name (usually ending in "er"—for example, Bernkasteler, a wine from Bernkastel) and/or a vineyard name (for example, Bernkasteler Doktor). If you want to get yet more precise, check the name of the vineyard owner/wine maker, since many vineyards (such as Bernkasteler Doktor) are divided among several owners, any or all of whom may bottle wine under their own label—which will, if you hunt hard enough among the squiggles, give you all this information.

Taste. Opinions tend to be more evenly divided about the taste of this wine. Usually a small minority actively dislikes it. Sugar-phobes, of course, taste nothing in it but sweetness and hate it for that reason: they are balanced out by sugar-philes, who agree with them about the taste but love it for that reason. Others don't feel as strongly but simply find it uninteresting; they will describe it as too light, or watery, or flaccid, or dull. Those who like it tend to praise its light fruitiness and moderate sweetness, which they will taste as complementing each other. They may specifically taste peach or pear or even crabapple in it. Usually they will call this Bernkastel soft; that softness seems to result from a deficiency of acid in the wine, an objective defect that for some palates can be an asset. Almost all tasters perceive a definite sweet finish to the wine and an apparent increase in sweetness as the wine opens in the glass.

The Bernkastel's companion wine in this flight comes from a very different part of the world: Friuli, in Italy's extreme northeastern corner, a region that formed part of the Austro-Hungarian Empire and its successor states until well into this century. Tocai is the most popular white wine in the region, where it is drunk with almost every conceivable sort of food on every sort of occasion. It is always vinified dry and should not be confused with the Hungarian Tokay, a sweet dessert wine, or Alsatian Tokay, made from another grape altogether. Just for the record, our wine is pronounced Toe-kigh (to rhyme with high); the other two wines are pronounced Toe-kay (to rhyme with hay).

Appearance. In appearance, this Tocai is very like the Bernkastel—a clean straw color, definitely a shade darker or more golden than the German wine, but still light and clear. Here, too, very dark colors would indicate a wine oxidized or oxidizing. Tocai should be drunk relatively young; but it can take some bottle age with advantage.

Aroma. Once again, don't be surprised by great diversity of opinion about either the intensity or the quality of the Tocai's aroma. Especially in a comparison with the Bernkastel, it is possible for some tasters to discern little more than a strong presence of alcohol—not because the Tocai has so much alcohol, but because the Bernkastel has so little: 8½ percent as opposed to the Tocai's 12½ percent.

But most tasters pick up a range of different scents in this wine. The one most commonly noted is a bittersweet nuttiness, which some tasters specifically discern as bitter almonds. Fruit, too, appears often in people's descriptions, and they tend to emphasize its ripeness or spiciness: comparing the Tocai's odor to spiced pears, for instance, is one possibility. Equally common descriptions cite the odors of flowers and spice and earth, the latter (for those who aren't happy with this wine) often shading over into the oppressively musky.

Taste. Often this wine feels slightly prickly or fizzy on the tongue, giving it a bit of an edge that different tasters sense as either a pleasing liveliness or an annoying sharpness. Those who dislike that aspect of the wine may also find it a bit on the sour side overall. Most tasters tend to remark on the wine's nice, bright fruit or its spiciness. Hazelnuts and pears are two specific flavors that many people taste in Tocai. Many also report tasting a good, somewhat almondy finish.

Whichever of these wines you may have preferred, tasting them side by side should have helped you to smell and taste more clearly important aspects of both.

Aromas, for instance: you should (if neither alcohol nor sugar interferes for you) be able to place the Tocai definitely in the spicy category and the Bernkastel definitely in the floral, even though one may have some flowery tones and the other some spicy ones. Also, you should be able to perceive that the bouquet of the Bernkastel is comparatively delicate and slight, while that of the Tocai is bigger and more assertive but somewhat coarser.

The taste comparisons work in similar directions. The Bernkastel allows you to see the good acid in the Tocai, which you might otherwise miss, while the Tocai underlines the charm of the Bernkastel's softness. You are, I think, also made more aware than you might otherwise be of the heft of the Tocai—not that it is a big wine, but its roundness and more aggressive fruit make its medium body feel more substantial on the tongue, especially when counterpoised by a low-alcohol, light-bodied wine such as the Bernkastel.

Overall, those things should add up to two wholly different styles, two distinctive modes of attack. The Bernkastel succeeds by charm and delicacy, reinforced by a touch of sweetness. The net effect is of lightness and grace, a wine that promises refreshment. The Tocai, on the other hand, is a bigger wine, fully dry, and more forward: not what you would call muscular (you wouldn't say anything like that, would you?), but definitely more energetic—bracing rather than refreshing. Your preference among wines as interestingly different as these should be beginning to blaze a pretty clear trail for you through the white-wine jungle.

A word about the makers of these two wines. Sichel is an old and highly respected shipper of German wines. Now part of Schieffelin & Company, it exports to the United States the whole gamut of German wine, from Liebfraumilch to estate-bottled rarities. Livio Felluga is a family firm rooted in Friuli. Felluga vinifies most of the important grapes of Friuli and is particularly notable for its white wines, especially those made from the traditional vines of the region. These are now imported to the United States by International Vintage Wine Company.

This is the conclusion of our fifth white-wine-tasting flight. There are several ways for you to proceed from here.

Following the lead of your own preferences:

If you liked the first wine better, Felluga Tocai, go to Flight 8.

If you liked the second wine better, Sichel Bernkastel, go to Flight 6.

Following the kind of grapes:

Wine 1: this is the only Tocai tasting.

Wine 2: go to Flight 6.

Following the wines of the country:

Wine 1: go to Flight 11.

Wine 2: go to Flight 6.

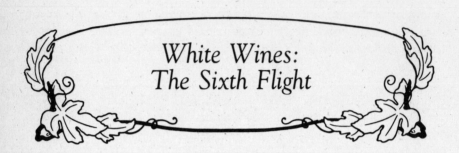

White Wines:
The Sixth Flight

PIESPORTER GOLDTROPFCHEN RIESLING KABINETT 1982 (WEINGUT JOS. MATHEUS-LEHNERT, MOSEL)
AND
DEIDESHEIMER HERRGOTTSACKER RIESLING KABINETT 1982 (DEINHARD, RHEINPFALZ)

This flight should certainly stretch your new skills, so taste carefully—especially those of you who have been pluming yourselves on your abilities to discern flavors even in the presence of residual sugar. These two are only lightly sweet wines, both of the *Kabinett* classification, but they embody the two broadest divisions in top-quality German wines. In the first place, representing the wines of the River Mosel, in the traditional long-necked green bottle, a single-estate wine (Goldtropfchen) from the town of Piesport. And in the second column, representing the wines of the River Rhine, a single-estate wine (Herrgottsacker) from the town of Deidesheim, in the equally traditional Rhine bottle of long-necked brown glass. The differences between the wines of the Mosel and the Rhine are significant, but they are also subtle. You will have to concentrate to find the regional differences among so many family similarities.

Okay, you've been warned: now perform the ritual and report back after you've talked over your findings.

Appearance. As usual, the appearance of these two wines presents no problems: both are the classic pale straw color, with occasional—and attractive—green or gold highlights.

Aroma. The first impression most people form of the scent of the Piesporter reflects its freshness: they may call it fresh, or clean, or refreshing, but almost all find it pleasing. Most also find it of delicate to moderate strength, and a great majority of tasters also detect in it distinct flowery tones. Fruit, too, appears often in descriptions of this aroma—peaches or, more often, pears—often with an exotic spicy element attached: woodruff or pepper, for instance, are both possibilities. Some people also report green tones as well—grass, or herbaceous odors, or green grapes. For most, this elaborate combination of elements is still delicate; but for others, it is just too sweet and too perfumed to be truly pleasurable.

The Deidesheimer strikes most people as having the more pronounced aroma of the two. Some tasters describe it as deep and pungent, somewhat reminiscent of a red wine's aroma (that's what they say if they like it), or almost cheesy or like damp wool (that sort of description usually comes from those who don't like it). As it sits in the glass, the Deidesheimer opens up to release more floral aromas and eventually fruit scents—bananas and especially the lemon smells commonly associated with the Riesling grape. Again, those who don't care for this wine will tend to find those fruit odors too strong: they probably will call them overripe.

Taste. The flavors of the Piesporter and Deidesheimer distinguish themselves from each other in much the same way. Most people taste the Mosel wine as delicate and light, fruity and pleasingly acidic. Different tasters, of course, will detect different fruit flavors, though pears and citrus—especially lemon—are the most common. But don't be surprised if you or one of your fellow tasters also pick up a hint of strawberry or black currant or a more floral element. A great many people find to their surprise and pleasure that this Mosel is drier than they expected, especially in the finish—probably the effect of its good acid balance. The possible objections to this wine are as varied as ever. For some it is too acidic; for others, too sweet; for others, too delicate—they taste

German Wine Grades

Kabinett is one of the grades of Qualitatswein mit Pradikat, *wines that must be vinified only with their own natural sugars. Since the German wine-growing areas are very northerly and the Riesling grape is a late ripener, the amount of QmP wine produced varies tremendously from harvest to harvest. In good years, grapes intended for QmP are left on the vines as late as possible to concentrate their sugars and acids, and sometimes there is help from Botrytis. Repeated hand pickings, often selecting individual grapes from a bunch, are the key to the greatest German wines. On the label, the varying degrees of sweetness achieved are indicated by the particular Pradikat (descriptive word or phrase): in ascending order of sweetness, Kabinett, Spatlese, Auslese, Beerenauslese, and Trockenbeerenauslese. The last two usually are referred to simply as BA and TBA, respectively, for obvious reasons. All these gradations sweeter than Kabinett usually are regarded as dessert wines, and some examples of them are among the very greatest wines of that category.*

nothing at all. But the majority of tasters seem to find it modestly sweet, light, fruity, and delicate, all within a small but pleasing range.

The biggest impression the Deidesheimer makes, after its initial rush of fruit and sweetness, is of liveliness: it seems to most people more forceful and more aggressive, a bit bigger and more mouth-filling than the Piesporter. The Deidesheimer, too, has a fine, bright acidity that balances its residual sugar, so this Rhine wine seems to dry somewhat in your mouth before it ends with a beautifully long, honeyed finish. Some people describe it as tasting of pears and/or apricots as well, with hints of thyme and lemon mixed in—a whole fruit stand of flavors mingling together. Its balance of sweetness and acidity and its sort of modulation or alternation of sweetness and dryness in the mouth are prominent features of this wine, and most tasters comment on them, though their language for doing so can run anywhere from confusion and frustration at being unable to pin this wine down to real satisfaction with its complexity.

Congratulations! You've now figured out the broad distinction between wines of the Mosel and wines of the Rhine.

No, I'm not kidding and no, it's not simply that Mosels come in green bottles and Rhines in brown (though it doesn't hurt to know that for quick identification at a distance). But the delicacy and the lightness and the floral qualities we talked about are all traditionally regarded as hallmarks of Mosel wines, which are probably among the world's lightest "serious" wines. And the greater liveliness and force, the bigger body and richer flavor of the Deidesheimer are precisely the characteristics that distinguish Rhine wines from Mosels. So you did it—you're capable of tasting that kind of quite subtle distinction; and if you can do that, the world of white wine holds very few problems for you. You're well on your way to getting a workable handle on it already.

Just to give you a better idea of what you've been drinking, here is a little extra information about these wines and their makers.

Piesport is one of the most esteemed wine towns in the district known as the Middle Mosel, and Goldtropfchen is the most prized vineyard within the denomination. Matheus-Lehnert, the wine maker, is a small firm that owns a particularly choice section of this vineyard. The wine is imported to the United States by Kobrand.

Deidesheim is one of the most esteemed wine towns in the Mittelhaardt district of the Rheinpfalz, the part of Germany bordering on Alsace. It is commonly known in English as the Palatinate. Its wines have long been popular in Germany and abroad. Herrgottsacker is one of several top-rated vineyards within the limits of Deidesheim. Deinhard is a long-established (since the 1700s) firm of German wine makers and wine dealers; it owns excellent properties in several of Germany's best wine regions. Its wines are imported to the United States by Deinhard & Partners.

This concludes our sixth white-wine-tasting flight. There is only one way for you to proceed from here.

Following the lead of your own preferences:

Whether you liked the first wine better, the Piesporter, or the second wine, the Deidesheimer, go to Flight 7.

Following the kind of grapes:

Go to Flight 7.

Following the wines of the country:

This concludes the German wines in these tastings.

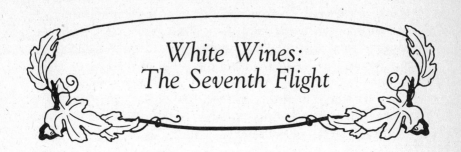

White Wines:
The Seventh Flight

DOPFF ALSACE RIESLING 1981
AND
CHÂTEAU STE.-MICHELLE WASHINGTON
JOHANNISBERG RIESLING 1982

You're not done with Riesling yet. This is a grape variety that rivals (many would say surpasses) Chardonnay as the premier white-wine grape of the world, and like the Chardonnay it is cultivated and vinified just about everywhere on the globe where serious winemaking is possible. And like Chardonnay, too, Riesling responds so sensitively to different soils and vinification techniques that it is possible to distinguish, in broad terms at least, what can genuinely be called national styles. So far you've been dealing with the classic German style in Riesling; in this flight you're going to be tasting to find out what France and the United States make of this grape.

Pour the wines, see, swirl away, then smell, sip, savor, and spit.

Appearance. In color, both these Rieslings are a clear straw yellow, a tone darker than any of the German Rieslings you've been drinking. This is a characteristic color range for non-German Rieslings other than late-harvest wines, which would normally be considerably darker and more golden than any wine we've yet dealt with.

Despite the fact that the Alsatian wine zone directly touches on the German and in geographical and climatic terms has to be considered virtually identical to it, most tasters find that the Riesling wines of Alsace differ quite markedly from those of Germany. So great is the difference, in fact, that Alsatian Riesling and Rhine Riesling (even though Alsatian Riesling grows along the banks of the Rhine, Rhine Riesling by universal practice always refers to German wine) are routinely cited by wine professionals as a textbook case of exactly the kinds of difference vinification techniques can make in a wine.

I think you can see this clearly right from the beginning, in that slight difference in color. The drier German Rieslings (the *Kabinett* classification) usually are paler, more delicate-looking; these two wines are comparatively more robust in appearance.

Aroma. Most tasters also notice big differences in the Alsatian Riesling's aroma. It smells drier, for one thing, and a bit deeper. Most people still smell fruit in it, but often now compounded with a whole range of other odors in the leafy-herbal-spicy group: mint and pepper and grass, for instance, and sometimes even woodruff. The Dopff's aroma still is not a big one, however, and for many people those specific elements are just too elusive. All they will report smelling is a general sense of dryness and depth, and their reactions to it can run from mildly pleased to neutral to mild dislike of its blandness.

As a handy reminder to you of previous flights, the Washington State Riesling turns out to be a wine much more in the Germanic style. Most people still find its aroma noticeably stronger and heavier than that of German Riesling (and, in fact, heavier than this Alsatian example), but they also tend to find a lot of the same components in its scent that they found in German Riesling. Most describe it as soft and fresh and mildly sweet-smelling, for instance. Many discern the same sort of fruitiness and spiciness they found in German Riesling: pears and apples and even mangoes are often mentioned, along with leafy odors and mint and pepper. For some tasters, of course, these odors are either indistinguishable (they are in that case likely to call the wine flowery or perfumed) or indiscernible (they're likely to call it dull) or overstrong (they'll probably call it cloying), but most of those who have been responding pleasurably to Riesling will find the Chateau Ste.-Michelle's aroma typical and enjoyable.

Taste. People tend to react in rather polar ways to the Dopff Riesling. Those who dislike it usually say it has too much acid, which causes it to taste tart or sour or bitter to them. Those who like it tend to admire its balancing of dry fruit and acid. They find strong citrus elements—especially grapefruit—and other more subdued fruit flavors—peach or pear, plum or apple—and a very slight spicy flavor in it, with a finish that they describe as dry or astringent (those who don't like it call it bitter).

The Chateau Ste.-Michelle Riesling strikes most tasters as a heavier wine, with more body and fruit. The specific flavors most likely to be mentioned fall into the by now familiar Riesling range—apple, peach, plum, spice. It may seem slightly *pétillant,* a little fizzy on the tongue. Its acidity catches almost everyone's attention; because of it, people will differ surprisingly on just how much sugar they taste in this wine, and their finding it sweet or dry doesn't seem to correlate with whether they like it or not. Frequently those who do like it describe it as bright, or live, or balanced. Those who don't like it say the fruit fades out too fast or that it finishes too bitterly or that it is badly structured.

These two wines as a pair are a fair example of the styles of their respective countries in vinifying Riesling. Both are bigger and fuller than German Riesling. Alsatian Rieslings, like this Dopff wine, tend to be fully dry and medium-bodied, with a slightly steely quality that differs markedly from the German soft touch. The American style runs toward greater fruit and higher alcohol than either Alsatian or German Riesling and has a rather full body that possesses neither the steeliness of Alsace nor the softness of Rhine. Both the United States and Alsace also make dessert wines from late-picked, very ripe Riesling grapes, just as Germany does. All of these very sweet wines are capable of reaching levels of extraordinary succulence, and they are never inexpensive.

Because of their expense and because also their extreme sweetness makes it impossible to taste anything else after them, we won't be dealing directly with the great dessert wines. You shouldn't hesitate to try them on your own, however. At their proper place in a meal, with—or better, as—dessert, they can be incomparable. All of the German QmP classifications of Auslese or sweeter are eminently qualified to serve as dessert wines. Equivalent classifications elsewhere bear designations such as Vendange Tardive or Sélections des Grains Nobles (Alsace) or Late Harvest (California). All should be deep gold in color, richly scented, lusciously sweet, but also with a wealth of flavors and nuances beyond simple sugar.

Dopff is an old family firm whose participation in the Alsatian wine trade began in the seventeenth century. It produces the full range of Alsatian white wines—Riesling, Gewurztraminer, Sylvaner, Pinot Blanc. Its wines are brought into the United States by Peartree Imports. Château Ste.-Michelle is one of the oldest and most important wineries in the Pacific Northwest. Headquartered near Seattle, Washington, the firm makes a wide selection of wines from many noble grape varieties, both white and red.

Here ends the seventh flight. There are several ways for you to proceed from here.

Following the lead of your own preferences:

If you enjoyed either the first wine, Dopff Riesling, or the second wine, Château Ste.-Michelle Riesling, go to Flight 8.

Following the kind of grapes:

This is the last Riesling tasting. Make sure you haven't missed Flights 1, 5, and 6.

Following the wines of the country:

Go to Flight 8.

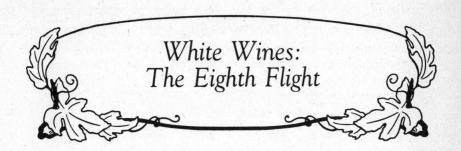

White Wines:
The Eighth Flight

HUGEL ALSACE GEWURZTRAMINER 1982
AND
SEBASTIANI SONOMA VALLEY GEWURZTRAMINER
1982

These two wines mark the transition between medium-bodied and full-bodied white wines. Depending on how they are vinified, Gewurztraminers will range from medium-bodied and highly aromatic to full-bodied and more restrained, from fully dry through lightly sweet to lusciously sweet, late-harvest-type dessert wines that can rival the finest Rieslings for succulence.

For our purposes, the Gewurztraminer qualifies as an almost perfect grape: it has a distinctive, quite easily rememberable aroma and flavor, and almost everybody likes it. I'm not trying to prejudice your opinion, but the Gewurztraminer—from the consumer's point of view if not the wine maker's—is a user-friendly grape.

The two wines you are about to taste have been chosen as fair representatives of the middle-of-the-road dry style of Gewurztraminer from its two currently most interesting areas of production, Alsace and California.

Enough preamble; taste the wines. Remember your full ritual—see, swirl, smell, sip, savor, and spit. And don't forget to try tasting both with and without a bite of food to see how it affects the wine. Go to it.

Appearance. For the first time in quite a while, we have some color variation to deal with. The Alsatian Gewurz is straw-colored, perhaps a bit deeper than you've been seeing among the Rieslings, with greenish-gold highlights. The California Gewurztraminer is still darker straw, a bit more golden perhaps, with a definite pinkish tinge to it; in some lights it will look like an onion-skin tinge. Both wines should be attractive, clear, and bright.

Aroma. As far as aroma is concerned, both these wines ought to give you something you can really grapple with; most people think of Gewurztraminer as an aromatic grape, and rightly so. A Gewurz without odor is a crippled wine.

Most tasters describe the aroma of the Hugel as clean and fresh. They find that it is made up of both fruit and floral elements, but when you search for more specifics, you wind up with a whole fruit stand. The possibilities include apples, figs, grapefruit, raisins, anise, grass, mint, pepper, and just generalized spices.

Many people have real difficulty pinning down specific components of this aroma, though they find the whole thing quite distinctive. Most tasters like it—they call it pleasant, intriguing, appetizing, and other words to the same effect. For some people, however, it is all a bit too much, and they find this aroma somewhat foxy or musky or musty, cloying or overly perfumed. Very few ever describe it as insignificant or delicate; when such a thing happens with a Gewurztraminer, it almost always means either nasal troubles or bottle troubles.

Most of the broader categories of things that people discern in the Hugel Gewurztraminer they will also find in the Sebastiani's aroma. It is similarly fresh, clean, and fruity, though most tasters report its scent as less forceful and slightly more fruity than the first wine's. It is *comparatively* more delicate and less intense; some will call it weaker. If you really press yourself and your fellow tasters and smell for all you're worth, you might pick up some specific aroma elements that distinguish this wine a bit more from the Alsatian. For instance, people sometimes discern scents of pear and citrus or almond in the California wine, as well as those scents it shares with the Alsatian Gewurz, scents such as flower and fruit and grass and mint (you might even find that the Sebastiani has a specifically spearmint odor). Objections and negative comments usually are pretty much the same here as for Wine 1.

Taste. The fruit, vegetable, and flower stand stays open for business during tasting as well as smelling, and the same cornucopia of specific elements usually appears here. Those who don't like this sort of wine tend to respond to the totality rather than to components, and they may simply call the taste of Gewurztraminer peculiar, or unpleasant, or strange, or—more rarely—too sweet.

What that last comment usually reflects, when it is made of dry Gewurztraminers like these, is a confusion of the flavor of intense fruit with sweetness. If you pay close attention, you can see that it is actually fruit flavor and not sugar you are tasting. This phenomenon happens occasionally with any number of different kinds of white wine. I've always wondered whether we're not the victims here of a bit of Pavlovian palatal conditioning: because our routine experience of intense fruit flavor is almost always in association with sugars as well, does it mean that the one taste automatically calls up the other for us?

Whatever the truth of that matter, it remains a fact that some tasters have trouble (especially with a spicy grape such as this) distinguishing between strong fruit and sweetness. There is not much one can do about that other than to be aware of the possibility and to practice making the distinction by drinking lots of dry, fruity white wine.

I warned you this was going to be a rigorous discipline.

Tasters who like this kind of wine spot a whole range of flavors at work in it. Of the Hugel version, for instance, in addition to simple, generalized fruit, they may report tangy fruit, licorice, pears, pepper, and spice, while the Sebastiani rendition of Gewurztraminer may elicit responses that include the omnipresent simple fruit, slightly sour fruit, apples, grapefruit, pears, cinnamon, and spice. Most people find the Hugel very crisp and acidic and tasting somewhat less fruity on the whole than its aroma led them to expect. The Sebastiani, on the other hand, usually surprises people by being—comparatively—very fruity, more so than its smaller aroma promised, and also—again comparatively—less acid. Depending on your reaction to the acid/fruit balance, you may find the Hugel too biting, perhaps verging on sour, or the Sebastiani too soft, lacking in bite, or perhaps verging on flabby. Or either one of them may strike you as a wine in perfect equilibrium, with just the right amount of acid and body to support a lively and distinct varietal flavor.

Characteristic varietal flavor is, in fact, what you're tasting in these two wines. No matter what words you've used to describe it, that conglomeration of fruit and spice we've been talking about in the aroma and the taste is typical of the Gewurztraminer grape. It may vary in intensity (as it does slightly in these two wines), but that spectrum of sensations is what Gewurztraminer yields everywhere it is vinified.

Regional differences occur, of course. For instance, the Hugel Gewurztraminer seems measurably more acidic than the Sebastiani, which has a fuller and richer (though softer and less bright) fruit flavor. That, I think, owes to the respective climates in which these grapes were grown. California grapes just routinely reach greater ripeness than Alsatian grapes. As a consequence, California grapes possess more developed flavors, higher sugars (which means higher alcohol in a completely dry wine), and lower acid. So the firmer, brighter style is typically Alsatian, and the softer, fuller style is Californian.

If you pay careful attention to the finish of these two wines, you'll probably notice that the Alsatian Gewurztraminer finishes drier and somewhat longer than the Californian and that it plants a little barb at the back of your throat before it goes down. For some people that finish is a little too bitter and raspy. For others it is pleasantly astringent. But whether it is enjoyed or deplored, it, too, is characteristic of the Alsatian style of slightly austere, acidic attack. Neither style, obviously, is objectively better than the other; it just depends on which pleases you, or which you're in the mood for at the moment. There is a time for steel and a time for velvet.

The name of the Gewurztraminer grape derives from the German word for spicy (*gewurz*) and the name of the town where it is believed this vine originated, Tramin, now Termeno, in what used to be the Sud Tirol but is now the Italian region of Trentino-Alto Adige. The grape still is cultivated there, where it produces for the most part rather light-bodied but intensely aromatic wines. Gewurztraminer is also vinified in Austria and Germany and several parts of the United States in addition to California.

The Hugel firm is one of the oldest and most respected in Alsace. It makes the full line of Alsatian white wines and is particularly famed for its late-harvest dessert wines. Its wines are imported to the United States by Dreyfus, Ashby & Company, a division of Schenley.

Sebastiani is a good-sized, family-owned winery producing an almost bewildering array of California wines in just about every price range. Quality levels are sound, and the wines are made with integrity throughout the line, so good value for your money is the norm with most of their bottlings.

This concludes the eighth white-wine-tasting session. There are several ways for you to proceed from here.

Following the lead of your own preferences:

If you liked the first wine better, Hugel Gewurztraminer, go to Flight 11.

If you preferred the second wine, Sebastiani Gewurztraminer, go to Flight 9.

Following the kind of grapes:

This is the only flight of Gewurztraminer.

Following the wines of the country:

Go to Flight 9.

QUEEN'S GAMBIT

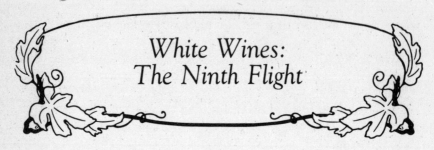

White Wines:
The Ninth Flight

SCHYLER ENTRE-DEUX-MERS 1982
AND
BEAULIEU VINEYARD ESTATE BOTTLED NAPA
VALLEY DRY SAUVIGNON BLANC 1982

With this flight you are starting to explore the fuller-bodied white wines. These sorts of wines are almost invariably vinified fully dry. Most of the wines you've tasted before this could be drunk equally happily as aperitifs or as dinner wines; most of the wines you are about to taste simply have too much substance to make a satisfactory cocktail. These are dinner wines par excellence, designed to accompany food of all sorts. Not that the greatest of them can't be enjoyed all by themselves; some of them deserve to be enshrined in a kind of splendid isolation and savored alone; as what in Italy is called a *vino da meditazione* (a wine for thinking both with and about). But that's getting more than a little ahead of ourselves: we're going to start a bit less exaltedly than all that.

Your focus of attention for the next two flights is going to be the Sauvignon Blanc grape. Let me underline that this is a distinct and important white-grape varietal. Many people have the false impression that wines labeled Sauvignon Blanc are just white-wine versions of

Cabernet Sauvignon, but that is not so, and you are now going to be able to one-up all such poor ignorants whenever the opportunity presents itself. There are in fact some white versions of Cabernet Sauvignon, just as there are from time to time rosé versions of it—why I will never understand, since it wastes a perfectly fine red grape. To my palate they are usually dreadful, but you can decide that for yourself if you are curious about them. They are always clearly labeled Blanc de Cabernet or White Wine from Cabernet Grapes, so there should be no reason ever to confuse them with the true white wine from the white grape Sauvignon Blanc.

The only possibility of labeling confusion you really need worry about stems from the fact that some American bottlings of Sauvignon Blanc call themselves Fumé Blanc. This is a practice that began some years ago with Robert Mondavi, who wanted to distinguish his then-novel dry vinification of Sauvignon Blanc from the at-that-time dominant sweet style. Nowadays few sweet versions ever find their way to the market, and the two names, Sauvignon Blanc and Fumé Blanc, are used almost interchangeably to designate a dry dinner wine.

One last piece of prologue: in this flight, the California wine, true to California practice, is a 100 percent Sauvignon Blanc varietal, while the French wine, faithful to the traditions of the Bordeaux area, mixes Sauvignon Blanc grapes with Semillon in proportions that will vary significantly from maker to maker.

Okay, now you're ready to work, so go to it and check back here after you've made all your comments and/or talked yourselves out about these two wines.

Appearance. The appearances of these two wines should be nearly identical. Both ought to be pale straw in color. In any given flight, one might look slightly paler than the other because of bottle variation, but the difference shouldn't be significant. And as you probably are tired of hearing by now, any darker colors—deep gold or especially brown tints—are sure to mean that that particular bottle is finished, either over the hill with age or destroyed by bad shipping or storage.

Aroma. Aroma may present some tasters with problems in the case of these two wines, because neither has what you could call a very pronounced or a very big bouquet. That's not a serious flaw in either wine, but it does qualify as a disappointment. Even though Sauvignon Blanc is not an intensely aromatic grape, some vinifications of it develop a very

Bordeaux Blancs

The Bordeaux region rests its vinous fame on its great red wines (from the Médoc, St.-Émilion, and Pomerol) and on its sweet white wines (from Sauternes and Barsac). It also produces enormous quantities of dry white wine, ranging in quality from dismal to quite extraordinary.

The largest AOC category, Bordeaux Blanc, is made up mostly of decent everyday wines, but it can include as well (as can any class of wine made anywhere) wines that are extraordinary for their price and wines that would be poor at any price. Entre-Deux-Mers is another large category of reliable white table wines. They are named for the specific place they are produced, the fat tongue of land lying between the converging rivers Garonne and Dordogne, the "two seas" of the name.

It is generally agreed that the finest dry whites of the region come from the area called Graves, southeast of the city of Bordeaux. Graves possesses its own AOC appellation and a ranking system similar to that of the red Médoc wines.

lively and very pronounced grassy aroma that is a real plus for the wine when present.

With these two wines we have aromas that most tasters describe as subtle or subdued, with the scent of the varietal Sauvignon Blanc being slightly more intense or powerful or marked than that of the Entre-Deux-Mers. Most people also call the two aromas faint, clean, refreshing, and pleasant. Those tasters who don't mesh with these wines tend to call the French wine slightly musty and the California a little acrid.

More specifically, the Entre-Deux-Mers is usually described as dry and soft-smelling, lightly fruity or spicy or floral, with herbaceous or applelike overtones. You may even detect a faint, lightly ammoniac smell, not unpleasant, that reminds some people of young, fresh cheese.

On the other hand, the Sauvignon Blanc smells sweeter and more flowery to most tasters, with an often-remarked-on leafy or grassy component fairly prominent. This latter element is an identifying characteristic of the grape variety. Some people may also pick it up as the scent of straw, or, at the other end of the spectrum, as a citrus odor.

Taste. In taste, even though once again neither wine has a big, overpowering flavor, they are usually much more readily distinguishable. Almost everyone tastes the Entre-Deux-Mers as the softer, the Sauvignon Blanc as the more acid—though as usual you can get sharp differences of preference about those tastes. The French wine is most often described as soft, mildly fruity, with a dry finish, straightforward and uncomplex.

The California wine, on the other hand, is usually felt as slightly fruitier, drier, and more lively on the tongue. Because of its greater acidity, many tasters experience a slight tingling sensation, almost as if the wine were *pétillant,* even though it is not. Some may report discerning a distinct grapefruit flavor in it. Most agree that it has a good, dry finish, but like the first wine is rather simple and uncomplicated.

Speaking as objectively as is ever possible about wine, I'd say that both wines are good, sound examples of their breeds.

The Schyler is to my mind the essence of what used to be (it seems centuries ago now) classic French carafe wine, designed not to call too much attention to itself but to partner quietly and well with almost anything on a menu. The worst you should be able to say of such a wine is that it is bland and inoffensive, the best that it is pleasant, with enough body to take food well and enough flavor to satisfy without requiring analysis. As an introduction to the dry white wines of Bordeaux, it shows well the kind of balance and body they strive for, though it gives you only a rudimentary idea of the complexity of flavor they can achieve.

Similarly, I find the Beaulieu Vineyard Sauvignon a good, middle-range representative of the grape's character as Californians handle it. It seems to me to have decent if not strongly accented varietal character, especially noticeable in those grassy/citrus/herbal scents and flavors. More important to me, it is not overly grassy, as some straight varietal Sauvignon Blancs can be. Some intense Sauvignon Blancs can make you feel you've been sent out to pasture. On the other side of the coin, it is not as rich in flavor and nuance as some other California Sauvignons either, though its fruit gives you some hint of what a more intense specimen might be capable of.

All in all, I would describe both as sound, well-made wines that are true to their materials and—what is most important for our present purposes—true to the style of their regions. The Entre-Deux-Mers is made by the firm of Schroder & Schyler, Bordeaux wine merchants since 1739 and the owners of Château Kirwan, a highly regarded classified-growth Margaux. Their wines are imported into the United States by The House of Burgundy. Beaulieu Vineyards is headquartered in the Napa Valley. This vineyard's many varietal wines are readily available throughout the United States. Beaulieu Vineyards' production is huge and quality obviously varies, but many of its wines are excellent, and very few are anything less than good drinking.

This is the conclusion of our ninth white-wine-tasting flight. There are several ways for you to proceed from here.

Following the lead of your own preferences:

If you liked the first wine better, the Entre-Deux-Mers, go to Flight 10.

If you preferred the second wine, the Sauvignon Blanc, go to Flight 12.

Following the kind of grapes:

Go to Flight 10.

Following the wines of the country:

Wine 1: go to Flight 10.
Wine 2: go to Flight 13.

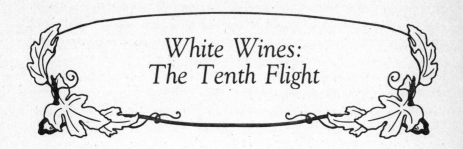

White Wines:
The Tenth Flight

CHÂTEAU CARBONNIEUX 1982 (GRAVES)
AND
DE LADOUCETTE POUILLY-FUMÉ 1982

In this flight you're still slugging it out with the Sauvignon Blanc grape. Once again you will be tasting the Bordelaise style, a blending of Sauvignon and Semillon (in this particular château, 65 percent and 35 percent), against a straight varietal vinification, in this case a Pouilly-Fumé, a wine from the northern reaches of the Loire, the region that provided the generally acknowledged model for California's current mode of handling Sauvignon Blanc.

Sancerre and Pouilly-Fumé (not to be confused with Pouilly-Fuissé, which is in another region entirely) lie far up the Loire in central France. This is almost exclusively white-wine country, and the Sauvignon Blanc is the dominant grape. Farther down the Loire, westward in the châteaux country of Anjou and Touraine, the Chenin Blanc holds sway, and farthest west of all, at the mouth of the Loire, lies the domain of the Muscadet grape. While the Rhône and the Gironde systems fight it out for the title of France's red-wine river, the Loire is its uncontested white-wine stream (unless, of course, you consider the Rhine a French river).

Once again, as so often in this book, you should be concentrating on tasting differences and similarities, or differences within similarities, subtle as that may be. Just pay attention as you smell and taste; that and practice are the only secrets of wine tasting.

It occurs to me it's been a while since I reminded you that your *analysis* of a wine—your description of the things you smell and taste in it—is not the point of this book, nor is it the point of the tasting you are about to perform. What matters most is your preference, your decision about which sort of wine gives you more pleasure. The analysis only helps you see what causes you to like or dislike a particular kind of wine so you can either seek out others like it or avoid it and its kin like the plague. So even if you find yourself smelling and tasting a particular wine very differently from the way it's described here, you're still attaining the object of your tasting.

Analysis and description are only the tools, never the goal. Taste fearlessly and trust your own olfactory and palatal impressions. Above all, don't be cowed by what anyone else (and this definitely includes me) says about the wine; nobody else can taste with your mouth any more than you can drink with theirs.

Are you ready? Okay, proceed with your full ritual of gauging appearance, aroma, and flavor, and don't forget to spit—you should certainly be doing that routinely by this point, without any lingering self-consciousness. The little bit you discard is negligible, and you can fully enjoy the wine better later for the small amount of it you "waste" now.

Appearance. Both these wines are a deep, clear straw shade, with the Château Carbonnieux perhaps a slight bit darker or sometimes showing traces of greenish-gold highlights. Both should be pleasing, clear, and live-looking.

Aroma. A few people might find these wines either elusive or overpowering, but most tasters are likely to describe both as fragrant but not intensely aromatic, meaning they both have reasonably distinctive but not powerful scents. The majority of tasters, by a very substantial margin, like the aromas of both.

The range of descriptions people provide for the Château Carbonnieux is pretty wide. It includes mineral terms such as "flinty," "chalky," or "limestone-smelling" as well as a more direct damp-stones or earth aroma. It also includes fresh grass and straw, herbaceous scents (sometimes mint is specifically mentioned), as well as fruit and spices (sometimes specifically cinnamon). Another sort of response emphasizes the fruit component of the aroma, describing it as a sort of peach with lemon-juice scent, very clean and lingering. Generally speaking, tasters find the aroma of this white Graves not big but complex and very composed.

The range for the Pouilly-Fumé is at least as great, but the emphasis is, for most tasters, quite different. The flinty tone some tasters observe in the Bordeaux wine tends to be more often and more prominently observed here (connoisseurs rightly or wrongly regard it as almost the defining characteristic of the Sauvignon Blanc wines from this part of France). Additionally, many people find the grassy, herbaceous, and fruity portion of the aroma spectrum more noticeable in this Pouilly-Fumé. Citrus especially (orange and grapefruit are possible as well as lemon)' and wood (oak often) and spice tones (cinnamon most commonly) are among the most frequently cited specific components.

Generally speaking, most tasters perceive the aroma of the Pouilly-Fumé as slightly less powerful but just as complex as the scent of the Graves wine. This usually causes some surprise, since tasters have a quasi-logical expectation that wine made from a single grape should be more intense but also more monochromatic than wine made from a blend of grapes. In this case, however, the Sauvignon Blanc grape brings to the blending a lot more aroma than the Semillon, which tends to subdue some of Sauvignon's more pronounced fragrance elements.

Taste. Most tasters react very favorably to this Château Carbonnieux. They tend to comment first on its balance: the first impression it makes on the palate is one of fullness, roundness, and elegance, all in one package. More specifically, they mention its nice, bright acidity and what seems to be a small but firm tannic bite coupled with its good, soft, and dry fruit. A few people may find its acidity a bit too high and talk about a tingly sensation or a sort of "hot lips" feeling, but the majority find it pleasing and lively.

Pushed for more specifics, tasters generally seem to describe the fruit of Château Carbonnieux as tasting predominantly of peaches, but subdued (by which they almost invariably intend a compliment: subdued as in well-bred or soft-spoken, not overblown). Mixed with that they also report a fairly distinct citrus component in the flavor. Most call it lemon, but some may call it lime, or grapefruit, or even pineapple. The wine is clean and extremely polished, with a good, dry finish. Food rounds and softens it a bit.

Almost everyone comments first on the fruitiness of the de Ladoucette Pouilly-Fumé, which most find very attractive. For only a few is it either cloying or, at the other extreme (and because of the wine's acidity), too sharp. Perhaps only a few tasters will explicitly notice or mention the Pouilly-Fumé's acid, but that is what really makes the liveliness of its fruit flavors possible.

The flavors that will almost certainly be commented on can include grass (meant as a compliment: a fresh, vegetal flavor), generalized fruit, exotic fruit (some say kiwi), and citrus (some may taste orange or grapefruit). This Pouilly-Fumé strikes most people as dry, clean, and refreshing, with a dry finish. It feels a bit lighter on the tongue than the Graves and seems a bit higher—a tenor rather than a baritone. Like the Graves, it rounds a bit with food but doesn't soften as much—its acid stays more forceful.

Preferences tend to be understandably pretty evenly divided between these two wines. This is, after all, a classic matter of taste. Both are very well made, sound, and flavorful wines, and the key differences between them are differences of style.

Most tasters will give the Graves the edge in complexity of flavor and nuance, the Pouilly-Fumé the lead in forcefulness and fruit. If I were choosing for myself, I'd want the straight varietal wine for drinking right now because I think its present brightness and freshness and vivacity are the acme of what this grape and this region have to offer and because I think the wine is at or near its peak at this age.

On the other hand, I'd be very happy to put away some bottles of the Graves to drink in a few years, because I think additional bottle age will bring out yet more flavors and subtleties in a wine of that type. At a guess, I'd say it would be at its best at about four or five years old and could probably hold well (properly stored, of course) for another five. That's a guess, mind you; I am not the oracle of Delphi. Part of the fun of estimates like that is putting away enough of the wine to check on your accuracy now and then. It's the wine lover's equivalent of looking in to see what the kids are doing.

Château Carbonnieux is a classified-growth Graves estate of great age and repute. It produces both red and white wines under the same name. It is distributed in the United States by Château and Estates Wine Company, which also imports a good many other excellent Bordeaux châteaux.

De Ladoucette Pouilly-Fumé is produced by Château de Nozet, a family firm headed by Baron Patrick de Ladoucette, and imported to the

United States by the International Vintage Wine Company. In addition to this wine, the house also markets a Sancerre Comte Lafond and its top-of-the-line Pouilly-Fumé Baron de L., made exclusively from very low-yielding old vines on one of the best vineyard sites in the region.

This concludes our tenth white-wine-tasting session. There are several ways for you to proceed from here.

Following the lead of your own preferences:

If you liked the first wine better, Château Carbonnieux, go to Flight 11.

If you preferred the second wine, Pouilly-Fumé, go to Flight 12.

Following the kind of grapes:

This is the last tasting of wines based on Sauvignon Blanc.

Have you tasted the earlier Sauvignon flights (3 and 9)?

Following the wines of the country:

Go to Flight 11.

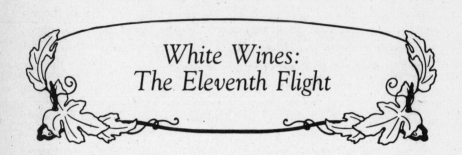

White Wines:
The Eleventh Flight

MASTROBERARDINO GRECO DI TUFO 1982
AND
LA BERNARDINE CHÂTEAUNEUF DU PAPE 1980
(CHAPOUTIER; CHARLES LE FRANC CELLARS)

This is a unique flight. Here you are confronting what is by rational wine terms an oddball pairing, one French white wine and one Italian, neither from an area famed for its white wines. In fact, the Italian wine comes from an area not famed for fine wines, period. I think that by the end of your tasting, however, you will understand the idea behind the pairing and I hope you will find both wines enjoyable. I'm pretty sure that at least you'll have seen a graphic demonstration of the fact that no one really interested in fine wine should ever write off any region without doing at least a minimal amount of fact-checking and tasting. Good wine is being made all over the world, and snap judgments and prejudices will only cheat you of pleasure in the long run.

End of sermon. Taste on: see, swirl, smell, sip, savor, and spit. See you back here in a few minutes.

Appearance. Not a great deal of problem here. Both wines are light gold, the Châteauneuf du Pape slightly stronger in color than the Greco di Tufo. These colors may deepen a bit more with more bottle age, but in all probability they will stay within the light-to-medium gold color range. However, these two wines could develop deeper coloration without being oxidized, so even if your two bottles (or either one of them) are considerably darker than I'm describing, don't *in this case* automatically assume they're bad; taste first. If the wine is inert, lifeless, flat, then return it to your dealer and get another bottle.

Aroma. I think it's pretty safe to say that most of you were surprised by these two. Their aromas are very different from what you've been smelling in white wines up to this point; in fact, they differ pretty markedly from the aromas of the great bulk of white wines. For many people, this divergence from what they may have been coming to think of and expect as normal can be a shock, and all shocks have a way of being unpleasant, so there may very well be a lot of *initial* negative responses or indecision about both these wines. I say initial because the majority of tasters find that these are aromas they can warm up to after a few minutes; a little adjustment is all it takes to start appreciating what Greco di Tufo and white Châteauneuf have to offer.

Greco di Tufo: Almost everybody remarks on the strength or intensity of this wine's aroma. Not its bigness, mind you; it isn't one of those almost mythical wines with an aroma so huge it fills the room as soon as you pull the cork. Strength is the right word; there's a kind of muscularity here (possibly owing to alcohol) that demands respect.

The next quality most people mention directly or indirectly is complexity—what they sense here is not just one thing but a medley of aromas, some of them very unusual in white wines. Here are some of the more commonly mentioned possibilities: flowers, especially strongly scented varieties; ripe or fermented fruit, especially apples and strawberries; herbs and spices, especially licorice or anise; cheese, especially parmesan cheese; and nuts, especially walnuts or hazelnuts. Any one or any combination of those may dominate a taster's impressions, and naturally like and dislike will vary tremendously. The majority of people, however, find Greco di Tufo's scent intriguing; "pungent but pleasing" was the way one particularly concise taster described it.

Châteauneuf du Pape: The remarks about strength and complexity that I made about Greco di Tufo apply every bit as accurately to this wine. The biggest difference between the aromas of this Châteauneuf and the Italian wine is not their attack but their components, the different elements you can discern in each. Three separate classes of scents seem to have almost equal shares in the Châteauneuf's bouquet: spices, grass, and mushrooms. More specifically, people mention a whole shelf of spices they smell in it: cardamom, cumin, mace, mint, and sesame (toasted seeds or oil). The grass smell comes across for some individuals as very intense—one taster reported it as smelling like arugola, which brings the grass scent right to the border of herbs and spices. So too with mushrooms: some tasters describe the clean earth smell of fresh mushrooms, others an intense fungous scent that borders on a slight odor of truffles. For some tasters, the combination of elements is strong and complex enough that they compare this aroma to that of some red wines; for others, it's strong enough to be unpleasant.

Taste. People tend to respond to Greco's flavor just as they responded to its aroma. Either by directly remarking on it or indirectly by the number of elements they will list, they show that the Greco's complexity has grabbed their attention once again. However, the range of flavor components people mention seems to be a bit narrower than those of the aroma. Most common are alcohol, noticed as a fiery or winey characteristic; fruit, again most usually apples or strawberries; and nuts, most often hazelnuts or almonds—almonds especially in the finish, which many tasters remark on. The great majority of tasters enjoy the taste of Greco, which they describe overall as pleasing, complex, balanced, dry, and round, with good body. Some people describe that last characteristic as a pleasing sense of weight on the tongue combined with a mouth-soothing oiliness. Tasters who have come to this flight directly from the wines based on Sauvignon Blanc seem to be particularly aware of this quality—Greco's rich "fatness"—as a dramatic contrast to the bright acidity of Sauvignon-based wines.

La Bernardine Châteauneuf du Pape: That fatness is one quality the Châteauneuf has in common with the Greco: it, too, is a rich, full-bodied wine, very round, with some of the same pleasing oiliness on the tongue. With both these wines, you know you've got something in your mouth; there is nothing frail or insubstantial about either of them. Of the two, this Châteauneuf seems somewhat more robust to most people, but that doesn't seem to imply any loss of subtlety. Tasters still remark on its balancing of fruit and alcohol, crispness and fruitiness. The elements they discerned in its aroma they tend to mention again in its flavor, particularly the spices, grass, and fruits. And many tasters are particularly pleased with the marked astringent finish of this wine.

Obviously, these are very different wines, but they share some likenesses that for me make this pairing very revealing. These are both warm-region white wines, the Châteauneuf from the southern Rhône, Greco di Tufo from Campania, not far from Naples. Both are big wines, full-bodied, sturdy, completely dry, with reasonably high alcohol for white wines, and yet fruity, flavorful, and above all, rich and complex. Both can take several years of bottle age with improvement. Nevertheless, they taste quite different from each other, operating in totally different segments of the flavor spectrum. Preferences will go as individual palates dictate, though I could be happy with either most of the time.

As you may have gathered by now, I'm a fan of both, and not just because after all those moderately light and fruity wines I really appreciate a wine with guts—though that's true, too. But the reason for my enthusiasm is more fundamental than that. For me these two wines exemplify something I call the southern style in winemaking. It's not very fashionable right now—in fact, when people talk about southern wine style they usually mean it as a put-down, implying the kind of sunbaked, high-alcohol, coarse wines that used to be the norm from Sicily or California's Central Valley.

What I mean by it I think you can figure out from these two wines: complexity of flavor coupled with fullness of body, a richness both of fruit and of nuance, all of which can be achieved only with fully ripened grapes and the most careful vinification. It makes for wines that, in these days of fashionable superslimness and light-mindedness, are unmodishly robust, wines that most rudely demand you pay attention to what you're drinking. In a world where everything seems to be in the process of being microminiaturized, Greco di Tufo and Châteauneuf du Pape and wines like them are uncompromisingly, untrendily big. I wish there were a lot more like them.

Needless to say (but I'll say it anyway), these wines are not at their best as aperitifs or cocktails, though they may perfectly well be enjoyed alone. They are wonderful dinner wines, not only with any of the dishes you would normally choose a white wine for but also with some you wouldn't. I would happily drink a white Châteauneuf with a steak or a Greco di Tufo with a bistecca pizzaiola or with a dish of bresaola or a Piedmontese veal tartare. These are substantial wines, and they will stand up to a wide variety of foods.

Mastroberardino is the name of a family-owned winery based in Atripaldi, high in the hills east of Naples. Its wine maker, Antonio Mastroberardino, is widely regarded as the best wine maker in the

Italian South and one of the handful of premier wine makers in Italy. The winery turns out a complete line of Neapolitan wines at the highest quality level. Most of these are imported to the United States by the International Vintage Wine Company.

Chapoutier is a 175-year-old firm based in the northern Rhône but owning properties throughout the whole valley. Chapoutier produces almost the whole range of Rhône wines, all of them made in a very traditional style. They are imported into the United States by Almadén Imports.

Here ends our eleventh flight of white wines. There are several ways for you to proceed from here.

Following the lead of your own preferences:

If you liked either the first wine, Greco di Tufo, or the second wine, Châteauneuf du Pape, go to Flight 14.

Following the kind of grapes:

There are no other flights tasting these grapes.

Following the wines of the country:

Go to Flight 12.

White Wines:
The Twelfth Flight

BOLLINI CHARDONNAY DI MEZZACORONA 1983
(NEIL EMPSON)
AND
MÂCON-LUGNY LES CHARMES 1982

You are now starting a series of tastings of wine vinified from what is widely considered the premier white-wine grape of the world, Chardonnay.

Whether it is the best is, like so much else in wine, definitely a matter of taste, but there is no doubt that Chardonnay is currently the hottest, the most glamorous, of the noble white grapes. It is enjoying a vogue among wine lovers and wine makers all over the world and is being planted in climates and soils very different from its native Burgundy, where it has been for centuries the heart of what are pretty universally thought of as the greatest white wines in the world. Again, whether white Burgundies are or aren't the world's greatest white wines is very much a judgment call—but in the world of wine connoisseurship, they serve as benchmarks for quality white wine in general and for any Chardonnay-based wine in particular.

That, however, should not mean a hill of beans to you, especially not with Chardonnay learning every day to "speak in accents yet unknown" when the Burgundian style was first formulated.

Chardonnay usually makes a full-bodied wine, but the grape is versatile and can be vinified in several different styles. The idea of the next few flights is to let you learn the basic taste of the Chardonnay varietal, to show you its different styles, and to let you choose the one that suits you best. To be honest, if money is an object, you had better hope you don't prefer the classic Burgundian style. Burgundian whites are right up there with red Burgundies in the retail-price stratosphere, and a real fondness for them could mean the start of your personal economic recession. I've been as kind to your pocketbook as I can in making the selections for this book, but the flavor of white Burgundy never comes really cheap. Be brave about it.

Your first flight comprises two of the most popular reasonably priced Chardonnays available in the United States, both imports: an Italian, Bollini, and a French, Mâcon-Lugny Les Charmes. In your tasting, try to pay attention both to similarities of the basic grape's flavor and to differences in style resulting from either the region in which grapes are grown or the methods of vinification. In other words, sameness and difference once again.

All set? Then work through your "infamous s's" and check back here when you're finished.

Appearance. Both wines should show a characteristic young Chardonnay color, a clear, clean straw with some gold or green highlights. Older Chardonnay wines, particularly those that have received some wood aging, will show deeper and more golden than these.

Aroma. Most people perceive the aroma of the Bollini as a bit on the delicate side—subdued but complex. It is in many respects a typical Chardonnay aroma, distinctive yet hard to describe. Tasters seem to be about evenly divided between describing it as fruity or as leafy. The fruit backers usually name pears and apricots, sometimes more exotic fruits. The leaf people usually just stick with that, though some will say freshly mown grass, some nominate mint, and some add fresh-turned earth as well. The great majority of tasters agree that this aroma is, overall, fresh, clean, and pleasing.

Les Charmes has an aroma of about the same magnitude as the Bollini, though different sniffers will rate it slightly bigger or slightly smaller. Almost all tasters describe it as predominantly fruity, though less defined than the Bollini's fruit: they will probably mention pears, perhaps also leaves or grass. Some tasters describe this Mâcon-Lugny's scent, in comparison with the Bollini's, as softer, damper, and weightier— more earthy, mushroomy-smelling. All of that, for those of you who may not be mycophiles, is definitely intended as a compliment.

Taste. Most tasters find that the flavors of these two wines match quite closely with their aromas, the Bollini fruity and lively, the Mâcon-Lugny fuller and rounder.

More specifically, the kinds of responses the Bollini elicits usually are in the nature of fresh, bright, and very fruity. People claim to taste in it things like apples, pears, and bananas. Traces of citrus fruits rarely are discerned in this wine (remember how frequent they were in Sauvignon Blanc, for instance?). There is a small trace of bitterness—some people love it, others are unmoved—that could be due either to the wine's fairly high acidity or to the Chardonnay grape itself. Most tasters pick out the bitterness particularly in the wine's finish; those who like it describe it as a good bitter-almond flavor; those who don't make small disparaging noises. Most tasters, however, find this wine very enjoyable if not particularly big or muscular.

By contrast, Les Charmes is fuller and weightier on the tongue; almost everybody can feel the real impression of heaviness it makes. Objectively speaking, this wine is not a true heavyweight: medium-bodied would be about the most accurate description. But just as its fruit seems subdued, minimized after tasting the Bollini Chardonnay, so, too, its body seems exaggerated and magnified. The fruit is still there, however, even if it is not so forward as the Italian wine's. As with Les Charmes' aroma, most tasters describe it as soft and somewhat unde-fined. They may suggest pears, and perhaps in this wine a slight touch of citrus—lemon or orange most likely—and maybe grass. Most people find an excellent long, dry finish in Les Charmes.

Both wines seem to respond very well to food, though the French wine's lower acidity and greater body may make it a bit more adaptable in that regard.

I think you have here a textbook illustration of the differences of national styles in handling the Chardonnay grape.

The Bollini Chardonnay is a very representative example of the dominant (but not exclusive) method of vinifying white wines in Italy today. Wine makers are striving for—and attaining—fresh, clean fruit, with a good but not overpowering taste of the varietal and a lot of acid to keep it all bright and lively. Italy is making oceans of sound, pleasing white wines like this from any number of grape varietals in several provinces. They are above all wines meant to be drunk young and enjoyed as aperitifs and with nonsolemn meals, though the best of them can be every bit as impressive as any good California varietal. The best examples, should you wish to pursue this branch of wine, seem to come from the two northern regions of Trentino-Alto Adige and Friuli-Venezia Giulia. They would include international varietals such as Chardonnay, Sauvignon Blanc, Pinot Blanc, Pinot Grigio, Gewurztraminer, and Riesling, as well as purely local varieties such as Verduzzo and Tocai.

This Mâcon-Lugny furnishes an equally fair representation of the French approach to white wine in general and the Chardonnay grape specifically. There is evidently less desire for fruitiness and a greater striving after body and balance. The wine has more roundness, more muscle, and probably a greater ability to survive in the bottle. I don't mean by that that this is a particularly long-lived wine, but it does show every sign that it will last essentially unchanged for about three or four years from bottling. On the other hand, I wouldn't plan to keep most Italian white wines around that long; that bright acid style doesn't seem to have that much staying power. The French seem to desire greater maturity from a wine and a more sophisticated, balanced attack rather than all that youthful *esprit* and *élan*. That, at any rate, is the style cultivated throughout the whole domain of the Chardonnay, from Dijon to Lyon, including Mâcon-Lugny's more famous sibling, Pouilly-Fuissé (not to be confused with Pouilly-Fumé, which is a Sauvignon Blanc wine), Chablis, and all the famous villages of the Côte d'Or.

You could argue—and you might well be right—that these essential differences in style stem from the differences between the two national cuisines the wines normally accompany. But what do you make, then, of French red wines, like Beaujolais, that are meant for quick drinking, or Italian white wines, such as Greco di Tufo or Torre di Giano, that are meant for laying down? There comes a point with wine where logic breaks down. That is the right point to think less about it and drink more of it. Onward.

Bollini Chardonnay is a non-DOC wine selected by Neil Empson, a *négociant* of Italian wines, and imported to the United States by Premium Wine Imports. Empson is one of the most famous and reputable wine dealers operating in Italy, and his name on the bottle is as good a guarantee as the DOC of the authenticity of the contents (just for the

Chardonnay's Kingdom

The realm of the Chardonnay grape actually encompasses a good deal more than what the wine lover thinks of as Burgundy, which tends to be largely the Côte d'Or, the thirty-or-so-mile-long strip that runs south from Dijon through Beaune to Chagny. Northeast of Dijon, near Auxerre and almost halfway to Paris, lies the Chablis district, one of Chardonnay's major fiefdoms. South of the Côte d'Or, lying beside the River Saône and along the direct route to Lyon, the Côte Chalonnaise produces important white wines as well as reds. The major townships for whites are Rully, Mercurey, and Montagny. And directly south of the Côte Chalonnaise lies the Mâconnais, where once again Chardonnay dominates the wine production. Mâcon wines appear on the market as simply Mâcon, Mâcon Villages, Mâcon with a specific village name attached (as our wine, a Mâcon-Lugny), or a single village name alone, such as St.-Veran, Pouilly-Fuissé (which for reasons known only to fashion often commands the same prices as the white wines of the Côte d'Or), or Pouilly-Vinzelles. South of the Mâconnais, red grapes take over again: the Beaujolais district runs almost to the Lyon city limits.

Just for the record (you never know when you're going to need the odd fact to break the ice), the town of Chardonnay, which gave its name to the grape, is located in the Mâconnais.

record, this wine hasn't been denied the DOC for any reason; the proper agencies just haven't acted yet. *Siamo in Italia.*)

Les Charmes is produced in the Mâcon by a cooperative of small growers called Cave de Lugny, and it is imported to the United States by Château and Estate Wines, which also brings in an extensive line of quality wines from most of the major wine-producing nations, with a strong emphasis on France and Germany.

This concludes our twelfth white-wine-tasting session. Paths begin to converge here.

Following the lead of your own preferences:

If you enjoyed either the first wine, Bollini Chardonnay, or the second wine, Mâcon-Lugny Les Charmes, go to Flight 13.

Following the kind of grapes:

Go to Flight 13.

Following the wines of the country:

Wine 1: This is the last flight including an Italian wine. Check to see if you have tasted in all the relevant earlier flights (3, 4, 5, and 11).

Wine 2: go to Flight 13.

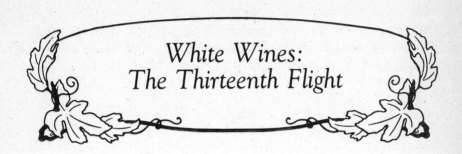

White Wines:
The Thirteenth Flight

CHABLIS PREMIER CRU FOURCHAUME 1982
(DOMAINE ROTTIERS)
AND
GALLO LIMITED RELEASE CHARDONNAY OF
CALIFORNIA NV
(THE WINE CELLARS OF ERNEST & JULIO GALLO)

In this flight you will start to move away from the simpler, fruity style of Chardonnay and toward its more complex, elegant, and fuller incarnation. Once again the comparison will consist of juxtaposing a French example with a different region's handling of Chardonnay—in this case, California. French vintners set the original standards for wines based on Chardonnay, and California wine makers really began to achieve international acclaim when, in the 1970s, some of their Chardonnays showed better than some French vintages in international exhibitions.

Despite the reciprocal emulation, imitation, and competition between French and American wine makers, it would be a great mistake for you to taste these two wines only to see which is better. Forget that idea entirely. Not only is "better" in an objective sense frequently indeterminable in wine tasting, but "better for you" is really all you should be interested in. Chardonnay grows differently in California than it does in France. The California way of vinifying Chardonnay has evolved in its own special direction. And American taste in wine is not necessarily, even at the level of connoisseurship, identical with French taste. What you should be thinking as you approach this flight is that you are about to taste two completely different wines that happen to share the same grape varietal, and what you should be looking for, once again, are the kinds of samenesses and differences that enable you to say (to yourself or anybody else who cares), "The thing I like about this wine . . ."

Got that? Okay, go for it: do the "infamous s's" and then check back at headquarters.

Appearance. Little or no problem: both wines should be showing a bright golden straw color, very attractive and definitely live. In any particular pair of bottles, one or the other wine could appear a slight bit more golden, but it should only be a very slight shading, not a marked difference.

If either is deeply golden, there is a fifty-fifty chance the wine has not gone wrong, so taste very carefully. Well-made Chardonnays can take a surprising amount of bottle age without harm and often with real improvement. When mature, such wines often show a deep golden tinge that can resemble the color of a maderized wine. (Maderization is the five-dollar word for spoilage of a particular kind, the sort of oxidation in the bottle that causes wines, particularly whites, to lose their flavor and turn brown. The color of a wine so spoiled sufficiently resembles the perfectly proper shade of the fortified wine Madeira for its name to be pressed into service—more accurately disservice, at least to Madeira.) Chardonnays like the two you are tasting here can sometimes undergo an accelerated development, going through what would normally be, say, a ten-year cycle of maturation in just a few years. So you might have a chance here to taste a more developed flavor than would ordinarily be available.

Aroma. Just about all tasters report small to middling aromas of some complexity in both these wines, with the balance tilting toward the Chablis as more complex and the Gallo Chardonnay as slightly stronger.

The great majority of tasters perceive a fresh, clean scent in the Chablis, though they may describe it in any number of ways: as lightly floral; as spicy or herbal (some people find thyme in there); as grassy or lemony or leafy; as delicately fruity; or as smelling like cool earth and stones or freshly shucked oysters. A lot of how that is expressed obviously depends on the individual taster's experience and associations. Many people pick up as well a vivid acid sharpness, which may or may not link for them with other elements to give the odor of flint that is traditionally associated with the aroma and taste of Chablis.

The Gallo Chardonnay smells stronger to most people, riper and deeper. It still is not what anyone calls a huge aroma, nor do people think it particularly complex. Most tasters pick up a compound of vinous, citrus, and alcohol scents that they may or may not separate from the kind of Chardonnay fruit aromas they described in the twelfth white-wine flight. The fruit aroma tends to be mixed up with a fresh wood scent that is definitely oak: this wine has been given some barrel age. Some tasters will describe a faint odor of toast or buttered toast: that, too, is Chardonnay fruit and oak in combination.

Taste. There are a lot of variables here, because the flavors of both wines contain enough diverse elements for different palates to respond to different stimuli. On the broadest level, most tasters react favorably to both wines, finding them pleasing and reasonably complex, the Chablis more vivid and the Chardonnay more composed.

Specific reactions cover a wide range. People remark on the Chablis' lively acidity (most discernible as a gentle prickle on the tongue) and its good fruit (grapefruit and not fully ripe pears). Despite its acidity, some detect a buttery quality and a bit of softness more usually found in white Burgundies from farther south. For many tasters, it hints at sweetness without actually being sweet, an effect both intriguing and enjoyable. Above all, for almost everyone this Chablis tastes fresh and clean, dry and fruity in what seems almost a perfect combination for a versatile dinner wine.

Tasters describe the Gallo Chardonnay first in terms of broad similarities to the Chablis: good fruit, good acid, a little bit tart, a little soft. The numerous differences follow. The Chardonnay is fuller, rounder, more tannic (from its wood aging). It has a buttery, toasty flavor most people pick up quite clearly, and its fruit is more subdued than the Chablis', more restrained or balanced by the amount of tannin present. It seems very complete and balanced, though on a relatively small scale.

Most people, tasting these two wines side by side, find it fairly easy to distinguish in the Gallo the basic varietal flavor of Chardonnay from the overlay of flavors that derive from the wood. Nevertheless, they may still find it hard to verbalize the differences they taste, a problem to which—at this point in this book—I am deeply sympathetic.

Loosely speaking, in this wine the range of sensations and tastes that includes tannin and the pucker it causes (try very hard not to confuse it here with acid prickle) as well as the flavors in the tea-and-toast range are all traceable to oak. Their interplay with the already rich flavors of top-quality Chardonnay grapes gives the best Chardonnay wines the complexity and layering of flavors that make them the nonpareils of the white-wine world.

Needless to say, there are lots of possible variations on the wood and fruit theme. You can probably by now guess all those due to the grapes—climate, soil, degree of ripeness, vinification method, etc.—but wood-aging introduces a whole new range: what kind of oak and from where, whether the cask is new or has been used and for what, how it has been treated (charring, for instance, can bring up that toasty flavor), and so on.

But the relation of wood flavors to grape flavors in this Gallo Chardonnay can pretty well stand as a decent example of how (in California, at any rate) those components are going to mesh. Move up and down from this Chardonnay on your imaginary intensity scale, shift the balance back and forth from fruit to wood: if you can taste for a while with your mind's tongue, you can find in this Chardonnay a very useful yardstick to measure your expectations and other wines' accomplishments by.

It is not belittling this wine in any way to describe it as a scale model of a top-flight Chardonnay: at its price, that is an accomplishment to put most other vintners to shame.

This Chablis, too, furnishes a good example of a whole class of wines, in this case the new style in Chablis. Old-fashioned Chablis used to be characterized as flint-and-steel, bone-dry wines with intense but austere fruit and plenty of structure. That may all sound a bit forbidding, but they were wonderful wines, among the most satisfying white dinner wines in the world, and quite capable of prolonged life in the bottle, too. Although a good number of Chablis makers continue to work in this old-fashioned style, you are more likely to encounter it among the Grands Crus than among the Premiers Crus.

The recognized AOC designations of Chablis are Petit Chablis, Chablis, Chablis Premier Cru, and Chablis Grand Cru. Among the last two designations you may find single-vineyard wines as well as shippers' blends. Generally speaking, Chablis Premier Cru most often turns up in the United States as dealer's wine from a single named township (such as Fourchaume), while Chablis Grand Cru appears as single-vineyard estate bottlings. The Grands Crus appellations are very limited in number: Blanchots, Bougros, Grenouilles, La Moutonne, Les Clos, Les Preuses, Valmur, and Vaudesir.

Thanks once again to modern technology, Chablis is now a much more consistent wine than before—if its highs were stratospheric, its depths used to be abysmal—and most of it is fresher-tasting and fruitier. The newer Chablis are made as is this Fourchaume: softer, with gentler and lusher fruit, more forward in development, and more accessible to the taste. They are very charming and enjoyable wines, of very high quality and—especially in comparison to other Burgundy whites—*very* reasonable price. And they are not in any sense a falsification of Chablis: the best of them have, as this Fourchaume does, a sturdy spine and a good, healthy, acid bite that identify them quite readily as Chablis.

I hope this flight pleased you. These are enjoyable wines and instructive ones: for my purposes (which I sincerely hope are your purposes as well), quite a perfect combination.

Fourchaume is a highly regarded Chablis Premier Cru designation. The maker, Rottiers, is a relatively new but quite respected dealer in the area. This particular Chablis and several others are imported to the United States by Paramount Brands.

This Chardonnay is one of Gallo's special "Wine Cellar" bottlings, limited releases of the most prestigious varietals vinified to very high standards. Most are nonvintage, like this Chardonnay, though occasionally the brothers Gallo do put out a vintage-labeled bottling (so far only Cabernet Sauvignon). It is anybody's guess whether the point of their not vintage-dating the bottles is (1) to retain the option of blending for a consistent and identifiable product, (2) to show all the California wine snobs that they don't need vintaging to make a first-class wine, or (3) sheer stubbornness and pride (since they built their success on humbler, nonvintage wines). Whichever point it is, they have made it resoundingly.

This is the conclusion of our thirteenth white-wine-tasting session. There is only one way to go from here—all roads lead to the final white-wine flight.

Following the lead of your own preferences:

If you enjoyed either the first wine, Chablis Fourchaume, or the second wine, Gallo Chardonnay, go to Flight 14.

Following the kind of grapes:

Go to Flight 14.

Following the wines of the country:

Go to Flight 14.

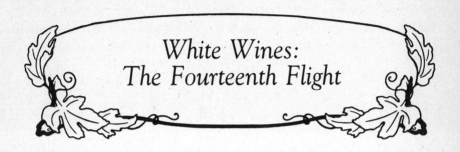

White Wines:
The Fourteenth Flight

CHASSAGNE-MONTRACHET 1981 (DROUHIN)
AND
CHATEAU MONTELENA ALEXANDER VALLEY CHARDONNAY 1982

In this last flight—yes, this is the last pair of white wines—you put your toe in the door of what is, in terms of price certainly and of prestige probably, white wine's biggest league. Once more, what you should be tasting for is to discern, at this high level of quality, the sameness provided by the basic flavor of the Chardonnay varietal and the differences caused by soil, climate, and winemaking techniques.

By this stage of the game, a task like that should be child's play for you. Go to it.

Appearance. Both wines should be showing distinctly yellow or golden straw, very clean, bright, and attractive. Slightly darker coloration is possible without necessarily indicating defect. In any given pair of bottles, one or the other may seem a bit lighter or darker. Such variation means almost nothing as long as both wines are within the same general color range; you have to start worrying only when there is a really marked difference between them.

Aroma. With these two wines, you have a chance to experience those scents that professionals regard as characteristic of Chardonnay. Actually, that is a complete misnomer, because the sorts of aroma that professionals and connoisseurs have in mind when they talk about "a Chardonnay nose" are typical only of the very highest levels of Chardonnay vinification. You've been smelling far more typical Chardonnay aromas in the two flights that have preceded this one. Unfortunately, a lot of people new to wine read about these ideal (and that is *really* what they are) aromas and then, because they can't perceive them in the less expensive Chardonnay they're drinking, wrongly conclude that they are insensitive or can't appreciate wine or that it's all a bunch of hokum anyhow.

I hope that you who have been working through these wines with me have by now gotten enough confidence in your own taste buds and your own judgment not to be buffaloed by that sort of thing, but it probably doesn't hurt to remind you once again that most wine writing describes the best that a grape or wine attains, not the average, while what most of us—and this includes wine writers, most definitely—drink most of the time is average wine. Great wine is almost by definition a special occasion for all save the wealthiest of us.

And just to eliminate the last possible confusion: the phrase "average wine" is emphatically not a put-down. We are lucky enough to be living in a time when the average level of winemaking skill turns out wines that run from pleasantly drinkable up to very fine, so "average wine" includes an awful lot of very enjoyable bottles, a lot of wines I personally would not want to be without.

I guess that was all preparatory to giving you your diploma. You are getting pretty near graduation, you know—but first we've got to finish these Chardonnays. Another tough assignment.

Reactions to the aroma of the Chassagne-Montrachet tend to be very uniform. The few differing reactions almost always come from tasters who simply do not like the Chardonnay grape, and their tendency is to find the aroma of this and many other Chardonnay-based wines synthetic-smelling and displeasing—a bit like acetone, in fact.

Most people, however, respond very favorably to the aroma of Chardonnay, and the majority will describe the scent of this Chassagne-Montrachet, at least in part, as recalling buttered toast. It's remarkable how many people spot butter in that aroma: some will say burned toast and butter, some butter and earth, some butterscotch, but the butter usually gets in there. Other elements frequently mentioned include alcohol, grass, fruit (especially pears), spices (especially cinnamon), and fresh sawdust or related woody odors.

Reactions to the Chateau Montelena Chardonnay seem to be less monolithic but nevertheless pretty regular also. Again, with the exception of people who just don't like Chardonnay, the great majority of tasters respond very favorably to this wine. Usually they will describe its aroma as similar to the Chassagne-Montrachet's, but with important differences. Some will say the Chateau Montelena smells more woody and tannic. Others perceive it as smelling more intensely fruity, even slightly sweet, as if the fruit were very, very ripe. Peaches, nectarines, and apriocots—sometimes even bananas—are what most tasters specifically mention. Others find grassy or herbal—especially minty—elements in it. And still others may pick up the scent of fresh mushrooms and wet woods, a clean earth-and-forest scent.

Just for your information, the trio of butter, fruit, and wood (especially oak) is pretty much the connoisseur's stereotype for Chardonnay's aroma.

Taste. The distinctions between California style and Burgundy style began to manifest themselves in the aromas of these two wines. Their flavors complete the lesson. Most tasters perceive these wines as markedly different not only in style but in flavor as well. Usually the minority of people who dislike Chardonnay entirely tend to perceive these two wines as similarly artificial-tasting and unpleasant.

Most tasters describe the Chassagne-Montrachet first of all as big: full-bodied, weighty, dry. They often remark on its perceptible alcohol or report a warmth or pleasant sting that could result from alcohol or acid or even tannin (most good Burgundies and many good California Chardonnays receive some wood-aging). For the most part, however, they find the wine very balanced and harmonious, even elegant. Specific flavors, for most people, follow very closely what they discerned in the aroma: butter, toast, butterscotch, fruit (pears can become very prominent), and spice (sometimes a new introduction here, such as clove). For most people the wine partners beautifully with food and finishes well, long and dry and slightly almondy.

The majority of tasters find that the Chateau Montelena also delivers on its aroma. Most of the specific elements that people will discern in its flavor are the same or related to those they found first in its bouquet—butter and toast again, fruit especially, and sometimes sweet fruit (peaches and apricots most often), alcohol, and often a strong tannic sensation (for some, reminiscent of oversteeped tea). The wine usually creates an overall impression of great fruit, big but soft body, and tannic dryness with an intriguing and almost paradoxical underlay of sweetness, as if the fruit were either incredibly ripe and deeply flavored or there was the smallest trace of residual sugar. Many tasters discern cedar in the finish.

Both wines seem to respond equally well—imperturbably—to food.

Most people find themselves pretty hard put to express a preference here, and for good reason. You're dealing here with excellent winemaking working with first-rate materials. The quality level is equal in both wines, so the only real point of preference is your reaction to their differing styles—the French wine big, authoritative, polished, and somewhat reined in, the California wine also big but more brash, spirited, with its fruit all up front. As the man says, you pays your money and you takes your choice—and you certainly apologize to nobody for your preference, not this close to graduation.

The Chassagne-Montrachet is made by Drouhin and imported by Dreyfus, Ashby & Company. The firm of Joseph Drouhin is an old and respected Burgundian house, dealing for many decades in almost all of the wines of the Côte d'Or, and at every level from a simple white Burgundy to wines from prized villages such as this to estate-bottled, single-vineyard wines.

Chateau Montelena is a Napa Valley winery noted particularly for the quality of its Chardonnay. It also produces fine Cabernet Sauvignon and Zinfandel. Chateau Montelena's wines are distributed by Vintage Wine Merchants.

This finishes our white-wine tastings, but there still are several ways for you to proceed from here.

Exploring other wines related to whites: go on to the rosé wines and the sparkling wines.

Following the kind of grapes:

Go to Flight 2 of the sparkling wines if you have already completed Flights 12 and 13 of the white wines.

Following the wines of the country:

Wine 1: go to Flights 2 and 3 of the rosé, Flight 2 of the sparkling wines.

Wine 2: go to Flight 1 of the rosé, Flights 1, 2, and 3 of the sparkling wines.

ROSÉ WINES

EN PASSANT

A rosé by any other name is a white wine. Surprised? Well, you're probably not alone. Most people assume—or have been led to assume—that rosé is a very distinctive kind of wine, made by some mysterious process that renders it (1) pleasing to everybody and (2) perfect with any food. Both are outrageous falsehoods.

In the interest of total honesty, I've got to tell you from the outset that I am a curmudgeon about rosé. I've rarely met one I've liked, and I think the public by and large has been sold a real bill of goods about them. Generally speaking, most rosé falls for me into the category of imitation wine, and I would much rather get on to the real thing. Nevertheless, I realize that there are good rosés in the world and that for many people they offer an attractive and engaging entry into wine, so we (that is to say, you) will taste a brief sampling of rosé wines, starting with some of the most popular varieties.

Before you begin, however (you didn't really think I'd let you off the hook that easily, did you?), you ought to know a bit about what rosé really is: how it gets that color, what grapes it's made from, what dishes it does go well with, etc.

Let's start with the grapes it's made from. Popular wisdom takes it for granted that rosé can be made only from a limited number of varieties. If you in your wine wisdom assume that popular opinion has once again committed a vulgar error, you're absolutely right. Pink wine can be made from any red grapes or a mixture of red and white grapes. Any. Anywhere. And it is: almost every spot on the globe that makes wine at all can and does make a rosé wine. If you look around any decent-sized wineshop you'll find rosé from California and New York, Chile and Argentina, Spain and Portugal, France and Italy. You'll find rosé of Grenache, rosé of Cabernet, rosé of Merlot, a white Zinfandel that's actually rosé. You'll find rosé that is in fact rose-colored, rosé that is cherry, rosé that is orange, rosé that is very close to colorless. You'll find rosé vinified still, crackling, and sparkling, sweet and dry.

Get the idea? Whatever rosé is, it is certainly not one thing. Rosé is every bit as varied and variable as any other kind of wine.

Another popular mistake about rosé is to think of it as a blending of red and white wines: add a little red and a little white and keep juggling until you get the color you want—*voilà!* rosé. Very definitely not true. The core of rosé—the thing that makes it rosé and not white or red—is a technique of vinification.

You start with red grapes or a blend of white and red grapes. You press them in the normal manner. At this point, if you were making a white wine, you would separate the musts and the solids immediately and proceed to ferment the musts by themselves. In wine jargon, this is known as vinification *au blanc*. If you were making a red wine, you would allow the musts and the solids to ferment together for anywhere from four days to four weeks. But if you are making a rosé, you will let the musts and the solids ferment together for a very carefully controlled and very brief time—often only a few hours, rarely more than a day.

This is because grape juices are mostly colorless when pressed: a red wine becomes red during fermentation, when color leaches from the grape skins into the musts. So early removal of the skins yields a lightly colored wine by shortening the dyeing process. That interruption curtails other processes as well, since the grape solids contribute many other things to red wine besides color—particularly tannin and other extracts that affect the wine's body and longevity.

After the skins have been removed, the musts are then fermented *au blanc*—that is, they are treated exactly as if they were going to make a white wine. These days this usually entails controlled, low-temperature fermentation to preserve fruit and freshness and the use of stainless-steel or Fiberglas tanks rather than wood to prevent the introduction of any other flavors than those the grapes themselves possess. So from the point of view of the finished rosé, therefore, the chief result of this whole process is to make a wine that, despite its reddish tinge, is structurally and palatally closer to white wine than to red. That is the most important thing you should know about rosé.

You've probably already figured out what follows from that. If rosé is actually more similar to white wine than to red and not, as the color suggests, something that stands midway between them, then it probably is going to taste better with the same sorts of food white wines accompany. That is in fact the way it is: you can only "drink rosé with everything," as folklore has it, in the sense that you can drink any wine you like with everything. Like any other wine, rosé goes better with some foods than with others, and the better the rosé itself is, the more important the wine-food combinations become—as with any other wine.

Okay, I think that's really enough preliminary. Sorry if I sounded a bit preachy, but as I warned you, I'm not a real fan of these wines. Anyhow, now's your chance to find out whether you are or not, so off you go to your first rosé tasting.

Rosé Wines: The First Flight

MATEUS ROSÉ NV
AND
ALMADÉN CALIFORNIA GRENACHE ROSÉ NV

I'm making things easy on you to start—two nonvintage rosés, both very popular, one Portuguese and one Californian. Nothing too complex here, so taste away—not forgetting the "infamous s's," all six of them.

Appearance. With rosé wines, there is somewhat more to say here than you're used to, isn't there? These wines will sharpen your eye if nothing else.

The Mateus normally shows quite a pale pink color with highlights of other tones throughout, gold or copper or peach, depending on your bottle and, to some extent, your lighting. The Almadén Grenache's usual color is a bright, vivid rose or thin cherry, a relatively pretty color reminiscent of—if this helps at all—grenadine.

Aroma. Reactions here tend to be pretty uniform. Almost all tasters find the Mateus's aroma quite faint. They chiefly discern an acidic, tart element linked with fruit, which they may describe as citrus or apple or coppery or even as a fresh-cucumber smell, all nevertheless faint. There is slightly more division of opinion about the Grenache. Some people find its aroma initially faint though growing stronger as it opens. Others find it strong from the beginning. Almost all describe it as fruity, but the range of fruits they discern is wide: cherries, mangoes, nectarines, peaches. For most people this fruit aroma has a definite sweet quality, and for some it is also accompanied by a clear presence of alcohol.

Taste. The greatest variable here is the individual taster's sensitivity to sugar and tolerance for it. The greater the appetite for sugar, the drier these wines will appear.

Responses to the Portuguese wine, for instance, can run the whole gamut from "pleasing dry/tart freshness" to "sweet and acid." Whatever the degree of sweetness perceived, most tasters describe a pleasant, generalized light fruit flavor (prunes or apples sometimes are mentioned) and a sweet finish.

The vast majority of tasters find the Almadén much drier, with a kind of vague sweet-and-sour fruitiness, the sour usually predominating. Some people report small herbaceous or grassy flavors as well as a salty, not unpleasant, seawater taste. Almost everybody agrees that the Grenache is rounder, softer, and slightly fuller than the Mateus, with a distinctly tart finish.

Just about everybody also agrees that these are not complicated wines. There isn't a whole lot more to say about them other than that both are surprisingly pleasant quaffing wines, especially when served as well chilled as their producers intend them to be. These wines do illustrate very nicely, however, the two basic schools of rosé: the light-bodied, often acidic, frequently sweet (even if only slightly so) style and the usually drier, fuller, more austere style. The choice between them is purely a matter of taste.

Mateus is one of the largest-selling brand-name wines in the world. It is produced by SOGRAPE, Portugal's largest wine company, from a mixture of Portuguese *vinifera* varieties.

Almadén is one of California's largest wine firms, producing everything from sound-value jug wines to vintage-dated bottlings of prestige varietals such as Cabernet Sauvignon and Chardonnay. Its Grenache rosé is probably the most popular rosé made in California. The Grenache grape also makes rosé wine in France, where it is grown widely along the Rhône and finds its way into red Châteauneuf du Pape as well as rosé.

Everything's Coming Up Rosés

Of course, Grenache is not the only grape that makes rosé in North America, and a good many wine makers all over the United States have for years been producing all sorts of rosé, usually from blends. Recently in California, because of the ever-increasing popularity of white wines and a temporary glut of red wines, more and more vineyards have been turning out blancs des noirs and rosés des noirs—white and rosé wines from essentially red-wine grapes. So you can now find Rosé of Cabernet Sauvignon and White Zinfandel side by side on the shelves. You're also likely to find them side by side in the color spectrum too: a lot of White Zinfandels are pretty pink.

Lots of these wines are coming out with highly imaginative and poetic names attached, and some of the wines even manage to live up to their names. But it is impossible to offer any useful generalizations about them to arm you for shopping. Each maker is going his or her own way with these wines, and you have to read each label carefully for clues even to such basic facts as sweetness or dryness. Let the buyer be wary is the best rule.

By the way, lest it be thought that all this sliding around the color scale was not well considered, you should know that a new name has been conferred on this new generation of rosé-type wines. They are now officially known as "blush wines." Whatever marketing genius invented that beauty deserves not one but two raises.

This is the conclusion of the first flight of rosé wines. There are several ways for you to proceed from here.

Following the lead of your own preferences:

If you liked either the first wine, Mateus Rosé, or the second wine, Almadén Grenache Rosé, go to Flight 2.

Following the kind of grapes:

Wine 1: there are no other tastings of these grapes.

Wine 2: go to Flight 3.

Following the wines of the country:

Wine 1: there are no other Portuguese wines in these tastings.

Wine 2: there is no other American rosé in these tastings. Go to the sparkling wines.

Rosé Wines:
The Second Flight

ZENATO CHIARETTO BARDOLINO
CLASSICO 1983
AND
MOC-BARIL CABERNET D'ANJOU ROSÉ 1983

Two European rosés this time, both well known among wine fans though neither is what you would call a chart-busting best seller (the wine world doesn't have very many of those). For the record, the Italian wine usually is referred to simply as Chiaretto, the French as Anjou Rosé.

These two wines are vinified from very different grapes, so there should be a lot of obvious differences for you to spot. The similarities ought to be subtler and more difficult, since they stem largely from the fact that these two wines have been vinified in a similar manner. They are distant cousins rather than kissin' kin, and that may or may not make your task tougher. In any event, I know that you are hardened to this arduous duty from the rigorous training you've been through, so get in there and taste!

Full drill: see, swirl, smell, sip, savor, and spit. Ask no quarter and give none.

Appearance. In talking about the exact shadings of different rosés, you probably will use more adjectives and get a wider spread of descriptions than you encountered in speaking of the appearance of all the red and white wines combined. For instance, this Chiaretto has been described as being deep rosy pink, as strawberry colored, and even as having golden or coppery highlights. The Anjou Rosé has been called simply a pretty pale pink, pink with a lavender tinge, and—clearly by a budding poet or a new parent—a baby-bottom blush tone. There is near unanimity that both wines are brilliant—that is, very clear and bright—and very attractive.

Aroma. About the aromas of these two wines there is an unusual level of agreement. Just about everyone credits the Chiaretto with a nice, light, fresh aroma, with marked but difficult to pinpoint fruit tones. Light fruits, such as berries or greengage plums or some citrus fruits, are the most popular candidates.

And just about everyone also finds the scent of the Anjou wine fresh but fuller and more savory. They name fruits less often, though apple sometimes shows up, and more generalized smells frequently—fresh cheese, vegetal odors, fresh wood (sometimes cedar). Often also they mention an elusive element they can't quite put a name to. The aromas of both wines rate as pleasing and/or intriguing with the majority of tasters.

Taste. More marked differences of opinion emerge in tasting these wines. Those who respond favorably to the Chiaretto usually find it light, markedly acid, and refreshing and describe its flavor as simultaneously sweet and sour or as good fruit on the borderline of sweet. Cherries, apples, plums, and citrus fruits, usually oranges and lemons, figure large among the specifics. Those who don't like it are usually responding to its acidity and consequently describe it as sharp, tart, or bitter, with a finish in the same vein.

Most tasters find the Anjou Rosé definitely sweet and rounder, fatter, and less acid than the Chiaretto. Usually they describe the Anjou Rosé as having more fruit—cherry seems to be the most popular candidate— and more perceptible sugar, with a small, pleasingly sweet finish. Those who don't react favorably to it usually fault its sweetness: they tend to find it too simple—sugar and water—and sometimes flabby.

In the wine world, both these wines are usually typified as charming, which is really meant both as a compliment to them (they *are* charming) and a condescension (that's all they are).

Both ought to be drunk as young as possible: bottle-age does not improve them. Both are meant to be served chilled, though not iced to numbness, and both are thought of essentially as hot-weather drinks or light aperitifs, roles in which it would be difficult to fault them. To my mind (though perhaps not to yours) they are less satisfactory as dinner wines, but I'd probably change my mind if I were having that dinner in the open air on a warm summer night somewhere on the banks of the Loire or of Lake Garda, where these wines hail from and where they seem not only appropriate but also practically inevitable in every situation.

Chiaretto is the general term used throughout the territory of the Veneto for what the French and we call rosé (*rosato* is the more common term elsewhere in Italy). Naturally, there are many different kinds of Chiaretto. This one is made in the Bardolino zone (Bardolino is a light, dry red wine from the eastern shore of Lake Garda, near Verona) from the standard Bardolino grapes; hence its full DOC designation is Chiaretto Bardolino. The word "Classico" here indicates that the wine has been produced in the heart of that zone.

Zenato is an important maker of Veneto wines, including the lordly Amarone. Zenato wines are imported to the United States by Winebow Incorporated.

Anjou is a province on the middle Loire, famous alike for beautiful *châteaux* and gentle wines. Rosé d'Anjou is perhaps the gentlest of them all. Usually it is made from a blend of red grapes, but the better examples, like this bottle, are vinified from the Cabernet Franc, which is the vinous aristocrat of the region. Moc-Baril is the trade name of the family firm of Albert Besombes, a long-established Loire *négociant*. It is imported to the United States by Kobrand.

This concludes our second rosé flight. There are several ways for you to proceed from here.

Following the lead of your own preferences:

If you enjoyed either the first wine, Zenato Chiaretto, or the second wine, Anjou Rosé, go to Flight 3.

Following the kind of grapes:

Wine 1: the grapes closest to this can be found in the second flight of red wines.

Wine 2: there is no other tasting involving a significant amount of Cabernet Franc.

Following the wines of the country:

Go to Flight 3.

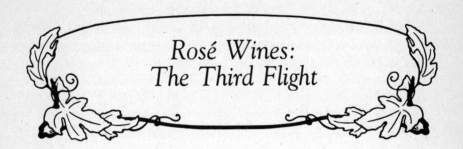

Rosé Wines:
The Third Flight

MASTROBERARDINO LACRIMAROSA D'IRPINIA 1981
AND
A. OGIER & FILS TAVEL 1982

Once more you face an Italian and a French rosé, but these are the big brothers of the last pair. In connoisseur circles, the two wines you are about to taste are thought of as being just about the highest that rosé reaches. So get ready to concentrate: taste carefully and—as always—be prepared to run into a surprise or two. Forward!

Do not, under pain of having your taste buds confiscated, omit the full ritual of tasting procedures.

Appearance. Marked differences leap to the eye (a grotesque phrase, don't you think?). The Lacrimarosa is very pale, barely rose. Usually it shows the color that some California vintners call "eye of the partridge" (another grotesque image). A better way to state it is to call it an onionskin shade, pale, coppery, bright, and pretty. The Tavel, on the other hand, shows a deep pink coloration, really a light cherry tone or a peach and pink combination—a strong hue, quite bright, almost electric.

Aroma. Here is where the surprises begin for most people.

The scent of the Lacrimarosa is very pronounced and very different from that of the other rosés you've dealt with, so much so that many tasters are a bit put off by it at first. Don't be thrown off by shock: let it sit, and come back to it a few times until you acclimate.

Everybody agrees this is a big and authoritative aroma, and most discern at least two main bodies of scent in it: cheese and herbaceous odors. By cheese most tasters do not mean fresh cheese, as we've had in some other wines, but the nutty, dry smell of mature cheeses like aged Parmagiana or aged Gouda. And by herbaceous elements they tend to mean rooty, stemmy, leafy underbrush scents—what one taster called "sawdust and soil"—as distinguished from more usual floral or herbal scents. On a more general level, many people notice an absence of acid components in this aroma and a presence of aromatic oils in their stead. Almost everyone agrees, too (whether it pleases them or not), that this wine has a quite complex aroma.

Almost all tasters also find the aroma of the Tavel both big and complex, though in a manner very different from the Lacrimarosa's. Most also find in the Tavel two main aromatic components: a kind of woody or oaky scent mixed up with leaves and grass on one hand, and a body of distinctly fruity odors on the other. The woody/grassy elements usually are described as very fresh and clean-smelling, the fruit as only hinting at sweetness and more marked by an attractive acid sharpness, even a little sourness. There is little unanimity about the specific fruit scents contained here: you might get peaches or melons or sour cherries or something as unusual as kumquats. Most people find this aroma more immediately appealing than the Lacrimarosa's and no less complex.

Taste. The surprises continue.

The first thing almost everybody reacts to on tasting the Lacrimarosa is its surprisingly big body, and the second is the presence of plenty of acid in the taste despite its absence from the aroma. Most find that acid very adequately balanced by something that they are prepared to call fruit but that doesn't seem to be fruit in the way they've become used to encountering it in white and rosé wines. Most say it *is* fruit (cherries, lemons, and even unsweet mangoes get mentioned), but fully dry and present more in the manner of a red wine than a white. Some tasters describe the sensation by saying that with your eyes closed you wouldn't know whether you were drinking a red or a white wine. Many also mention a lingering, astringent finish that adds to the mixed impression of austerity, complexity, and elegance the wine makes on them. Almost everybody finds this wine very balanced and very impressive. For a small percentage of tasters, it's just too big and powerful. Generally, all agree that this is by no stretch of the imagination a delicate aperitif wine but rather a first-class dinner wine.

The Tavel has some surprises for most tasters as well. Few expect it to be as fully dry as they find it, and many discover a little tannic pucker in there that catches them off guard. Most describe the wine as fruity and acidic—sour cherries and citrus fruits, especially grapefruit, are often mentioned—with its balance just beginning to take hold: it gives the impression that it has further evolution in front of it. Most tasters call it medium-bodied, a bit lighter than the first wine and softer in the finish, though every bit as intriguing and perhaps a bit more attractive. As with the Lacrimarosa, most also agree that this is a more substantial wine than any in the first two flights of rosé and that it should definitely be used as a dinner wine rather than as an aperitif.

Tavel and Lacrimarosa are very close to, if not at, the ceiling for rosé wines: they just don't make them much better than these, and only in a few places do they make them this good. Rosé is a limited option in wine. It reaches its apotheosis (for my palate, at any rate) in pink Champagne, where the additional body extracted by fermenting Pinot Noir on its skins raises an already superb wine a notch higher on the pleasure scale. Interestingly enough, that's also one of the very few cases in which a rosé wine is made by blending fermented red wine with separately fermented white.

Lacrimarosa d'Irpinia is an extremely localized and unusual wine. It is made primarily by one house, Mastroberardino, in a small growing area not far from Naples and vinified from the Aglianico grape, which otherwise yields a full-bodied red wine (Taurasi) of great breed and longevity. Mastroberardino's wines are imported to the United States by International Vintage Wine Company.

Tavel is the much more famous name of the two. Produced on the west bank of the Rhône near Châteauneuf du Pape, Tavel uses almost the same grapes as that big red wine, but particularly Grenache. A. Ogier & Fils is a long-established firm of Rhône *négociants*. The importer is Joseph Victori.

This finishes the rosé section. You may either move directly on to the sparkling wines, or you may

Follow the lead of your own preferences:

If you liked the first wine better, Lacrimarosa d'Irpinia, go to its cousin in white-wine Flight 11.

If you preferred the second wine, Ogier Tavel, try its burlier kin in red-wine Flight 19.

Following the kind of grapes:

Wine 1: There is no other tasting of the Aglianico grape.

Wine 2: See rosé Flight 1.

Following the wines of the country:

If you liked the first wine better, Lacrimarosa d'Irpinia, go to sparkling-wine Flight 3.

If you preferred the second wine, Ogier Tavel, go to sparkling-wine Flight 2.

SPARKLING WINES AND CHAMPAGNES

END GAME

If it is possible for one kind of wine to be the victim of more disinformation and confusion than all the others combined, sparkling wine is my candidate for the dubious distinction. With regard to the difference between sparkling wine and Champagne, more fuss has been made and more words written by more people (myself among them) about these mere words than most others in my long memory. *C'est la vie.*

Champagne is a sparkling wine made in the Champagne region of France; thus Champagne is a geographical name, like Bordeaux or Burgundy, so it stands to reason that "real" Champagne comes only from Champagne.

Any sparkling wine anywhere in the world can be made by the Champagne method if the wine maker is willing to go to the trouble and expense of doing so, but that shouldn't—and within the European Common Market doesn't—allow that wine to be called Champagne any more than a blend of Cabernet Sauvignon and Merlot made in the Napa Valley should be called Bordeaux.

The problem arises simply because words like "Champagne" and "Chablis" and even "Burgundy" have been used outside France as wine names rather than as geographical identifiers. To speak of the wines of Burgundy is one thing, but to talk of California Burgundy is quite another. But if you are willing to risk exactness—an increasingly bold

Turn on the Bubble Machine

The steps of the méthode champenoise are as follows. First the grapes are carefully selected. Each village in the Champagne growing area is rated, and Champagne makers compete strenuously for the best grapes. Further selection and elimination of unsound or unripe berries occur just before pressing. After pressing, the juices are fermented in the ordinary white-wine manner, and in the following spring they are bottled off. At the same time, each bottle of still wine receives a small amount of sugar and yeast solution. It is then tightly corked.

The yeast and sugar cause a second fermentation in each bottle, which, because it occurs in a completely closed environment, generates gases that are forced into suspension within the wine. This is both the origin of Champagne's characteristic sparkle and the reason Champagne is always packaged in heavy bottles with mushroom-shaped, wired-down corks: the pressure inside a Champagne bottle is five times greater than that in the normal atmosphere.

Champagne is then aged for whatever period the maker's policy determines. Before shipment, however, the sediments thrown by the second fermentation must be removed. This is accomplished by a process called riddling. The bottles are placed neck downward in specially perforated boards called pupitres. These are gradually raised to steeper and steeper angles until the bottles are almost standing on their heads. In addition, the bottles are regularly rotated to move the sediments down the neck and against the cork. Finally, the necks are plunged into a freezing brine solution and the corks quickly extracted (in some firms, still by hand). This, if all is going well, extrudes the wad of sediment, leaving the wine clear for topping up and recorking.

Along with topping up, each bottle receives a final dosage, an addition of a sugar solution that will determine the final dryness or sweetness of the Champagne.

undertaking in the final quarter of the twentieth century—the case is simple. Here is all you need to know about it: All Champagne is sparkling wine, but sparkling wine is a category that includes much more than Champagne. Or, if you prefer the snobbier formulation: Champagne comes only from Champagne—all the rest is only sparkling wine.

The difference between the Champagne method (*méthode champenoise* is the technical phrase you will usually see on labels) and other ways of making sparkling wines, however, amounts to considerably more than a matter of words. The Champagne method is painstaking, costly, slow, and laborious, and to this point in history it results in sparkling wines that are almost always perceptibly better than those made by other methods.

Time was when the Champagne method was practically a monopoly of the Champagne region. Now, however, wine makers in a good many other parts of the globe have learned and are utilizing its techniques, with the result that Spain, Italy, and the United States at least are presenting increasingly impressive challenges to Champagne's hitherto unquestionable supremacy among the world's sparkling wines.

The tastings that follow in this section are designed to give you a chance to explore the range of styles possible within the broad category of Champagne-method sparkling wines. As a preliminary, it would be just as well to unfreight yourself of either or both of the two most widespread (and, interestingly enough, contradictory) prejudices about sparklers, should you happen to believe them.

The first prejudice says that all sparkling wines are just too la-di-da, too snooty or pretentious or serious. The second prejudice states that they aren't serious at all, that they are pure fun wines to be tossed down without thought or appreciation. The first prejudice misses all the pleasure of these wines completely; the second gets only half of what they have to offer, like smelling a rose but never looking at it, or sniffing freshly baked bread but never eating any.

Sure sparkling wines are fun. All wines are fun. Why else bother to drink them? The world is filled with lots of other things that are good for you. The factor that puts all wines miles ahead of cod-liver oil is the pleasure they give, and that pleasure is definitely heightened in sparkling wines. There is something indefinably and undeniably festive in their simple appearance, and that quality is amply reinforced by the power of custom and tradition, which have made sparkling wines the irreplaceable centerpieces of all major celebrations. Weddings, births, anniversaries, graduations: all lose their sparkle when they lack a sparkling wine.

But that isn't all there is to these wines. In fact, that's mostly the power of our own associations and our own attitudes. The most basic fact to remember about sparkling wines is that they start out life as still wines like any others, and each one is just as good—or as bad—as the wine it's based on. Good grapes make good wine make good sparkling wine, and you can and should taste sparkling wines for the same things you would look for in still wines—*plus* the added lift that a well-orchestrated sparkle should give them.

Okay, those are your general orders. Now get down to the nitty-gritty: get in there and taste.

Sparkling Wines:
The First Flight

TAYLOR BRUT NEW YORK STATE CHAMPAGNE NV
AND
CODORNIU BRUT CLASICO 1982

Neither of these two sparkling wines is a true Champagne in the sense that it comes from Champagne, though the New York wine, like others from other parts of the United States, freely uses the Champagne name, to the outrage of French growers. Only one of them is made completely according to the Champagne method (the Codorniu, which says so explicitly on the bottle). And neither uses any of the grape varieties from which traditional Champagne is made. In fact, these wines use such a diversity of grapes that they don't even have one variety in common. So your mission is to go boldly where your palate has gone many times before, but this time with a little twist. Try to discern here, while you are tasting the big differences due to grape varieties and climates and soils, what similarities of flavor or style you can trace to the similarities of the wines' treatment. That should keep you occupied for a bit.

The best glasses for serving Champagne or any sparkling wine are not those broad, shallow fruit-dishy-looking things that tradition in the

United States seems to hallow. Anything that wide and shallow simply dissipates the bubbles, so why bother with a sparkling wine at all? Rather, choose a tall, narrow glass, flute- or tulip-shaped, with enough of a stem so your hand won't warm the wine, and pour your sparkling wine deep enough in it so you can appreciate fully its special charm.

Real purists never use any kind of soap or detergent to clean glasses intended for Champagne (or any other wine, for that matter), and they use only the finest-quality, lint-free towels to dry them. Other equally knowledgeable wine drinkers regard all that as preposterous affectation. It all depends on just how sensitive your nose and eyes really are.

Okay, wine trekker, taste away: see, swirl, smell, sip, savor, and spit.

Appearance. Right away, being the wily bird you are, you noticed that sparkling wines have introduced a new element into what used to be the most routine part of your tasting procedure, checking the appearance of the wine. Bubbles. Bubbles change everything, don't they?

The color of these two wines is not radically different from anything among the white wines you've been looking at till now: both are, or should be, a deep shade of straw, the Taylor perhaps a little yellower than the Codorniu. But the bubbles completely alter the appearance of the wine and make what would be a perfectly ordinary-looking wine seem very gay and lively.

Since that appearance and impression of liveliness in a sparkling wine is highly desirable, whatever contributes to it is good, and whatever detracts from it is bad. So if one of your glasses is showing a steady, rapidly ascending stream of fine bubbles while the other is making only a few sluggish, large, and vulgar-looking bubbles, it doesn't take an advanced degree in aesthetics to tell which is more pleasing and attractive to the eye and which, therefore, is the better-made sparkler.

Among connoisseurs, that stream of bubbles usually is referred to by one of the nicer pieces of jargon in the wine trade: it is called *perlage,* which is a French term denoting, loosely, the quality of the beading or the pearling of the wine.

Under ideal circumstances, both these wines should generate a persistent, lively stream of what are, in the range of wine sparkles, just about medium-gauge bubbles. Remember, however, that there can be great variation not only from bottle to bottle but even from glass to glass, depending on the glass's shape and how it was cleaned.

Okay, now that you have picked up some new pieces of technical language and data and increased your sophistication enormously thereby, let's get on with the tasting.

Aroma. Most tasters find a readily identifiable broad distinction between the aromas of these two wines. The Taylor strikes most people as smelling fruity (apples, often) and ever so slightly sweet, with some acute sniffers also discerning grassy, leafy, or minty overtones—all relatively light and subdued. The great majority of tasters describe the Codorniu, on the other hand, as smelling faintly of fresh or toasted bread, or as having a good yeasty or sourdough aroma. Very few detect fruit here.

A small note of caution: It is possible with almost all white wines but especially with sparklers to smell a trace of sulfur when the bottle is first opened. Almost always this passes off within a few moments. Obviously, if it persists it is a serious flaw in the wine.

Taste. For most tasters, the broad differences indicated by their aromas continue into the flavors of these two wines.

People are likely to describe the Taylor as some combination of light, dry, lively, and/or fruity (but not sugary), and they may taste in it apples or apricots or peaches or white grapes: They may term it acidic (many people find it strongly so and taste a nearly unpleasant sourness because of it) or aggressively carbonated, with a "sticky" or sweetish finish. Overall, the most common responses depict a light, bright, active wine, which most people tend to like.

On the other hand, most tasters find the Codorniu markedly dry by comparison, slightly fuller and weightier, with high acid and very subdued fruit. The most frequently discerned flavor seems to be toast or a nonspecific, very lightly sweet fruit. The overall impression is of a somewhat austere, restrained and balanced wine, more elegant than zestful.

Some people may summarize the differences between the two by seeing the Taylor as starting from a more interesting and fruity base wine and the Codorniu as being the better-constructed sparkling wine, a distinction that goes to the heart of a great deal about these wines.

That is because the Taylor wine is vinified from a handful of native American or French-American hybrid grape varieties. Those grapes may lack the breed and delicacy of *vinifera* varietals, but they possess plenty of fruit and flavor that, when it is well handled, makes interesting wine.

Taylor follows the Champagne method up to a point. You will notice its label says "fermented in the bottle," not "fermented in this bottle." That indicates that the second fermentation has been induced in the individual bottles in the orthodox Champagne manner but that the costly riddling and Champagne-process disgorgement have been side-stepped: instead, the bottles are opened into large tanks where, under constant pressure so the sparkle isn't lost, the wine is filtered and then rebottled. This is called the transfer process.

Codorniu also made its sparkling wine from native grapes, Spanish *vinifera* varieties, which seem to possess some of the delicacy the American grapes lack but only a shadow of their fruit. Codorniu has, however, followed every step of the labor-intensive Champagne method right to the end and is therefore entitled, as you can see, to describe its wine as "Champagne method sparkling wine" and "fermented in this bottle."

Both Taylor and Codorniu make what are among the least expensive sparkling wines on the American market, and both offer sparkling wines at several levels of quality. Codorniu probably is the largest maker of Champagne method sparkling wine in the world and has been producing such wines since the 1870s. It is imported to the United States by Joseph Victori Wine Company. Taylor began business in the 1880s and has been an important New York wine maker ever since. It was the firm that introduced hybrid varietals to the area; they have since become a mainstay of the New York wine industry.

This concludes our first flight of sparkling wines. There are several ways for you to proceed from here.

Following the lead of your own preferences:

If you enjoyed either the first wine, Taylor New York State Champagne, or the second wine, Codorniu Brut, go to Flight 2.

Following the kind of grapes:

There is nothing else like these grapes in these tastings.

Following the wines of the country:

Wine 1: go to Flight 2.

Wine 2: the only other Spanish wine in these tastings can be found in red-wine Flight 5.

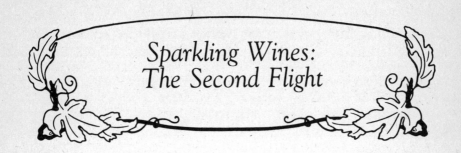

*Sparkling Wines:
The Second Flight*

KORBEL BRUT CALIFORNIA CHAMPAGNE NV
AND
BOLLINGER BRUT CHAMPAGNE SPECIAL CUVÉE NV

In this flight your challenge, once again, is to taste for regional and stylistic differences in two wines made from the same sorts of grapes and in exactly the same manner. Both of these wines are nv, nonvintage, a category that constitutes the major portion of the production of any Champagne or sparkling-wine house. Because of that, all wine makers take special pains to preserve a continuity of flavor and body and attack in their nonvintage bottlings and to create in them a readily recognizable house style.

That makes this class of sparkling wines ideal for the sort of sophisticated comparison at which you've become so expert, so go to it.

Don't forget to perform the whole ritual: see, swirl, smell, sip, savor, and spit. Meet you back here in a few minutes.

Appearance. The Korbel Brut should show a pale straw color, rather delicate-looking, with a persistent stream of middling-sized bubbles. The

Champagne Vintages

In Champagne, vintages do not simply occur: they are declared. The norm in Champagne is nv, a blend of wines from different grapes (Pinot Noir, Pinot Meunier—both red—and Chardonnay), from different vineyards and areas (for example, Montagne de Reims or Côte des Blancs), and from different years. Each house maintains reserves of wine for blending to be able to preserve a continuous and recognizable flavor and style from year to year. The wine so produced constitutes the bulk of each house's line. Vintages are exceptional and are declared only in those years when the house decides it has access to enough superior grapes to make a wine sufficiently distinct from its nv to warrant separate labeling. This is an individual decision, and not all Champagne makers choose to bottle a vintage wine for the same harvest. In 1975 and 1976, most Champagne makers bottled a vintage wine. In 1978, many did so; in 1979, a few. In 1982, almost all declared a vintage. In 1983, some (but by no means all) will make a vintage wine.

Bollinger Brut ought to be a little deeper yellow than that, with a fine, steady *perlage*. Both are good-looking wines.

Aroma. Both wines fall into the category of light or delicate aromas: no blockbusters here, nor are they very common anywhere in the world of sparkling wines.

Tasters seem to divide pretty evenly about what they smell in the California sparkler: one group picks up mostly yeast and alcohol, the other group largely discerns delicate leafy and fruity scents—sometimes as specific as mint, but usually more generalized than that. Almost all find the aroma of the Korbel clean and fresh.

There tends to be more unanimity about the Champagne: almost everybody discerns yeast, or freshly baked bread, or buttered toast, or some other variant on that class of aromas, once again delicate rather than powerful. The only major departure from that—and it is not really very big—is the occasional mention of something like a warm, earth smell. As with Korbel, most tasters find the aroma of this Bollinger fresh and clean.

Taste. Here, of course, is where the real differences in style between these two wines are going to show most strongly. The Korbel strikes most tasters as lively, bright, and acidic, with a relatively light body. Most people taste it as fully dry, perhaps even a little austere, with very restrained fruit—a little generic fruit on the tongue, a little suggestion of peach in the finish. Some people describe it as a lean wine. Some call it steely.

By contrast, most people feel the Bollinger as heavier: they may call it anything from medium- to full-bodied, but what they almost invariably mean is a greater sense of weight on the tongue and a genuine sensation of fullness, almost roundness, in the mouth. They tend to describe it as softer and more giving than the Korbel, with a definite wheaty element in the flavor as well as some medium-strong fruit—peach, maybe. Many tasters also report a lovely long finish, dry and distinctly nutty.

Not everybody likes these wines, of course. For some, all sparkling wines are just a dead issue and they taste nothing but acid or a little prickle on the tongue. Others find the Korbel too hard or too one-dimensional. Yet others find the Bollinger too heavy and insufficiently zestful—a little too old-and-tired-tasting for their palates. But most people, by and large, respond favorably to both wines, though perceiving large differences between them. Overall, consensus gives the Korbel an edge in muscularity and liveliness, the Bollinger a lead in composure and complexity.

Speaking as objectively as one ever can about wines (which, of course, is still very subjectively), I would say that the Korbel Brut has been vinified in a style I would call hard Blanc de Blancs.

What on earth do I mean by that? I'm so glad you asked.

Let's start with some Champagne basics that usually surprise people. Three grapes go into Champagne, and two of them are red: Pinot Noir and Pinot Meunier (the red grapes) and Chardonnay. What happens to the color? Well, except for pink Champagne (about which more later), the musts from the grapes for Champagne are fermented off the skins— that is, the liquids are separated from the solids immediately after pressing. Most grape juice is clear: the color in red wine leaches from the skins into the musts over a period of time. This is not allowed to happen with Champagne.

Fascinating, no doubt, but what has it to do with anything we're talking about? Well, it is the red grapes that give body and flesh to Champagne, and the blending of the different kinds that provides Champagne with its complexity. Nevertheless, some houses make (it is very popular right now) a Blanc de Blancs Champagne, a white wine made exclusively from white grapes—in this case, Chardonnay. Such a Champagne is almost always paler in color, lighter in body, more delicate, and less complex than conventional Champagne. If you'll forgive a pun, Blanc de Blancs is monochromatic.

Nevertheless, within the limitations of Blanc de Blancs, there is still room for house style to express itself. The wine can be soft or hard, very fruity or very restrained, delicate or assertive. This Korbel, which I would bet has a very high percentage of Chardonnay, reminds me of a Blanc de Blancs Champagne in the hard style: its bright, steely muscularity is to my palate characteristic of that particular kind of Champagne.

The Bollinger, on the other hand, shows just exactly the kind of complexity and balance I would expect from a very well made Champagne containing the usual three grape varieties. In fact, just because this particular wine is rather full-bodied and weighty, I would expect that it contains a substantially higher percentage of red grapes than white. They (especially Pinot Noir) provide the grounding for Champagne: they give it its bass notes.

That is why, by the way, a genuine pink Champagne is no airy, effete drink. Pink Champagnes, which derive their color from allowing some Pinot to ferment for a while on its skins, usually are among the most full-bodied and robust of sparkling wines. A Brut Rosé from a good Champagne house usually ranks as one its special *cuvées* (*cuvée* is the term used in Champagne for any blend). Such a sparkler can teach you a lot of respect for pink wines.

That's an awful lot of Champagne lore for you to digest at one sitting, so pour yourself a glass of bubbly and read through it again to make sure you've got it straight. Then go on out and swank the neighbors.

Korbel is a California winery specializing in sparkling wines and brandies. It probably is the largest producer of *méthode champenoise* wines in California. It also markets a Champagne-method wine labeled "Nature," which is even drier than its Brut.

Bollinger is one of the *grandes marques*, the great Champagne houses upon whom so much of the prestige of Champagne rests. It produces wines that are highly regarded examples of the big, full-bodied style in Champagne. In addition to this nonvintage Special Cuvée (a brand name), Bollinger markets in the United States both vintage Champagnes and its great speciality, Tradition R.D., which indicates wine that has been allowed to rest and mature for many years on its lees and only *Recently Disgorged* prior to sale. Bollinger's wines are imported to the United States by Buckingham Wile.

Needless to say, both France and California (not to mention Spain and Italy) are rich in producers of fine *méthode champenoise* wines, so if this sort of sparkling wine appeals to you, there is a whole world for you to explore. Here are some names to work with:

- *California:* Domaine Chandon, Hanns Kornell Cellars (interesting wines reminiscent of the best German *Sekt*), Schramsberg Vineyards
- *Spain:* Codorniu, Freixenet
- *Italy:* Cinzano, Equipe 5, Ferrari, Fontanafredda, Gancia, Riccadonna
- *France:* Charbaut, Deutz, Charles Heidsieck, Heidsieck Monopole, Krug, Lanson, Laurent-Perrier, Moet & Chandon, Mumm, Perrier-Jouet, Piper Heidsieck, Pol Roger, Ruinart, Taittinger, Veuve Clicquot

Most if not all of the French houses (and some of the others) in addition to their regular nv bottlings produce vintage Champagnes, pink Champagnes, Blancs de Blancs, and special *cuvées* of various styles and ages.

This is the conclusion of our second sparkling-wine-tasting session. There are several ways for you to proceed from here.

Following the lead of your own preferences:

If you liked either the first wine, Korbel Brut, or the second wine, Bollinger Brut, go to Flight 3.

Following the kind of grapes:

See the Chardonnay flights among the white wines and the Pinot Noir flights among the red.

Following the wines of the country:

Wine 1: go to Flight 3.

Wine 2: this is the last flight of French wines.

Sparkling Wines: The Third Flight

SCHRAMSBERG NAPA VALLEY CRÉMANT DEMI-SEC 1981
AND
GRANDUCA ASTI SPUMANTE

The two flights before this have been your hors d'oeuvre and entrée. This now is the dessert course: two sparkling wines that are less than bone dry. With white wines, no matter how you duck and dodge, the sugar always comes back at the end.

Before you start your tasting ritual, let me take a minute to explain why a wine labeled Demi-Sec (half dry), as is the Schramsberg, is likely to be anywhere from slightly to distinctly sweet. It isn't just part of the International Wine Conspiracy to keep you confused and feeling inadequate.

It came about because, in the nineteenth century and in France especially, Champagne was made very sweet. Public taste (English taste in particular) began to demand drier and drier Champagnes, and as the makers gradually reduced the sugar in their wines, they evolved a series of names indicating increasing degrees of dryness. They obviously thought they had gone about as far as common sense would take them when they created *sec* (dry), but they were quickly pushed beyond that to *extra sec* and finally to *brut*. To give you some idea of what some more conservative Champagne makers thought of all this, the French word *brut*, which we now use unthinkingly to mean dry Champagne, literally translates as rough or raw.

Almost all of these grades of Champagne are on the market today. Just remember that if it says dry or *sec* at all, it's got some sugar in it, and if it admits to *douce* or sweet, it's got a lot. The sweeter Champagnes usually are served with dessert (though some people, especially in France, also take them as an aperitif), the dry with a dinner's earlier courses. And just for your information, some Champagne and sparkling-wine houses also make a wine drier than *brut*: usually it is called *nature* or *dosage zéro* to indicate that it has no sugar whatever.

Crémant, by the way, is a Champagne term denoting a wine having about half of Champagne's normal internal pressure and therefore producing a rather gentle creamy foam when poured, rather than Champagne's more explosive fizzing. The word implies nothing about a wine's sweetness or dryness. In some sparkling-wine-producing areas outside Champagne, the term Crémant is beginning to be used to distinguish top-of-the-line bottles from more ordinary sparkling wines.

Appearance. Both wines are very pretty—limpid, straw colors, with fine, persistent *perlage*. The Schramsberg Crémant is visibly a bit more golden than the Asti Spumante, and its *perlage* is a trifle more irregular.

Aroma. Everybody describes the aroma of the Schramsberg as light in comparison with the Asti. Almost everybody calls the Schramsberg fresh and fruity (some say apples) as well, and a few tasters may even find it reminiscent of Riesling, with a delicate floral aroma and hints of spice. Many also pick up in the aroma a distinct scent of yeast, sometimes even of toast—all very like the Brut Champagne of the last flight. Practically all tasters (except those who abominate even the slightest trace of sweetness) agree that this wine's nose is complex, clean, and refreshing.

The Asti Spumante's aroma is, it almost goes without saying, very different from the California wine's, absolutely unmistakable for any other wine scent and nevertheless very difficult to describe. It is first of all a strong aroma, about as deeply fragrant as you will ever find in a sparkling wine. It is a deep, heavy aroma, a baritone to the Schramsberg's tenor. And it is markedly fruity, even sweet-smelling. About 99 percent of the people who try Asti will agree to all of that without any trouble. But how do you describe what that scent is like to someone who's never encountered it? What you are smelling in the Asti is the characteristic scent of its single grape, the Moscato or muscat grape. The best that most tasters can come up with to define it is to compare it to the aroma of concentrated fruit essences, such as pear or apricot leather or prunes or other dried fruits. Most people love it and find it almost intoxicating, but for some it is overpowering and cloying.

Taste. Tasters may encounter a few surprises here.

The California sparkler strikes the majority of people as lively and fresh, very bright and acidic—an essentially and surprisingly dry wine with an accompanying, almost peripheral sensation of light sweetness. Its fruit is unexpectedly big and vivid, much more pronounced in flavor than the aroma seemed to most people to predict. That fruit hits different tasters in different ways: some will taste ripe peaches in it, some orange or other citrus flavors, some apricot. Some even claim to discern ginger. But whatever they taste, most will describe the total flavor as rich, hardly sweet at all, and finishing like an organ blast, with everything evident and echoing long afterward.

With regard to the Asti, all but unanimity reigns. Practically everyone gets an enormous burst of fruit on the palate, strongly flavored but very clean: some describe it as golden raisins, others as intense berry flavors. The wine strikes most tasters as soft and—choose your word—fat, big, round, full-bodied, rich. For all its opulence and all its sweetness, however, most people don't find this sparkler at all cloying or sugary. Its sweetness seems in balance with the intensity of its fruit, and there is a lot of acid to keep the whole mass animated, even though it is not acidic in the way the California wine is. Many tasters remark on its excellent finish, which they describe as surprisingly dry and giving a final burst of pure muscat flavor. Most tasters, even if they don't care for this sort of wine, find this example very well made and very interesting. Many get enthusiastic about Asti, but some just find it all too much— too rich, too aggressive, too sweet.

There can be little argument that these are both very well made wines in totally different styles, the Schramsberg fruity and muscular in a half-Californian, half-French style, the Asti Spumante lush with fruit yet balanced in a very typically Italian fashion. Most sparkling wines labeled Demi-Sec will show their sweetness a lot more readily than this particular Crémant does, but for my money this kind of wine or one the merest touch sweeter makes the best accompaniment to dessert.

A really sweet wine on top of a sweet dessert is not simply too much of a good thing; the two sweets also in effect cancel each other out, and you lose the effect of at least one and maybe both of them. In my opinion, you don't serve a wine like this Asti Spumante with dessert; you serve it *as* dessert, and you bless the day you dried out your palate sufficiently to really appreciate the wonder of a well-made sweet wine.

The Granduca firm, under the direction of its highly regarded president and wine maker, Michele Chiarlo, produces the whole range of traditional—and mostly red—Piedmontese wines, from fine Barbera up to noble Barolo. Its wines are imported to the United States by Kobrand.

Schramsberg Vineyards make only *méthode champenoise* wines and probably has the highest reputation for them among California vineyards. Most use the traditional Champagne grapes, but this Crémant is vinified from a grape called Flora, a cross between Gewurztraminer and Semillon.

Coda

Well, boys and girls, men and women, you've made it. Here you are at the end of the book, with all those wines under your belt, all those notes in your files, and all that knowledge in your head. I can't give you a degree or anything like that, not even a certificate, much as I would like to and much as I think you deserve it for your perseverance. (You did persevere, didn't you? You're not just skipping over a lot of wines and sneaking a look at the end, are you?)

But if you've really been working with me through all these pages, you can give yourself something that will show just how much you've profited from all this effort: You can go out and buy yourself a special bottle of wine that you'll really enjoy. If this book has done its job well, you'll now know exactly which one that is.

Happy days!

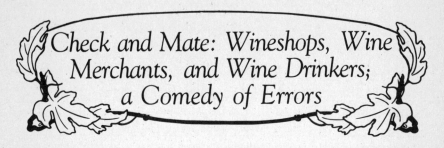

Check and Mate: Wineshops, Wine Merchants, and Wine Drinkers; a Comedy of Errors

My intention in writing this little note is simply to try to give you some information that will, as you get more involved with wine, help you recognize a good wineshop or wine merchant and avoid bad ones. That should be straightforward enough, but the buying and selling of any alcoholic beverage in the United States is so surrounded by federal, state, and local regulations (not to mention taxes) that most citizens can acquire marijuana with greater ease than they can a specific bottle of wine.

If you are so miserably unfortunate as to live in a state where all wine sales are handled through state stores, nothing I have to say here is going to help you. I can say only that I grieve for you. Most states impose merely primitive and incommoding conditions on the wine drinker; state stores and their concomitants are not even up to the level of Neanderthal. I have had the dubious pleasure of watching a selection committee for one state's alcohol control board tasting wines. Is anyone going to be the least bit surprised when I say that they knew nothing about wine and were, moreover, the only individuals at the tasting who got rip-roaring drunk? So much for alcohol control.

How do you know a good wineshop? How can you tell a really knowledgeable wine merchant from a glib salesperson? There are ways. They are not infallible, but there are things to look for, both good and bad, that can save you time and trouble and shorten your quest. The really great wineshop, with terrific selection and reasonable prices, and the really fine wine merchant, knowledgeable and helpful but not hard-sell, are the holy grail of every wine enthusiast. Unless you are stupendously lucky or very well friended, you are not going to stumble on them right away. But they do exist, so be patient.

Keep your expectations realistic. Don't enter a small neighborhood shop that does most of its business in vodka and Scotch to search for a specific vintage of a specific vineyard, and don't go into a rage when the shop doesn't have it. Remember, you're dealing with businesspeople who have to move their stock to pay the rent.

If the shop is really conveniently located for you and you honestly believe you might do a lot of business there, talk to the owner or manager. Tell him or her what you mean by a lot of business. See how cooperative he or she is. Some shopkeepers are interested in increasing their wine sales; others don't want to be bothered. If this one falls into the latter camp, just move on—don't waste your energy trying to make a convert. If he or she is interested, try to set up something on a trial basis so you both can see how it works out.

Remember, in a small shop every new wine the merchant brings in means something else he or she no longer has room for, and it means cash out of the merchant's pocket, so don't be surprised if a shop owner doesn't clap hands with delight every time you suggest a wine you think you'd like to try. In any event, you have to reconcile yourself to the fact that there are real limitations to what a small, neighborhood shop can provide for an increasingly serious wine enthusiast.

There are exceptions to this, of course. Sometimes (especially in smaller towns where cellar space comes cheap and competition may not be so intense) you find a merchant who is a wine enthusiast, too, and who has been able to turn a neighborhood shop into a specialty store. That sort of place can be a treasure trove if you recognize it and treat it properly.

First, some obvious things to warn you off.

If the window display is filled with flavored wines and pop wines, the odds are not strong that you'll find what you want inside. The window display pitches to the customer the shop caters to, or wants to cater to. If the window holds a display of what you consider good wines but they are all standing upright in full sunlight, be dubious. If they look as if they have been that way for a long while, be very distrustful. If you enter the shop and all the wine is standing upright on all the shelves, with not a single horizontal display or storage shelf to be seen, run, do not walk, to the nearest exit. Wine drinkers patronizing such a place deserve the spoiled wines they will almost certainly get.

Other warning signs come from the personnel. Don't even bother to attempt to explain to the clerk or merchant who wants to sell you a five-year-old Beaujolais or Pinot Grigio. The odds are that he or she already knows that those wines are supposed to be drunk young but just doesn't care. Be suspicious also of the dealer who always tries to move you up the price ladder from your initial interest: the dealer may be trying to steer you to a better wine, but if it happens all the time, he or she probably is only trying for a better mark-up, whether the wine is actually better than what you requested or not.

Above all, avoid like the plague the shop where the owner or manager is constantly marking up the prices with each new edition of *Beverage Media.* Very few places move stock that fast, and what you're witnessing, in many cases, is simply gouging a bigger margin out of old stock, a practice that is immoral at best and in some places downright illegal—but it happens, so watch for it.

So what are you looking for, then? Let's talk about the ideal, and you can scale down from that to a realistic model for your region and your needs.

First, personnel. The staff—whether it consists of the owner or owners alone or of a whole group of clerks, stock people, and delivery people—is crucial to the success of a wineshop. The people in the store have to know about wine beyond the rudimentary level of responding to queries for a light white wine or a dry red one. This doesn't mean that every individual has to know everything there is to know about wine (it isn't possible, anyway) but that somebody on the floor should be able to respond accurately to questions like "Were the Rhône reds any good in the '77 vintage?" or "Isn't this '78 Chianti over the hill already?"

And certainly the floor people should know their own stock. You should get very suspicious of a store with a lot of wine that nobody on the premises has ever tasted: that often means that it was stocked only because the price was advantageous. That, in turn, does not mean that you won't be able to get good buys in such circumstances, but you'll have to rely on your own knowledge and luck entirely, because no help will be forthcoming from the staff.

Attitude is a good indicator, too. Serious wine merchants realize that a wine drinker has to start somewhere, that even a great connoisseur once couldn't tell the difference between Bordeaux and Burgundy. Knowing that, they usually are patient with beginners and thoughtful in answering questions, insofar as time and the pressure of business will allow. Naturally, if you walk into a shop on a busy Saturday afternoon or right before a major holiday and present the dealer with a list of questions the length of *War and Peace,* you are not going to receive all the deference and courteous respect that is, no doubt, your birthright.

But at slower times (which is when you should appear if you really have a lot of questions) you will be able to recognize a good wineshop by the thoughtfulness with which your queries are answered.

Finally, the staff should show a certain amount of pride as well as knowledge, a bit of enthusiasm as well as information. They should be able to show you wines you won't get just anywhere, and they needn't be the costliest rarities, either. A good wine staff should be just as happy to be able to offer a good, sound, everyday wine as a noble vintage.

That brings us to stock, which probably is what you're most interested in.

The first criterion is completeness. No single shop could stock even one bottle of each of the world's wines, so exhaustiveness is out of the question. Who would want all of them, anyway? Completeness in this context means that our ideal wineshop would stock the major kinds of wines of the major producing areas of the world and at a good mix of price ranges. I would say also that it wouldn't hurt a bit if in addition to that sort of completeness the shop or its owner or its staff also possessed a specialty, an area of wine in which its stock and their expertise were exceptionally strong.

The second criterion is accessibility. That marvelous selection of wines should be so displayed that you can see what's there to choose from, pick up the bottles, read the fine print and the back labels. I find very unsatisfying (not to say uncomfortable) the system of some European shops where you sit in antiseptic splendor and choose your purchase from a catalog. I want literal hands-on experience of the wines I'm going to buy. I'm not even happy with (though because of space limitations I sometimes can see the necessity for) the practice of keeping only one vintage of a particular wine on the floor and holding the others in storage.

Especially for people just starting out in wine, I think it is important that they familiarize themselves with the different bottles, the labels, the vintages, the different data given on each. Not that they're going to memorize all this for some giant wine quiz—say the right vintage and a foie gras comes down—but simply to get comfortable with such things, to build up a level of easy recognition. Besides, there is also a bit of romance that no catalog can supply involved in actually handling a rare old bottle, and romance is one of the attractions of wine for the enthusiast and one of its selling points for the dealer.

The third criterion is pricing. A shop can meet those first two criteria and still be a nightmare rather than a dream if its prices are always pegged at maximum mark-up. You as a customer must feel you're getting good value for your money. Your enjoyment of wine and your satisfaction in it are diminished if you think you've overpaid. You want to feel you've made a good buy, not ransomed a hostage from terrorists.

That doesn't mean every wine has to be steeply discounted, either: good merchants are entitled to their profits. A reasonable balance between all-that-the-market-will-allow and no-frills-no-services-plain-pipe-racks is the ideal. The quickest way to assure yourself that a particular shop is dealing fairly with you in this regard is to watch its sale offerings. Are the items quoted really on sale, or merely lightly discounted from prices inflated to begin with? Are there genuine bargains in the sale, or do these prices merely bring the merchandise into a range regularly or frequently available elsewhere in your region? Are there only one or two spectacularly discounted items—loss leaders—and the rest not a sale at all?

Those are the questions to ask, and if the answers you get start turning up in the wrong column, you are probably dealing with a robber baron rather than a real wine merchant. And don't be intimidated at this stage by prestige or reputation either: some wine dealers count on both to justify preposterous prices—but you can't drink pretension, so neither should you pay for it.

Once you have found a wineshop to your liking, introduce yourself to at least one of the regular staff. Let someone in the shop get to recognize you, and fill in him or her on your circumstances and your taste insofar as you can. Pick your times right—not in the middle of a busy spate— and genuinely confer with this person about the wines in the shop. Exchange opinions and information and enthusiasms. This will enable your regular clerk to help you better and give you a basis for judging how likely it is for a wine that he or she enjoyed to please you. And don't just go back to the shop with complaints. Stop by occasionally and let them know how much you enjoyed that *petit château* they recommended or how well the Barolo went with the leg of lamb, just as they said it would. You're building a relationship that could go on for years, to both your benefits, so try to think about it not just in a business context but in a human one as well. That's where wine belongs, anyway.

Good buy, and good luck.

APPENDICES

How to Read a Wine Label:
or,
When the White Knight's Talking Backward, the Chessmen Tell You Where to Go *

Now that you've cut through all the mumbo jumbo and mystic rites of wine lore and found that wine is really pleasurable, there is still one last obstacle in the way of your simply enjoying it. That is penetrating the arcana of the wine label to find the wine you're looking for, or a reasonable facsimile thereof. And it ain't easy. Wine labels seem to be the last refuges of untrammeled self-expression. No two are alike: facts are put in different places, sometimes prominent, sometimes hidden. Different type sizes and faces emphasize or disguise different things. The same sort of wine can go under several aliases: varietal name, type name, regional name, brand name. The purchaser confronts forests of print, spiky legions of gothic letters, an octopus wriggle of copperplate script, not to mention illustrations ranging from antiquarian to avant-garde, classic to commercial. In all that, figuring out what is the essential information looks more like a task for a CIA-trained cryptographer than for a hapless wine lover.

Take heart, however. Things aren't as bad as they seem: those labels only look like pure anarchy. Legally, certain minimal and fairly precise kinds of information must appear on the label, and once you know what you're looking for, it usually can be found lurking somewhere. The thing to be aware of is that the requirements of truth in labeling and the

---

*With apologies to Grace Slick and the Jefferson Airplane.

requirements about the kind of information to be conveyed vary from country to country just as winemaking practices and wine tastes do. So on a French wine label you will look for different data than you would seek on an Italian label, which in turn will be different from a German or a Californian.

Already, from your many wine tastings throughout this book, you know a lot of the items to look for in the different nations' wines. For your convenience, what I'm going to do here is pull that information together in one place and fill in any gaps that may be left. To make this really useful, I'll risk a certain amount of repetition and talk about typical wine labels from the four areas that have absorbed the greatest part of our attention in the tastings: California, France, Italy, and Germany.

California

We'll start at home. Most of what there is to say about California wine labels will be true for other U.S. winegrowing regions as well.

First, take a look at a typical label.

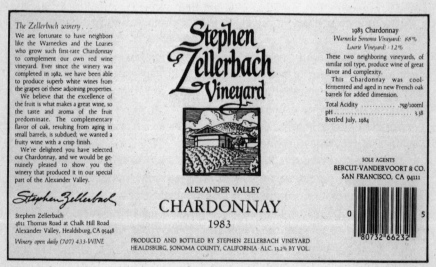

The Zellerbach winery...
We are fortunate to have neighbors like the Warneckes and the Loanes who grow such first-rate Chardonnay to complement our own red wine vineyard. Ever since the winery was completed in 1982, we have been able to produce superb white wines from the grapes on these adjoining properties.
We believe that the excellence of the fruit is what makes a great wine, so the taste and aroma of the fruit predominate. The complementary flavor of oak, resulting from aging in small barrels, is subdued; we wanted a fruity wine with a crisp finish.
We're delighted you have selected our Chardonnay, and we would be genuinely pleased to show you the winery that produced it in our special part of the Alexander Valley.

Stephen Zellerbach

Stephen Zellerbach
4011 Thomas Road at Chalk Hill Road
Alexander Valley, Healdsburg, CA 95448
Winery open daily (707) 433-WINE

ALEXANDER VALLEY
CHARDONNAY
1983
PRODUCED AND BOTTLED BY STEPHEN ZELLERBACH VINEYARD
HEALDSBURG, SONOMA COUNTY, CALIFORNIA · ALC. 13.2% BY VOL.

1983 Chardonnay
Warnecke Sonoma Vineyard: 88%
Laurie Vineyard: 12%
These two neighboring vineyards, of similar soil type, produce wine of great flavor and complexity.
This Chardonnay was cool-fermented and aged in new French oak barrels for added dimension.
Total Acidity .... .75g/100ml
pH 3.38
Bottled July, 1984

SOLE AGENTS
BERCUT-VANDERVOORT & CO.
SAN FRANCISCO, CA 94111

This label is a model of clarity. They won't all be this easy to read, but this one is practically a schematic diagram of what an American wine label can and can't tell you.

Here are the relevant data, from top to bottom.

Stephen Zellerbach Vineyard. Usually the first and most prominently displayed item on the label is the brand name or winery name or vineyard name. With the proliferation of would-be quality wineries in California, this information is not always as useful as it might be to the consumer, especially to the new wine-drinker. Nevertheless, many California wineries have already achieved a level of recognizability and reliability, and more—in California and all over the United States—are doing so every year. So this piece of information will matter more and more to you as you learn more and more about American wine.

Logo. Every label has one. Sometimes they convey real information (what the winery looks like, the lay of the land); sometimes they bear very little relation to reality. This one looks like a simplified view of the vines and winery itself. Attractive but neutral for adding to your information.

Alexander Valley. Somewhere on the label every wine has to indicate its place of origin. The general rule of thumb is this: the more precise the designation of origin, the greater the wine's potential for excellence. That is a theory to which, alas, there often are exceptions, but use it as a working principle nevertheless. U.S. labeling law requires that 100 percent of the grapes from which the wine was vinified must have come from the area named; no alien infusions are allowed.

In California, there are many possibilities of geographical designation:

- California, simply indicating that all the grapes are from within the state;
- North Coast counties, or some similar indication that the grapes originate in a single but broad growing area;
- Sonoma or Napa or Monterey or similar county name, indicating that all the grapes were produced within that one county;
- Alexander Valley or similar, indicating a very restricted growing zone. Alexander Valley happens to straddle two counties; about half of its growing area lies in Sonoma County.

The Bureau of Alcohol, Tobacco, and Firearms (believe it or not, that is the agency with jurisdiction over wine) is in the process of approving areas as specialized wine zones, so you can expect to start seeing even more precise growing-area designations appearing on labels (names such as Carneros Region, for instance, will be strictly controlled and applied only to wines grown and produced within very tightly defined limits). In effect, this marks the serious beginnings of an American system to parallel the European AOC and DOC: legally controlled names of the regions of origin.

Chardonnay. After the name of the winery, the second most prominently displayed piece of information on the label is the name of the wine. In this case, following normal practice for California's quality wines, it is the name of the grape varietal. By law, any wine labeled for a grape variety must contain at least 75 percent of that variety. Almost all makers in California far exceed that minimum, and many would not consider making anything other than a 100 percent varietal wine. Some go so far as to report on the back label when they have mixed batches of the same varietal from different fields, giving percentages of each in the crush. For the average consumer that amount of information constitutes overkill, but if you reach the point of connoisseurship where you are tasting and enjoying such slight differences, you will no doubt surprise yourself by just how interesting you'll find data of that sort.

One final word about straight varietals and blended wines. There is, of course, nothing intrinsically wrong with blended wines; many of the world's most sought-after wines are blends. Californians seem to have succeeded very well with varietal wines, but their blended wines generally have gotten a comparatively bad press—largely because of the dominance in the market of inexpensive California blends bearing the names of European wine regions (or wine kinds) to which they have no relation at all. Chablis and Burgundy are good examples of this type, which are known in the trade as generics. To distinguish their wines from these generics, back when California wines of quality were struggling for proper recognition, many wine makers reacted by going to the opposite pole and refusing to blend their grapes at all. Interestingly, more and more serious U.S. wine makers now seem to be experimenting with quality blends—mellowing the asperities of Cabernet Sauvignon with small percentages of Merlot, for instance, or modifying Zinfandel with Petite Syrah, or in white wines blending varying percentages of Sauvignon Blanc and Semillon, as is done in Bordeaux. Blends of that sort may well be the next wave of fashion in California wine.

The back label gives even more precise designations of origin than Alexander Valley. It indicates the exact vineyards in the Alexander Valley from which the grapes came. Not all wine labels will give this information, of course, since not all wines, even at the very highest levels of quality, come from single growers or farms. But if the vineyard is a prized one and if its grapes have been vinified and bottled separately, as is the case here, those facts will be clearly presented. Of course, such wines will cost more than simpler, less restricted bottlings.

1983. The vintage year, not the bottling year or the year of release. Many wines rest in barrels and in bottles for several years before becoming commercially available. Vintage information can be of crucial importance in determining not only the quality and value but also the readiness or unreadiness of a wine for drinking.

Alc. 13.2% by vol. American law requires a statement of alcoholic content on the bottle. This usually is done by volume, a measure that includes both the actual and the potential amount of alcohol in a wine. Potential alcohol means the amount of unfermented grape sugars remaining in the wine. The sugar measure most commonly used in the United States is Brix; a rough formula holds that 2 degrees of Brix yield 1 percent of alcohol. In a dry wine such as this, the alcohol-by-volume measurement is going to be very close to, if not identical with, the actual alcohol in the wine. In a sweet dessert wine, where a good deal of unfermented grape sugar still survives in the finished wine, the difference between alcohol by volume and the amount of alcohol actually present in the wine can be quite substantial.

France

Here you have a completely different visual layout from that of the preceding California label. Nevertheless, this fairly typical French label presents much the same information; only its arrangement is different.

For example, the center of the label is almost completely filled by the logo, the estate's motto and seal, and its name, *Château Gruaud-Larose*. This is a very prestigious estate, ranked as a Second Growth (*Deuxième Cru*) in the 1855 classification of the wines of the Médoc. That information you'll find at the top, where it says *Grand Cru Classé*. Bordelais custom dictates that only the top-ranked wines (*Premiers Crus*) proclaim their specific rank on their labels; all others band together as *Grands Crus Classés*.

The bottom third of this label gives you the broad regional information and vintage as well as the alcoholic strength of the wine. Below the eye-filling logo, you are informed that this wine has been estate-bottled (*Mis en Bouteille au Château*), a distinction that used to mean more than it does now, when almost every small farm throughout France seems to be dubbing itself a *château* and bottling its own wine. In the days when many wines were shipped in the barrel and bottled on arrival at their market, estate bottling served as a preventative against adulteration. The owner's name was on the bottle and his or her reputation rested on its contents, so if the owner wanted to continue to get the best possible price for the wine, he or she was unlikely to stretch the harvest by additions of lesser wines. Today the estate-bottled designation serves mainly as a reassurance that the entire production of the wine has been watched over by the proprietor, who still has a vested interest in preserving the quality and integrity of his or her product. The name *Cordier* here indicates the name of the family firm, Bordeaux wine merchants long and fine repute, who own this and several other estates and make and ship this wine.

St.-Julien: Appellation St.-Julien Controllée. This is the wine's precise AOC designation, its controlled appellation of origin. St.-Julien is one of the prized townships of the Médoc that was included in the 1855 classification (the others were Margaux, Pauillac, and St.-Estephe). In most regions of France the township or village is the most precise level of origin indicated. There are a few exceptions in Burgundy, where a few extraordinary estates have been granted their own AOC, but this is rare. Normally the appellations follow a pattern similar to California's. A broad regional designation is the largest and most inclusive appellation (Bordeaux, Bourgogne). A narrower geographical appellation (for example, Médoc or Côte de Beaune) is the next smaller unit, succeeded by a township appellation (for example, St. Julien or Aloxe-Corton), followed finally by a precise vineyard designation (Château Gruaud-Larose or Le Corton).

Some further confusion can present itself for Burgundy buyers in that a single vineyard in Burgundy may be shared out among several owners, all holding the right to use the vineyard name on their own bottles. Nevertheless, the basic data appear on French wine labels very much as they do on Californian. The major difference is that whereas the finest California wines most often bear the name of the grape they are made from, the finest French wines usually bear a regional or vineyard name. The only serious exception to that is Alsace, where varietal wines are the norm throughout the region.

Italy

Italy's wine legislation, like that of the United States, is young and yet evolving, despite the fact that Italy is one of the oldest wine-producing regions in the world. Italian winemaking, too, is going through a period of intense change and modernization, and the consequence can be, from the consumer's point of view, very confusing. Add to that the fact that Italian wine labels may bear the traditional names the wines carry in their region (for example, Lacryma Christi) or commercial names (for example, Rubesco), or place names (Chianti), or varietal names (Pinot Grigio), and many people conclude that no sense can be made of the chaos.

There's no need to despair, however. The labels still tell the truth about the wine, and they are no harder to read than any others. Here, for instance, is an Italian wine label that is a model of clarity:

The vintage appears elsewhere on the bottle, usually in the form of a subsidiary label. This principal label gives you just the basic facts: wine name, *Barolo*, the same as its area of origin (*Denominazione di Origine Controllata*, just below the word Barolo); maker, *Pio Cesare*; and the fact that the wine is not estate-bottled, but rather is "produced and bottled in Italy." In the lower left-hand corner, the alcoholic content; in the right, Alba, the name of the township from which Barolo originates. Very honest, very straightforward, very unconfusing.

There can be further data, even on a label as clean as this one. For instance, though most Barolo continues to be blended from the produce of several vineyards as Piedmont tradition dictates and as this wine apparently is, you will find Barolo produced and bottled from a single site. This usually will appear on the label as *Localita* X or *Tenuta* X or

Vignete X, or sometimes simply with another place name prominently displayed. The Prunotto Barbaresco Montestefano you tasted in Flight 18 of red wines is a good example of that.

Italian varietal wines invariably bear a regional DOC as well as the grape's name, so you will find Cabernets that are DOC Friuli or DOC Trento, Trebbiano from Tuscany or Lazio, Chardonnay from several provinces.

The great number of wines Italy produces is both its blessing and its curse, just as it is for the consumer. For people just beginning to learn Italian wine, the maker's name often is the most useful and most reliable piece of information. A good rule of thumb is to stick with a maker whose wines please you, try all of that maker's varieties, and use them to measure others. Reputable wine makers, in Italy as anywhere else in the world, work hard to keep their quality up and their product consistent. Where there are so many other variables and such a great profusion of wines to choose from, that is one very comforting constant.

Germany

Wine drinkers probably have more difficulty with German wine labels than any other. Even seasoned wine shoppers have been known to lose their way among the swirls and curlicues of German labels. But the information contained on those labels is quite precise, if you know what you're looking at. Here's a typical example.

The very top line of the label tells us two important facts—the wine's grade (*Qualitatswein*) and broad region of origin (*Rheingau*). The simple designation *Qualitatswein*, you remember, places it at the doorstep of Germany's ascending ladder of sweetness grades, which are called *Qualitatswein mit Pradikat*—*Qualitatswein* with a descriptive word attached. Those descriptive words correspond to the levels of sweetness: *Kabinett*, the driest, followed by *Spatlese* (late harvest, in effect), *Auslese* (selected picking—of very ripe bunches is understood), *Beerenauslese* (picking of very ripe grapes), and *Trockenbeerenauslese* (picking of ripe, partially raisined grapes). In terms of establishing a German wine's price range, these grades are the single most important factor.

Toward the bottom of the label, in a relatively legible scroll, you can see some more important facts about the wine. First, the varietal—*Riesling*—is announced. Second, the vintage is clear: *1981*. Surrounding the vintage (and less clear to non-German speakers) are the wine's township of origin (*Eltviller* translates as "from Eltville") and the vineyard from which it comes (*Sonnenberg*—literally, the sunny hill). That is the usual pattern for revealing these facts on German wine labels: the village or township name, almost always ending in "er" to make it into an adjective modifying the following vineyard name.

There is other valuable information, much more obscurely presented, in the words surrounding the elaborate heraldic device that fills the center of the label. *Erzeugerabfullung* means that this is an estate-bottled wine (*abfullung* means "bottling"). *Freiherr Langwerth von Simmern* identifies the owner of the estate and the maker of the wine, in this case an ancient family estate long known for wines of the highest quality.

Essentially, that same sort of information must be present somewhere on the label of every German wine, and the absence of various pieces of it moves you regressively down the line of prestige. If there is no

Pradikat, that is one step; if no vineyard name, but only a village, another. If there is not a village name but a *Bereich* designation (a *Bereich* is a much larger region), that is yet another step. And finally, if there is only the broadest regional designation—Rheingau or Moselle, for instance—that is yet another step. As with all the other labels we've looked at, the greater the degree of particularity about origin, the greater the potential quality of the wine.

There are other niceties about German wine labels that can illuminate or confuse the buyer, but I've given you the basics here. They ought to see you safely through your first few forays into German wine. After that, if you're hooked on Hock or Moselle, you'd better invest in a German pocket dictionary.

That just about covers what I can tell you about label lore in anything shorter than an encyclopedia. No doubt you'll come across some exceptions to the general explanations I've given you, but don't let that throw you. One of the real charms of wine, you discover after a while, is that it is more or less all exceptions, and the "rules" are the first things you throw away after you've found out what you like.

Happy hunting!

Possible
Substitutions

You should regard this list of substitute wines as a last resort, although there is nothing at all wrong with any of the wines I list here. Indeed, in their own right many of them are splendid wines that you would very much enjoy drinking. But for the purposes of our tasting lessons, you should abandon the wines listed in the main sequence only when absolutely driven to it. Why? Because the variations that naturally occur from vintage to vintage, plus the variations that occur in fermentation, plus the variations that result from each different house's or *château*'s or country's individual style all add up to the fact that no two wines are ever exactly alike, no matter how closely related they may be.

Your first choice as a substitute for any of the wines in this book should always be a younger vintage of the very same wine. If that too should be unavailable, I've listed here some wines that should give you a reasonable approximation of the tastes and sensations described in the tasting notes. But remember: an exact duplication is impossible. So if you use any of these substitutes (and by all means do so rather than leave out a tasting you're really interested in), be prepared for some divergences from my descriptions, and be prepared to use your palatal imagination a bit more than usual.

Where no alternative is given for a particular wine, it means that a younger vintage of the same wine is the only possible or acceptable substitute.

Red Wines

The Second Flight   38
Bolla Valpolicella 1982 and Jaboulet "Parallèle 45" Côtes du Rhône 1982
Folonari is a possible brand to substitute if Bolla is completely unavailable. A simple AOC Côtes du Rhône from another good Rhône shipper, such as Chapoutier, is a possible alternative for the Parallèle 45.

The Third Flight   47
Jadot Beaujolais 1983 and Paul Masson California Zinfandel 1983
Good alternatives for the Jadot are: Latour, Duboeuf, Maufoux, or Bouchard; for the Paul Masson, Almadén or Gallo.

The Fifth Flight   62
Federico Paternina "Banda Azul" Rioja 1981 and Almadén San Benito Gamay Beaujolais 1982
Try Marques de Caceres or Domecq for a Rioja and an equivalent bottling from Paul Masson or Gallo for the Gamay Beaujolais.

The Seventh Flight   74
Pedroncelli Sonoma County Gamay Beaujolais 1982 and Latour Beaujolais Villages 1983
If necessary, you could use a Gamay Beaujolais from Monterey Vineyards or from Robert Mondavi, and a Beaujolais Villages from Bouchard Père & Fils or Georges Duboeuf.

The Eighth Flight   80
Château de La Chaize Brouilly 1983 and Jadot Moulin-à-Vent 1982
For the Moulin-à-Vent, you might try a different shipper: Latour, Bouchard Père & Fils, Maufoux, and Drouhin are all possibilities.

The Ninth Flight   85
Cordero Dolcetto d'Alba 1983 (Monfalletto) and Bersano Barbera d'Asti 1982

For the Dolcetto d'Alba, consider Prunotto or Fontanafredda. For
the Barbera d'Asti, try Granduca.

The Eleventh Flight   98

Château de Sales Pomerol 1981 and Gundlach-Bundschu Merlot
1981
To change estates is to alter radically the tasting experience, but if
you must, go to Château La Croix or Clos l'Église or Château
Nenin for a Pomerol, and to Sterling Vineyards or Buena Vista for
Merlot.

The Twelfth Flight   111

Prosper Maufoux Côte de Beaune Villages 1979 and Zaca Mesa
Santa Barbara County Pinot Noir 1981
For the Prosper Maufoux wine you might substitute Bouchard Père
& Fils Côte de Beaune Villages of the same vintage, or the 1981
vintage of either. For Zaca Mesa, use a fresher vintage or sub-
stitute a Washington State Pinot Noir of 1981 or 1982.

The Thirteenth Flight   116

Domaine Dujac Morey St.-Denis 1980 and Prosper Maufoux Pommard
1981
Not very satisfactory alternatives are the same villages from other
shippers.

The Fourteenth Flight   122

Villa Antinori Chianti Classico Riserva 1979 and Brusco dei Barbi
1979
The vintage here is very important, so if substitutions must be
made, for the first wine try Fossi or Badia a Coltibuono Chianti
Classico Riserva of the same year. The Brusco dei Barbi has no real
equivalent: the closest you can come is a young (under five years
old) Rosso dei Vigneti di Brunello from Altesino or Caparzo.

The Nineteenth Flight   148

Château Fortia Châteauneuf du Pape 1979 and Masi Amarone 1977
If you must substitute, stick with these vintages. For the French
wine, try Château de Beaucastel or the Domaine du Vieux
Télégraphe; for the Italian wine, Santa Sophia, Tommasi, Bolla, or
Allegrini.

White Wines

Because most white wines are meant to be drunk reasonably if not very young, the freshest vintage available is always a completely satisfactory alternative to the wine described in the tasting notes. You may assume this to be true for all the white wines. Exceptions will be noted below along with any other viable substitutes for a particular wine.

The Third Flight   178
Bolla Soave 1983 and Oliver de France 1983
Folonari Soave could be used in place of the Bolla and Prats' Maitre d'Estournel Blanc could be used instead of Oliver de France.

The Fifth Flight   185
Livio Felluga Tocai Friulano 1982 and Sichel Bereich Bernkastel (Mosel Qualitatswein) 1982
If the Felluga Tocai is unavailable, try a Tocai from Jermann or Borgo Conventi or, less satisfactory, Duca Badoglio.

The Sixth Flight   192
Piesporter Goldtropfchen Riesling Kabinett 1982 (Weingut Jos. Lehnert-Matheus, Mosel) and Deidesheimer Herrgottsacker Riesling Kabinett 1982 (Deinhard, Rheinpfalz)
Newer vintages of either wine will do, but be aware that 1983 was an exceptionally fine vintage in Germany.

The Seventh Flight   197
Dopff Alsace Riesling 1981 and Chateau Ste Michelle Washington Johannisberg Riesling 1982
If Dopff is unavailable, try another Alsatian house such as Hugel, Trimbach, or Dopff & Irion.

The Eighth Flight   201
Hugel Alsace Gewurztraminer 1982 and Sebastiani Sonoma Valley Gewurztraminer 1982
If Hugel is unavailable, try another Alsatian house, such as Dopff,

Trimbach, or Dopff & Irion. In the unlikely even that Sebastiani is unavailable, try Almadén or Souverain.

The Ninth Flight 206
Schyler Entre-Deux-Mers 1982 and Beaulieu Vineyard Estate Bottled Napa Valley Dry Sauvignon Blanc 1982
You could try another shipper's Entre-Deux-Mers if Schyler is not available. Failing Beaulieu, try Buena Vista.

The Tenth Flight 211
Château Carbonnieux 1982 and de Ladoucette Pouilly-Fumé 1982
Château Olivier is a possible replacement for Château Carbonnieux. A bottling from a good producer/*négociant* such as Caves St.-Vincent could stand in for Ladoucette.

The Twelfth Flight 221
Bollini Chardonnay di Mezzacorona 1983 (Neil Empson) and Mâcon-Lugny Les Charmes 1982
If you can't get Les Charmes, try a Mâcon from shippers such as Latour, Jadot, or Duboeuf.

The Thirteenth Flight 227
Chablis Premier Cru Fourchaume 1982 (Domaine Rottiers) and Gallo Limited Release Chardonnay of California nv (The Wine Cellars of Ernest & Julio Gallo)
A different shipper's Chablis Fourchaume (also sometimes spelled Fourchaumes) could be used.

The Fourteenth Flight 233
Chassagne-Montrachet 1981 (Drouhin) and Chateau Montelena Alexander Valley Chardonnay 1982
A Chassagne-Montrachet from another of the great Burgundian *négociants* could be used: Bouchard Père & Fils, Jadot, Latour, Maufoux.

Rosé Wines

As with white wines, a fresher vintage of any of these rosés is always an acceptable substitute.

The Third Flight   249
    Mastroberardino Lacrimarosa d'Irpinia 1981 and A. Ogier & Fils
    Tavel 1982
    Another makers's Tavel could be substituted for Ogier.

Sparkling Wines, and Champagnes

Since most sparkling wines, including Champagnes, are not vintaged, no substitutions should be necessary for them. If a wine is vintage-dated, a fresher vintage will be acceptable as a substitute.

Index